Financial Planning for Nonprofit Organizations

Nonprofit Law, Finance, and Management Series

Financial Planning for Nonprofit Organizations

Jody Blazek, CPA
Blazek & Vetterling, LLP

John Wiley & Sons, Inc.
New York • Chichester • Brisbane • Toronto • Singapore

Library of Congress Cataloging-in-Publication Data:

Blazek, Jody.
    Financial planning for nonprofit organizations / by Jody Blazek.
      p. cm. — (Nonprofit law, finance, and management series)
    Includes index.
    ISBN 0-471-12589-X (cloth : alk. paper)
    ISBN 0-471-41285-6 (paper : alk. paper)
    1. Nonprofit organizations—United States—Finance. I. Title.
    II. Series.
    HG4027.65.B55   1996
    658.15'9—dc20   96-19863

Printed in the United States of America

10 9 8 7 6 5 4 3 2 1

About the Author

Jody Blazek is a partner in Blazek & Vetterling, LLP, a CPA firm focusing on tax and financial planning for exempt organizations and the individuals who create, fund and work with them. Her concentration on nonprofits began in 1969, when KPMG Peat, Marwick assigned her the task of studying and interpreting the Tax Reform Act of 1969 as it related to charitable organizations and the creation of private foundations. She is author of *Tax Planning and Compliance for Tax Exempt Organizations, Second Edition,* also published by John Wiley & Sons and supplemented annually.

Blazek is a founding director of the Texas Accountants and Lawyers for the Arts and continues to serve as board member and program chair. She is also a director of the Anchorage Foundations, Houston Artists Fund, River Pierce Foundation, and Planned Giving Council of Houston. She is a speaker for the National Health Lawyers Tax Conference, the University of Texas Nonprofit Organizations Institute, the Institute for Board Development, the Texas Society of CPA Nonprofit Organization's Institute and Annual Tax Expo, the Funding Information Center's Nonprofit Legal and Accounting Institute, the United Way Management Assistance Program, and other nonprofit symposia. For Tax Analysts' *The Exempt Organization Tax Review,* she serves on the national editorial board.

Blazek received her BBA from the University of Texas at Austin in 1964 and attended South Texas School of Law. From 1972 to 1981, she gained nonprofit management experience as treasurer of the Menil Interests where she worked with John and Dominique de Menil to plan the Menil Collection, The Rothko Chapel, and other projects of the Menil Foundation. She and her husband, David Crossley, nurture two sons, Austin Blazek and Jay Blazek Crossley.

Preface

Financial planning contributes significantly to the success of a nonprofit organization and allows it to better accomplish its mission. The planning tasks are challenging and are too often overlooked. In this time of shrinking governmental support for nonprofit organizations, astute use of available resources following a well-developed financial plan may be the key to a nonprofit's survival.

The concepts and techniques presented in this book can *simplify* the efforts of financial managers and board members to be fiscally responsible, or accountable, to the organization's private and governmental funders, to its clients, to the community in which it operates, and to the society benefiting from its work.

The nonprofit world to a great extent embodies selfless groups of people working to help others in a wide context. The groups through which they work are clustered in three distinct types:

1. the charitable organizations—the church, the soup kitchen, the university, the museum, and the research institute;

2. the associations and community organizations—the civic league, the business league, the labor union, and the social club, and

3. the public section—governments, municipalities, agencies, and public boards that work with nonprofits.

I hope that many people working in this broad range of nonprofits will find in this book a good and often essential prescription for their organizations' fiscal health.

My experiences as an accountant serving nonprofit organizations inspired me to develop checklists and forms to encourage the use of financial planning. When my firm is engaged to perform traditional accounting services for a nonprofit organization, such as preparation of the annual Form 990 or performance of an annual audit, we often find the organization needs financial management assistance beyond the specific task we are engaged to perform. When we are engaged to help overcome unexpected financial problems, we too often find the nonprofit managers could have averted the crisis with adequate advanced planning.

In Chapter 1, I seek to dispel myths that can hamper a nonprofit's financial success. Nonprofits can profit, or accumulate revenues in excess of expenditures, so long as such resources are devoted to improving the fashion in which the nonprofit accomplishes its exempt purposes. Although surpluses should not exceed that amount reasonably needed to assure financial stability, funds can be saved to finance future plans. A nonprofit can set aside funds to expand programs, self-insure risks, build a new building, establish a new location, or simply provide adequate working capital. The primary distinction between a for-profit and a nonprofit is that the latter has no owners. The nonprofit does not distribute its profits, if any, to any private individuals—its creators, insiders, or those that govern it. It can, however, and should accumulate sufficient working capital from surplus income to assure uninterrupted and viable program delivery.

In pursuit of financial stability, a nonprofit can conduct its financial affairs in a businesslike fashion as long as its managers understand the ways in which it is different from a for-profit business. Both need strategic plans based upon clearly defined goals with a focus on accountability, productivity, and profitability. To be fiscally successful, both need skilled financial managers. In evaluating a nonprofit's staffing budgets, it is interesting and can be useful to observe whether the organization considers financial personnel equally important as its program officers. Seeking probono volunteer financial services is not always cost effective in the long run.

The fiduciaries of a nonprofit have special responsibilities. Whether labeled as directors, trustees, elders, or commissioners, they are the financial stewards ultimately accountable to those constituents the nonprofit is organized to serve. The common denominator for this stewardship role is selflessness. The beauty of the U.S. philanthropic community is its extensive network of generous volunteers who expect no monetary compensation in return for their efforts. The challenge, however, is to design an organizational structure for the nonprofit within which this great human resource can efficiently function.

Chapter 2 explores the roles of the board members, the staff, and the volunteers. The objective is to define tasks clearly and to establish an adequate financial management structure with checks and balances and built-in warning signs to spotlight problem areas. A checklist of issues a fiduciary should consider in fulfilling his or her duty to oversee and guide the organization and its managers is provided. Most importantly, the distinction between inside and outside accountants is explained to aid in understanding the need for separation of their roles to achieve suitable fiscal oversight and controls. This book should prove particularly useful to the many well-meaning volunteer accountants, lawyers, and other professionals who have little or no experience with nonprofit organizations.

For some years, I have collected examples of poor financial planning by nonprofit organizations. Fund-raising events are perfect specimens for such analysis. My favorite example, found some years ago in a now-yellowed and undated newspaper clipping, is the story of a small college in Massachusetts. The school spent $400,000 printing 100,000 copies of a cookbook with recipes contributed by local and state politicians; the idea being to raise money and bring some attention to the college. Instead of selling the hoped-for 100,000 copies, only 6,000 copies were sold and the college reportedly was forced to curtail its academic programs.

How could financial planning have improved this situation? First and foremost, the college could have applied the concepts discussed in Chapter 3; it should have prioritized its mission and balanced its available resources. It allocated funds needed for academic programs to invest in a risky publishing venture. One can imagine its budgeting procedures were inadequate so that no marketing feasibility study or forecast was conducted in advance and no follow-up promotions were budgeted, as suggested in Chapter 4.

Too many times I see fund-raising events run by well-meaning volunteers with little or no advance planning for financial feasibility. Consider whether fund-raising events would actually show a profit if the value of the volunteer time devoted to organizing and presenting such events was quantified. It is amazing to me, now that the IRS requires nonprofits to calculate the value of fund-raising events, the narrowness of the margin between the cost of such events and the gross proceeds.

Poorly planned expansion plans can also wreak havoc with a nonprofit's financial situation. A good example of this problem was reported recently in the February 5, 1996, issue of *Time* magazine. The American Center in Paris announced it was forced to close its doors 19 months after the opening of a new $41 million building designed by American architect Frank Gehry. The building construction costs used up the center's entire endowment, leaving nothing for running the literature, language, and dance classes that had made the center the pre-eminent showplace for American artistry in Europe.

Investment of the organization's savings, working capital, and permanent funds is a significant and often troublesome issue for nonprofit managers and board members. Chapter 5, entitled Asset Management, addresses the questions involved when a nonprofit accumulates resources beyond its immediate operating needs. In seeking restricted funding and longer-term endowment gifts, a nonprofit must be prepared to respect the covenants and safeguard the property. The Prudent Investor Rules can be applied to safeguard the assets. If one doubts the need for financial planning, remember the bankruptcy of Orange County, California, and the losses suffered by the Common Fund, an investment management company advising some 1,400-plus universities in 1994. If that is not enough, talk to a professional whose clients invested in the Ponzi scheme of the New Era of Philanthropy. Some lost a lot of money and some who received the unreasonable returns have now been asked by the bankruptcy judge to give the excess profits back.

In addition to checklists and models to be used in setting financial priorities and allocating precious resources, the reader will find a brief, but thorough, description of the elements of an accounting system in Chapter 6. This chapter should be required reading for all new board members and trustees. To meet their fiduciary responsibility to judge the organization's fiscal condition means they must be able—at least once a year—to read the financial statements. It is not sufficient, in my opinion, for the board treasurer to simply report to the assembled board members, "Everything is OK, so you need not bother to read the auditor's report."

Yes, I understand many nonprofit managers and volunteer board members lack financial training and have a fairly high level of avoidance or denial of their ability to understand a balance sheet or cash flow report. To dispel this lack of basic knowledge, Chapter 6 explains the fashion in which financial information is accumulated and presented. Understanding basic terms like accrual method , restricted funds, and receivables can lead to improved financial decisions. I've noticed the attitude of persons newly trained to understand financial statements is similar to the mood of clients who deliver their annual income tax data to the firm—a necessary evil has been conquered and overcome.

Beyond basic accounting lies financial analysis applied with the Special Financial Tools explained in Chapter 7. Before approving the cookbook project mentioned above, for example, the board or finance committee members would ask to see the projected sales analysis and have the opportunity to recognize it was grossly inaccurate. When asked to approve a proposed increase in the annual tuition, a private school trustee would ask what the direct per-student cost is and want to know the amount of unapplied variable overhead costs that must be covered. After studying Chapter 7, a financial planner will know why cost accounting is useful in answering such questions. Once one knows how to read the financial statements with an understanding of what makes up each category, ratio analysis can be applied to compare and analyze the numbers. Some financial disasters can be averted when more board members know how to measure the nonprofit's acid-test and other financial ratios explained in Section 7.1.

Financial pressures on nonprofits are growing. To balance the federal budget, Congress has begun to reduce funding for federal programs, and state and local governments consequently may have to reduce spending. As all begin to search for alternative sources of funding, some nonprofits may be caught in the crossfire. Income-producing activities designed to replace funding cutbacks may be subject to constraints and taxes by the governments causing the need to raise new funds. Some say there is a war being waged on nonprofit organizations. Proposals recently introduced into the United States Congress certainly present serious challenges to the long-term financial stability of many nonprofits. A few examples include the following:

- Billions of dollars in federal appropriations cut from labor, health, and human services, and education budgets in 1995.

- Congressman John Mica proposed advocacy groups and nontraditional charities be eliminated from the Combined Federal Campaign. The CFC raises about $200 million from federal employees and serves as a model for the over 200 state and local employee funding drives that raise money on behalf of non-United Way charities.

- The Istook Amendment proposed that eligibility for federal grants be denied to any organization that has advocacy programs.

- Proposed structural tax reforms, either through a flat tax or national sales tax, remove favorable income tax incentives provided by charitable income tax deduction and below-market tax-exempt-bond financing rules and could adversely affect many nonprofit organizations.

- Reduced tax on for-profit competitors may allow them to lower prices and remove the advantage of nonprofits' exempt status.

- Consumption tax may be tied to the type of product sold rather than the seller's form of organization. Thus nonprofit sellers may be required to charge tax for the first time on services or products now exempt from tax, such as hospital charges. Correspondingly, some or all nonprofit purchasers may find themselves paying tax for the first time.

PREFACE

Nonprofit organizations can take positive steps to replace resources lost in the budget fray. *The New York Times* on Sunday, February 18, 1996, reported that the New York City Parks and Recreation Department had turned Central Park's drives into a test road for BMWs, was renting out another park to a dinner-theater production, and had sold advertising space on park basketball backboards to a sporting goods company. The headline for the article was "A Parks Department Aggressively Pursues Business." On the same day in the *Houston Chronicle,* the headline read "Texas to Promote Nature, Adventure Tours." The story reported a plan for the state to team up with private tour operators, outfitters, and guides to promote tourism. The plan is part of an initiative by the Texas Parks and Wildlife Department to pay for itself by the year 2000 through fees and other earned income.

Those who govern and manage nonprofit organizations must always be cognizant of the reasons why nonprofits are permitted tax exemptions for federal and local tax and other purposes. Chapter 8 explains the rationale behind granting tax exemptions and requirements for maintaining the special status. Someone with each nonprofit organization should regularly use Exhibit 8.1, "Suitability Checklist for Tax-Exempt Status," to test for ongoing qualification. Before undertaking income-producing programs, such as those described in the previous paragraph, the impact of the activity on tax status should be examined.

In completing a marketing questionnaire for this book, I was asked to choose my favorite parts of this book and to describe those that could prove most useful to a nonprofit's financial managers. My answer is the most unique information that is contained in Chapter 1—the notion that a nonprofit organization must profit to be financially successful. This concept alone can improve the fiscal health of a nonprofit. Adopting the attitude that the organization can function in a businesslike fashion with efficient fiscal systems, well-paid personnel, and balanced resources and vision can improve the results. Certainly to wage what some are calling the war on nonprofits, the organization's managers can arm themselves with the tools and techniques of financial planning presented in this book.

JODY BLAZEK

March 20, 1996

Contents

CONTENTS

CONTENTS

List of Exhibits

LIST OF EXHIBITS

LIST OF EXHIBITS

Introductory Concepts

The key to the financial success of a nonprofit organization is the use of traditional management tools—forecasts and budgets, well designed and timely financial reporting system, clearly defined line of business (mission), cash flow charts, fiscal controls, and a lot of goodwill.

Financial planning for nonprofits, like a nonprofit's very purpose for existence, is based upon the philosophical aspirations of persons joining together to accomplish mutual goals. The very purpose for existence of a nonprofit is based on hope, sometimes on prayer, and almost always on dreams. Dreams can be unrealistic and can make financial planning a risky venture. The challenge is to stretch and balance precious resources to best accomplish the dream. Together, the two functions—performing the mission and providing the requisite resources—work in tandem to sustain the nonprofit's existence.

Although idealistic aims guide the planning process and dictate a nonprofit's priorities, accomplishment of the goal can be enhanced with astute planning. Readers familiar with business management will recognize the planning processes discussed in this book. Similar to the income tax rules concerning nonprofits discussed in Chapter 8, financial planning requires the special character and language germane to nonprofits be understood alongside language and concepts applicable to for-profits. When working with a nonprofit organization, it is useful to ask what would make it prosper and flourish like a business? You can ask how an entrepreneur would respond if the same situation arose in his or her successful business? You should wonder whether the stockholders, if the nonprofit had any, would ratify the recommendations being proposed by management? If there is any doubt about the need for good financial management and planning, remember what happened to the United Way of America. Even in what one would think was one of the best run organizations in the United States, money was misappropriated by an executive director reportedly for personal gain.

1.1 HOW TO USE THIS BOOK

This book provides step by step solutions to the dilemmas involved in keeping financial resources and the mission in balance. Financial management tools and techniques for nonprofits are explored and reviewed in some detail with illustrations, examples, checklists and model forms. As this chapter explains, the concepts and planning methods used by businesses are germane and can be tailored to suit a nonprofit's needs. The financial planning checklist at the end of this chapter is designed as a comprehensive survey of financial planning issues that face a nonprofit.

Planning for a nonprofit's fiscal health and effective operation is an ongoing and continually evolving process. The mission statement is not necessarily revised monthly, but the current financial data must be. Exhibit 1.1 illustrates the overlapping circles of financial management activities. As a first planning step, the organizational structure is evaluated. It should be clear from the rules of governance and procedures who is in charge, as discussed in Chapter 2. All should understand the function of the board, volunteers, and staff, and the roles of the internal and external accountants in the financial affairs.

Exhibit 1.1. Financial Management Activities in Nonprofit Organizations.

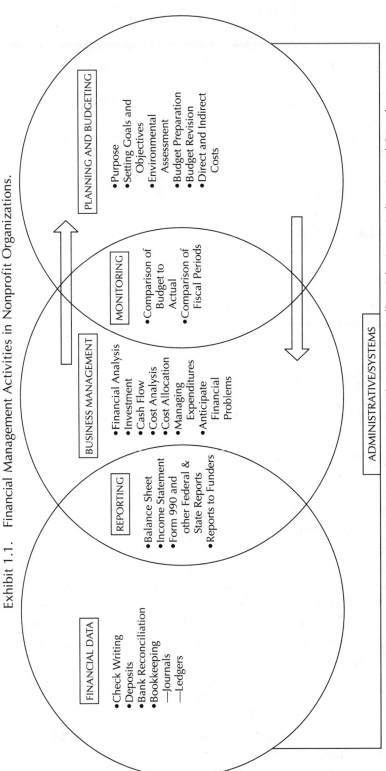

FINANCIAL DATA
•Check Writing
•Deposits
•Bank Reconciliation
•Bookkeeping
  —Journals
  —Ledgers

REPORTING
•Balance Sheet
•Income Statement
•Form 990 and other Federal & State Reports
•Reports to Funders

BUSINESS MANAGEMENT
•Financial Analysis
•Investment
•Cash Flow
•Cost Analysis
•Cost Allocation
•Managing Expenditures
•Anticipate Financial Problems

MONITORING
•Comparison of Budget to Actual
•Comparison of Fiscal Periods

PLANNING AND BUDGETING
•Purpose
•Setting Goals and Objectives
•Environmental Assessment
•Budget Preparation
•Budget Revision
•Direct and Indirect Costs

ADMINISTRATIVE/SYSTEMS

Tax Compliance; Accounting Procedures Manual; Computers; Filing Systems; Staffing; Selecting an Auditor; Internal Controls

Copyright 1986 The Support Center

■ 3 ■

Next comes planning and evaluation of organizational objectives as shown on the right-hand side of the circles in Exhibit 1.1. Before spending a penny, the board members and major supporters in concert with staff define the mission and develop specific performance goals. How can funders or members understand the nonprofit's vision without a description of its activities and financial goals? What will provide the volunteers with a source of direction? Dreams and aspirations must be explored, examined, and written down in a mission statement. This "what if" segment of the planning process facilitates an evaluation of alternatives. Chapter 3 explores these concepts and provides suggestions for utilizing critical analyses to test the means of accomplishing the mission.

Once the basic philosophical ambitions are understood, financial management translates the mission into financial terms. Aspirations are expressed in numbers as budget planning begins. The end result should be a financial blueprint for achieving mission-oriented goals. Fiscal performance goals are, after all, merely a means to successful program achievements. Chapter 4 explores the process of preparing (and adjusting) budgets, incorporating staff participation in the process, and fostering staff support of financial goals. Operational as well as capital-addition budgets are discussed.

Although budgeting is designed to allocate the organization's current resources to achieve program goals, effective asset management maximizes the value of those resources. Plans to increase the yield on cash and other investment assets are formulated in Chapter 5. The investment policies and decisions concerning permanent funds are explored. A checklist for managing and monitoring endowment and restricted funds is provided to serve as a tool in protecting these important resources.

Reporting and monitoring financial transactions as they occur is critical. Chapter 6 discusses financial records and the decisions an organization makes in establishing its accounting systems. Useful journals and ledgers are defined and suggestions made regarding design of charts of accounts. The difference between—and when to use—the cash method rather than the accrual method of accounting is considered. The meaning of FASB and GAAP is explored with an outline of currently applicable pronouncements. A checklist is provided as a guide to computerization and selection of appropriate accounting software.

Control and evaluation complete the cycle of financial planning. The task is to monitor, to manage the problems highlighted, and to be aware exactly how well the reality measures up to the nonprofit's aspirations. The financial planner will want internal controls, such as those described in Chapter 6, installed with the help of the outside accountants to safeguard the nonprofit's resources on a daily basis. The ratio analysis techniques presented in Chapter 7 will be useful in pinpointing any weaknesses and identifying hidden trends. Financial evaluations for purchasing and leasing decisions, employee compliance, and agency agreements implementing strategic alliances are provided. Other financial evaluations can be made using the comprehensive checklists and sample forms presented throughout the book.

Because not all nonprofits qualify for tax-exempt status, Chapter 8 explores the criteria for, and the means of obtaining, special tax treatment. Confusion arises because the activities of nonprofits and for-profits are often the same or very similar. Financial planners need to understand the breadth of activity permissible to an exempt organization. Issues pertaining to the use of unrelated business income to support exempt purposes are also discussed. A glossary of tax and financial terms unique to nonprofits precedes the index at the end of the book.

1.2 ATTRIBUTES OF NONPROFITS

The world of nonprofits includes a broad range of institutions: charities, business leagues, political parties, schools, country clubs, cities, cemeteries, employee benefit societies, social clubs, united-giving campaigns, and a wide variety of other pursuits. For financial planning purposes, it is useful to distinguish between organizations that direct their efforts outwardly, or externally, and those organizations whose work is focused internally, or toward benefiting their members. Nonprofit organizations share the common attribute of being organized for the advancement of a group of persons, rather than particular individual owners or businesses. Sometimes it is useful for the organization to think of its beneficiaries as clients for planning purposes. Applying this concept, nonprofits can be divided into different groups as follows:

- *Type 1.* Nonprofits that operate to serve the public good by providing health care, education, culture, and social welfare service to the public (hospitals, schools, libraries, and homeless shelters, for example).

- *Type 2.* Organizations that serve both the public and their members (churches, public interest groups, and civic leagues).

- *Type 3.* Nonprofit membership organizations that are member oriented or that focus their activities on fulfillment of member services (social clubs, business leagues, and labor unions).

INTRODUCTORY CONCEPTS

A nonprofit can utilize the same tools as commercial businesses that perform essentially similar services or sell goods. Likewise, the nonprofit can and should patronize its constituents or customers who fall into basically two groups:

- *Patrons or Investors:* Those who provide resources or money to the nonprofit.

- *Constituents or Customers:* Those to whom services and goods are provided.

Type 1 and Type 2 organizations as described above have both investors and customers. Type 3 organizations usually only have customers. All three types must focus on keeping its investors and customers happy.

Investors want a return on their money. The return that investors in Type 1 and 2 nonprofits receive is mostly intangible and the investment is inspired by compassion for the mission. Their benefit comes through their conscience and knowing they help someone else. Volunteers who invest time must feel important and useful and be shown that their contribution of time is valued. Hiring a volunteer coordinator can be an important choice in attracting and maintaining this vital source of financial support.

Types 2 and 3 nonprofit customers must choose whether to accept or reject services or goods proffered. These NPOs must make every effort to attract customers and give them top priority. The old adage, "Make new friends but keep the old," is a suitable refrain for a membership campaign. Whether one is silver or the other is gold, new and renewing members are an invaluable resource to a wide variety of nonprofits. A nonprofit's attitude towards them can significantly impact its success, although it is not easy to measure this intangible in the annual budget.

For those customers receiving the nonprofit's free or low-cost services, there is an invisible interaction with the investors or contributors. How the nonprofit is perceived or evaluated by its customers can impact the attitude of its investors. The financial planners should ask if the organization treats those to whom it provides services with the highest respect. Does it instead dispense its handouts to the sick, poor, uneducated, or homeless person in a demeaning fashion? How does the general public, particularly the nonprofit's contributors, view the value of its services to the community.

In deciding what to call its investors, some organizations cause confusion by choosing the term *member*. As explained in Chapter 8, a membership organization is one whose members elect the governing board. Contributors should only be called members if they actually have this voting right. The name *member* is also tainted by several tax limitations on the income tax deduction of membership dues.

1.3 CAN NONPROFITS *PROFIT?*

The pursuit of profit in the normal sense is not the primary motivation of nonprofits, but there are no specific constraints or sanctions prohibiting the accumulation of excess funds, or capital, as long as the mission, or exempt purposes, are served. For many, the term *nonprofit* implies a prohibition against the receipt of revenues in excess of expenditures. Such a view suggests that a nonprofit cannot have a profit and is expected, instead, to lose money. Whatever the result is called, a nonprofit can generate revenues in excess of its expenses and accumulate a reasonable amount of working capital or fund balances. It can save money to build a building, to expand operations, or for any other valid reason serving its underlying exempt purposes. It can borrow venture capital to establish a new project. Basically, a nonprofit can operate without a profit motive and still produce what many think of as a profit.

(a) Meaning of *Profit*

For nonprofit organizations profit can mean many things, including bringing good, making progress, or being gainful, useful, advantageous, or productive.[1] These terms connote benefit to others and the selfless activities of the organization. Profit for a nonprofit does not always come just from the bottom line. Instead, profit may be measured in terms of the number of books published, increases in attendance or test scores, or enhancement of the profession's public image. Although not necessarily measurable in financial terms, discovering a cure for a disease is the yield, return, or reward for a research organization's efforts.

When a hospital buys a magnetic resonance machine to offer better healthcare, it may reasonably expect the machine to pay for itself plus provide a steady stream of excess revenue, or profit. The hospital may use such profits to improve its diagnostic capabilities or use them to purchase a building, to expand other departments, or for any other valid reason serving its underlying nonprofit purposes. The distinguishing factor is the motivation for undertaking the activity that might generate

---

[1] *Webster's Deluxe Unabridged Dictionary, Second Edition,* Simon & Schuster, New York, 1982, p. 1437.

the profit. Did the hospital buy the machine simply to make a profit or instead to better improve the health of its patients?

An accurate perspective on the term *nonprofit* focuses on the lack of self-interest in the financial results of the operations. The directors or trustees serve as stewards of the funds to assure they are devoted to meeting the socially desirable goals. The income, or profit, is not distributable to its members, directors, or officers. Just like a for-profit business, the nonprofit can pay salaries and employee benefits to its workers (including its directors), as long as the pay is reasonable in relation to services performed. There are two things it cannot do: (a) distribute the net profit as a return on capital to the people who fund and control the organization, or (b) accumulate profit or capital resources in excess of that needed to accomplish the mission.

(b) Profit Prohibitions

There are few, if any, reasons—legal, ethical, or otherwise—why nonprofits should not accumulate excess funds, or capital, as long as such funds are devoted to the mission. Consider two authoritative interpretations of the term *nonprofit*. The State of Texas says a "nonprofit corporation means a corporation no part of the income of which is distributable to its members, directors, or officers." Similarly, the State of New York provides two tests for determining whether a corporation is qualified to be treated as a nonprofit entity:

- New York nonprofits must be formed for a nonpecuniary purpose *and*

- No part of their assets, income, or profit is distributable to, or may inure to the benefit of, its members, directors, or officers with certain exceptions otherwise permitted.

The word *pecuniary* simply means "that which relates to money."[2] Clearly a nonprofit must receive, hold, and use money to operate. The nonprofit's purpose or reason for having money must not be to generate more money. Money can be its means, but not its end. Without specifically saying so, the New York law requires that the nonprofit focus on accomplishing its mission and that mission must be something other than receiving, spending, and accumulating money.

[2] Ibid, p. 1420.

Note that the second test anticipates the nonprofit may produce a profit; the test simply prohibits insider benefit. The American Institute of Certified Public Accountants' Audit Guide for Not-for-Profits states that the term *not-for-profit* is not intended to imply that a voluntary health and welfare organization cannot obtain revenues in excess of expenses in any particular period; rather it implies that the organization is not operated for the financial benefit of any *specific individual or group of individuals.*[3]

A nonprofit organization receiving excess revenues, or profit for the year, must decide what level of balances it should reasonably accumulate. Must the money be expended during the coming year? Can instead the money be set aside or saved for a rainy day? A number of different factors influence the answers. For federal tax purposes, the question is whether the organization's nonprofit purposes are served by saving the money rather than spending it on programs. The tax code contains no numerical constraint on the amount of fund balances a tax-exempt organization can maintain. The only specific spending mandate applies to private foundations and requires that 5 percent of the average fair market value of the investment assets be distributed annually for charitable purposes.

Another factor in the decision is the attitude of the organization's funders. A successful nonprofit with money in the bank may meet some resistance to its requests for gifts. It may have to justify its need for funding as compared to a nonprofit whose programs may be curtailed unless it receives the funding. The National Charities Information Bureau standards (reprinted in the Appendix) provide an organization should "have net assets available for the following fiscal year not usually more than twice the current year's expenses or the next year's budget, whichever is higher." Note temporarily or permanently restricted funds may not be treated as "available for this purpose." See Section 5.6 and 5.7 for consideration of such funding and Section 6.7 for new accounting definitions.

(c) Why Seek a Profit?

The belief that a nonprofit organization must lack profit motive can limit its success—and ultimately its existence. True enough, an organization's top priority is not to produce profits—it dedicates itself to carrying out a

---

[3] Industry Audit Guide: Audits of Voluntary Health and Welfare Organizations Including Statement of Position 87-2, 2d ed, American Institute of Certified Public Accountants, New York, 1988.

mission to benefit others. Yet, profit can enhance the ability to perform its mission just as the year-end profit distributed as dividends to shareholders influences a for-profit common-stock market price.

Consider what happens when a nonprofit never generates revenues in excess of expenses. Such an organization cannot finance the expansion of its activities, accumulate a decent level of working capital, retire debt, or meet countless other financial capital needs; its existence might be tenuous, to say the least. Certainly, a newly established nonprofit should plan to generate revenues in excess of expenditures—profit—in its first few years to accumulate sufficient working capital.

1.4 DIFFERENCE BETWEEN NONPROFITS AND FOR-PROFITS

A nonprofit organization is distinguishable from a for-profit business in many respects. One distinguishing factor between them is the motivation for undertaking an activity that generates revenue. The fact that a nonprofit charges for the services it performs is not evidence of profit motive. A hospital may pay all of its costs with patient charges. Whether such a hospital is a nonprofit depends on why it was created and how it operates. Is its purpose to promote the general public's health or solely to earn a profit? In other words, does it exist to support an ideal—or particular individuals?

A nonprofit decides to adopt a project because of its value to society or its members rather than its potential to generate monetary profits, although one worthy project may be chosen over another based on revenue expectations. Accordingly, the challenges in achieving financial success are considerably more daunting for nonprofits than for for-profits.

(a) Capitalization: Philanthropists versus Investors

A nonprofit's need for capital, or resources, to commence and to continue operation is similar to a for-profit's: Capital provides the financial underpinnings to bridge gaps in the flow of funds and to ensure that financial obligations can be paid in a timely fashion. Consider, for example, a social club's capital requirements. The typical club has a physical site for its members to congregate and socialize. Whether the club buys and maintains its own building or leases facilities, the club needs capital to do so. Before agreeing to provide the property to the club, the landlady/lord or building seller will require evidence of the club's financial viability, or capital available to finance acquisition and upkeep. The capital may come from the membership assessments or from existing club funds accumulated from profitable club operations in the past. It may also use borrowed capital to buy and operate the property.

The economic rewards customary in business—dividends, interest, and capital appreciation—are not available to those who invest in nonprofits. The standards used by a nonprofit supporter to measure returns on their money are very different from a for-profit investor's. The tools for measuring success, however, are similar. Financial indicators that evidence goals accomplished can be used as a measure. The prosperity of a nonprofit can be evaluated by counting the number of children clothed and fed during the year, by comparing the per patient costs this year with last, or by studying the number of new professionals qualified due to a business league's training efforts.

Philanthropists who donate capital funds to a nonprofit to obtain buildings or to establish endowments certainly expect the organization to "profit" or benefit from the gift in a sense. In donating capital, the donors are investing in the mission. They recognize and intend their capital to be an unselfish gift directed outward in service of a public purpose. In effect, nonprofits operate on a one-way street. Much of the money they receive is just such one-way money—donations made out of pure generosity, for which nothing is provided or expected in return. Privately owned businesses, in contrast, operate on a two-way street. For-profit organizations generally receive funds from investors who expect something in return.

On a limited basis, a tax-exempt organization is allowed to compete directly with nonexempt businesses. Revenues from unrelated business activities comprise a major source of funding for some nonprofits. The Internal Revenue Code places such a nonprofit on the same footing as competing businesses by imposing a regular income tax on profits they generate from a business. If the unrelated business activity becomes too substantial, the organization can lose its exemption.[4] Chapter 8 considers the question of when a business is "unrelated" and described the level of business activity allowed.

---

[4] See the author's book entitled, *Tax Planning and Compliance for Tax-Exempt Organizations*, Chapter 21, for a discussion of the unrelated business income tax.

(b)   Revenues: Constituents versus Customers

Recipients of a nonprofit's goods, services, or monetary grants in aid are distinct from, but similar to, a for-profit's customers. A prosperous nonprofit most likely treats its program-service constituents—the poor, the sick, the culture seekers, the students—as a business would its customers. It values their patronage and caters to their needs. Whether the nonprofit charges for the goods and services provided or furnishes them on a reduced or no-fee basis, the methods used by a for-profit in purveying similar goods can be observed.

Traditionally some nonprofits charge for the goods and services they provide to their program service recipients; hospitals and universities are good examples. Churches certainly encourage their congregants to tithe. Many nonprofits provide free services that are financed by a complex variety of donations, grants, and other income sources. Some operate with volunteer labor and sell or distribute donated goods. One important distinction is the fact that it may be impossible for some organizations to charge for the services provided. The public depends on immediate and free response from its firefighters or policemen and women, for instance. Having library doors open in the evening for students to do research is expected.

When a nonprofit does charge, the charge may not necessarily cover costs of the service; for-profits only sell things for less than cost if forced to do so by market apathy. Obviously it is more difficult for nonprofits to raise prices, partly because of the public's expectations and partly because of the economic need of the organization's constituents. Ironically, the tight budget situation created by cuts in government funding typically comes during depressed economic periods or when new tax rules reduce or remove the tax benefit of contributions, thus discouraging philanthropy. Suffice it to say, a nonprofit is significantly different from a for-profit in many ways, even though its operations and financial decisions may often appear to be similar.

1.5   FOR-PROFIT TOOLS

Although businesses do not often show movies for free or feed the poor, they do operate schools, hospitals, theaters, galleries, publishing companies, and conduct other activities that are also carried on by nonprofit organizations. The nonprofit's reason for conducting the activity and the ultimate benefit from the capital are definitely different. Nonetheless, the financial issues look much the same; both types of organization can use similar financial tools. Just as discussed above under the profit issue, there is no reason why a nonprofit cannot use a for-profit model to manage its financial affairs. A nonprofit that operates in a businesslike fashion may be more likely to succeed. Some of the tools that might be useful include:

- Business Plan. To achieve idealistic goals, nonprofits can develop a long-range plan that looks like what is called a business plan, complete with market surveys, cost projections, and strategic goals. Like a for-profit, a nonprofit can:

  - Accumulate reasonable reserves by earning more than it spends,

  - Be clear about who makes decisions, and

  - Follow sound financial practices for both planning and reporting.

- Critical Analysis of Decisions. A nonprofit considers how a for-profit would make a similar financial decision. In considering a question, the nonprofit might ask:

  - What would make this nonprofit prosper and flourish?

  - How would an entrepreneur respond if the same situation arose in his or her business?

  - Last, but not least, if the nonprofit had stockholders, would they ratify the recommendations being proposed?

- Traditional Management Tools. The management tools for achieving organizational objectives are the same whether the objectives are business-oriented or mission-oriented. Like for-profits, a nonprofit's management tools include:

  - Forecasts, budgets, and ratio analysis,

  - Well-designed and timely financial reports,

  - Defined lines of communication and responsibility,

  - Cash-flow monitoring system,

  - Efficient organizational structure with fiscal controls,

  - Identification of the target served, i.e., the customers or constituents, and

  - Clearly defined line of business (mission).

1.6 PURSUIT OF FINANCIAL SUCCESS: SOME OBSERVATIONS

However different the nonprofit is from a business, the methodology for measuring and achieving success is conceptually the same. Before launching into the technicalities of financial planning for nonprofits, readers may wish to consider the following observations regarding the pursuit of financial success.

(a) Be Realistic about Expectations

Nonprofit organizations are created from dreams. Rational, even scientifically determined, projections can be wrong. The polls may say people are worried about feeding children, but they may not respond with contributions. The compassion felt toward those with a disease may wane. Fund-raising is often successful because of the energy and influence of board members. The nonprofit organization, however, is seldom their top priority; having a great fund-raising chair one year does not assure the success of next year's campaign. See Section 4.7.

As an example, the New Era Philanthropy investors were tempted by the promise of unusually high returns on their investments. The scheme, however, apparently violated the prudent-investor rules. The investors who lost money now wish they had tempered their desires for an unrealistically high return with a critical evaluation of the risks inherent in such a now-worthless investment. Expecting modest but reliable returns on the organization's savings could have protected the nonprofit's money and avoided loss of the money as well as public confidence in boards that approved investment of funds in New Era. See Section 5.5.

(b) Make Use of Intangible Resources

A nonprofit's goodwill can be a highly valuable and useful resource. Opportunities abound today for a nonprofit to allow a credit-card company to use its logo for an "affinity card." Scientific discoveries or symphony performances can be licensed for public distribution. Tangible resources, such as museum spaces, gardens, football stadiums, auditoriums, and similar facilities may also have value outside their use by the organization. The resourceful nonprofit rents or otherwise creates revenues from these otherwise idle assets. Care and careful planning is required. The mailing list madness that has infected the United States is apparently beginning to lose its luster as the financial returns evaporate and environmentally conscious mailees ask that their names be removed from the lists. See Section 5.2.

Forming strategic alliances to leverage the nonprofit's know-how can also be lucrative. Cooperative research projects, educational conferences, and publications, for example, can spread administrative costs and maximize potential for return for all the partners working together on the projects. The business league that recognizes its need for a skilled financial manager it cannot afford to hire might try to find one or more similar leagues with whom to share such a person.

Merging two or more organizations can yield operational efficiencies and enhance the long-term financial viability of the nonprofits joining forces. A photographic exhibition space, sculpture garden, and a children's art center might fare better together rather than in competition with each other. A host of factors might indicate suitable candidates—nature of services provided, economic size, staff skills and longevity, board composition and organizational structure, and so on. See Section 7.4.

(c) Nonprofit Mentality Is Often "Penny Wise and Pound Foolish"

The financial success of some organizations stems from their ability to recruit cadres of volunteers and pounds of donated goods. They tap a wealth of support and goodwill and run on the belief that intangible assets can sustain them. Such resources must, however, be supported by a management structure capable of relieving overworked volunteers and underpaid staff members. Too many nonprofits suffer from classic burnout inefficiencies: lost grants from missed application deadlines, penalties and interest for failures to file returns or deposit payroll taxes, poor program performance, and high employee turnover. Some of a CPA firm's most troublesome clients (and often those with the highest fees) will be those organizations who sought volunteer help from somebody's friend who, unfortunately, had little or no experience with nonprofits. In most cases, a nonprofit operates much more efficiently with well-paid staff empowered to hire reputable experts as necessary.

(d) Financial Accounting for Nonprofits Is Different

A nonprofit should engage independent accountants who are both familiar with and experienced in providing accounting services to nonprofits. Expect the CPAs to be responsive to the organization's particular needs, to evaluate fiscal recordkeeping systems, and to make suggestions. Ask the CPAs to design readable financial reports that can be understood by nonaccountants. Expect them to translate the meaning of the numbers and the footnotes. Always ask if they have prepared a management letter and if so, follow up on the implementation of the suggestions included. Be sure the financials are presented using fund accounting, the preferred system for nonprofits to distinguish restricted and permanent funds from unrestricted moneys as discussed in Section 6.6.

Volunteer service organizations formed to provide assistance to nonprofit organizations exist in many cities throughout the United States. An organization in need of an accountant, lawyer, or other financial advisor experienced in nonprofits should identify such local volunteer groups. The CPA society, the bar association, and the united giving campaign organization typically have such public service programs. Such groups are a good resource for referrals to professionals who work with nonprofits, for educational materials, and information regarding resources available to nonprofits in the area. Some of them provide probono or sliding scale financial management services. Many sponsor educational classes and maintain a library of useful information. Public libraries in many cities have a special section devoted to nonprofits established in coordination with the Council on Foundations.

(e) Respect the Organizational Structure or Change It

People managing a nonprofit should read and understand the organization's charter and bylaws and then see that the rules are followed. Find out if the board of directors or trustees hold regular meetings documented with reasonably detailed minutes of its decisions? Are new board members and officers chosen annually in accordance with the bylaws? Is proper notice of meetings communicated with responsible parties in a timely manner? Does a board executive committee hold regular meetings with the organization's managers? See Section 2.2.

Determine whether the organization has a special relationship with another nonprofit; specific rules govern the activities of nonprofits established to support another organization. Does the organization use fund accounting to identify and maintain segregation of restricted funds?

(f) Know Who's in Charge

Separation of duties is a cardinal rule for fiscal responsibility. Know who's in charge and who's responsible for what. Financial management is more successful when the right mix of people are operating with a full knowledge of their job and the interrelationships between those jobs. The hierarchy established will depend on the form of organization. Most commonly, a nonprofit is managed by its Board of Directors which is either chosen by its membership or the existing board members themselves as a self-perpetuating body. The board sets policy; the staff carries out the programs and manages the organization according to the policies. The board must be sufficiently involved so that the staff does not function as the board. Board governance policies, expressed in written procedures, make it possible for all to know their role and work in concert. The written procedures can also facilitate certain tasks that are difficult, for example, firing an ineffectual but well-loved executive director. Does the board set policy or make daily operating decisions? See Chapter 2.

(g) Know Why the Nonprofit Organization Has Tax-Exempt Status

Ask to review Form 1023 or 1024, the original application seeking tax-exemption, to find out why the IRS decided the organization qualified for tax-exempt status. Look at a few years of operational history, such as the annual reports or Forms 990, to see if the purposes of the organization have changed or evolved. Identify the exempt constituency—those persons the organization was formed to serve. Ask whether exempt constituents are in fact being served or if, instead, the private interests of specific individuals are benefited to the detriment of the intended beneficiaries. Find out who's in charge of whatever reports are required by local, state, and federal authorities regulating the nonprofit and be assured they are timely filed. See Chapter 8.

(h) Enhancing Computer Capabilities May Not Cure Financial Ills

Late, incomplete, or irrelevant financial reports are not necessarily due to technological deficiencies. The learning curve for new hardware and software is often steep. If the lack of financial information is due to poor organizational structure, low personnel skill levels, or volunteer distraction, the problem will not be solved with new technology. Although computerized checkbook programs, such as Quicken, are not accounting programs, they may provide a good alternative for the modest nonprofit that lacks a staff person trained in bookkeeping and accounting.

On the other hand, the nonprofit should not skimp on the computer acquisition budget. A lot of valuable human resources are wasted on inadequate or ill-suited software. A donor database system is an invaluable fund raising tool that can also enhance volunteer efforts. Better yet (and correspondingly more costly) is an integrated financial reporting system that allows the donor data to be simultaneously entered in the accounting records and the donor database. See Section 6.2.

Getting on the World Wide Web to convey the nonprofit newsletter to members may quickly recoup the computer costs. In view of the ever-rising cost of mail and paper and the environmental bonus of the eliminated waste paper, this issue deserves special attention.

(i) Economic Conditions Must Be Anticipated

Economic conditions influence the nonprofit's revenue and expenditure flows and must be considered during the planning process. An inflationary or deflationary period may have a significant impact. The banking and real-estate price collapse in Houston during the 1980s certainly caused hardships for many nonprofits and the demise of those that were not properly prepared for the resulting economic changes.

The country's fiscal situation impacts those nonprofits receiving governmental funding. Following the 1994 elections, the political climate and demands for balanced Federal and state budgets caused significant changes in the way nonprofits are financed.

When reviewing a nonprofit's financial information, ask if the resources are reflected at current market values. In spite of the impact of inflation or deflation on asset values, many financial statements are issued with historical cost figures, with present values reflected only in the footnotes, if at all. Decisions based upon past numbers might be flawed. Reports issued by CPAs now are presented with current values of readily marketable assets. See Section 6.7.

(j) Producing an Audit Trail Benefits the Organization in Many Ways

Being able to connect the source document (for instance, an admission ticket) with the accounting reports provides the detail required for good budgeting and also facilitates information retrieval (in case the ticket buyer calls six months later for a copy of the receipt). Fiscal assets are safeguarded by such connections. It only takes a moment to indicate that an invoice has been paid with a particular check number on a particular day. Such a simple step prevents overpayments and provides the answer to many questions.

Well-meaning volunteer bookkeepers and treasurers may not be capable of or have the time to maintain proper records. Although hiring a part-time accounting clerk recommended by auditors may strain the budget at first, overall operational improvement may easily recoup the cost. Knowing who does what is particularly important for an organization with few or no staff members performing all the accounting tasks. It is critical to develop methods of checks and balances by establishing a good system of internal control. The person who opens the mail and records the financial transactions should never, for example, be permitted to sign the checks. See Section 6.8.

(k) Long-Range Planning Is Indispensable

Plotting the future of the organization according to agreed goals and objectives and converting them into definitive steps over a period of three, four, five, or more years greatly improves chances for success. Each program a nonprofit initiates requires energy and financial resources that are more economically recouped when the program functions successfully over a period of years. In other words, a decision to expend funds to launch or even continue programs should be made in view of their impact over a period of time. Thought of in business terms, the nonprofit invests its resources in each program it sponsors. One of the objectives of long-range planning is to evaluate the return on such investments over a number of years. Similarly, an important part of the planning process plots annual revenues and expenditures. Such budgets approved by the board prior to the beginning of each fiscal year and regularly monitored throughout the year can contribute immeasurably to a nonprofit's financial stability.

1.7 COMPREHENSIVE FINANCIAL PLANNING CHECKLIST

As a prelude to the book, the following checklist (Exhibit 1.2) presents a series of issues with specific questions to be asked in evaluating the financial well-being of a nonprofit organization. Chapters of the book in which the issues are explained in detail are noted. Some issues that are beyond the book's scope, such as insurance and investment manager performance, deserve attention with other references.

Exhibit 1.2.   Financial Planning Checklist for Nonprofit Organizations.

This checklist poses questions a nonprofit's chief financial officer in concert with the board treasurer or finance committee might review each year. Most answers should be yes, but some questions deserve a no answer or specific information. The objective is to comprehensively survey financial-planning issues that face a nonprofit organization at least annually.

A. Organizational Issues (Chapter 2)

  1. Is the organizational mission clearly defined? ☐

    a. Is the mission statement printed? ☐

    b. When was it updated? ☐

    c. What does IRS Form 1023 or 1024 say purposes are? ☐

  2. Does the nonprofit organization have a functioning board with members that exercise their fiduciary responsibilities? ☐

    a. Are board meetings regularly scheduled and well attended? ☐

    b. Does the executive committee supervise interim decisions? ☐

    c. Do minutes of directors' meetings reflect efforts to be responsive to exempt constituents by considering the best interests of the community (members or general public) served? ☐

    d. Are decisions made with the view that funds belong to public or members? ☐

  3. Should a finance committee of the board be established? ☐

  4. Do board and organizational policies insure management and control of the organization's resources? ☐

    a. Are prudent-investor rules followed? p. 2

    b. Are personal financial interests monitored? p. 2

    c. Is there short- and long-term financial and program budgeting? p. 3

    d. Are approved plans evaluated systematically? p. 4/5

    e. Is satisfaction of funding requirements monitored? p. 5

    f. Is proper risk management assured? p. 5/6

    g. Must information be disclosed to the public? p. 6

  5. Are government reporting requirements satisfied? p. 6

Exhibit 1.2. *(Continued)*

B. Monitoring Self-Dealing (Chapter 2)

1. Are there written policies governing financial transactions between the organization and its insiders (and families)? ☐

2. Should board members sign a formal conflict-of-interest statement? ☐

3. Were there any financial transactions with insiders this year? ☐

   a. Are compensation levels reasonable? ☐

   b. How do salaries compare to similar organizations? ☐

   c. Was anything brought from or sold to an insider? ☐

   d. If so, was fair market paid? ☐

   e. Was the value determined by independent parties? ☐

4. If such a transaction occurred, did private inurement result? ☐

5. Does the organization sell products or goods produced by volunteers or members? ☐

6. Did the NPO accept gifts that require other organizational funds to manage or conserve (a bailout)? ☐

C. Short- and Long-Term Budgeting (Chapter 4)

1. Is the budgeting process timed properly? ☐

   a. Do officers of the board change prior to budget approval? ☐

   b. When is the annual meeting? ☐

   c. Is budget approved after major funding requests are filed? ☐

2. What type of budget is appropriate for this organization? ☐

   a. Would zero-based budgeting allow critical evaluation of priorities to allow cutback in spending? ☐

   b. Would a functional expense or line-item budget allow for review of program goals? ☐

   c. Are budgets required for fund-raising events? ☐

3. Are the proper steps taken in the budget preparation process? (Chapter 3) ☐

   a. Are goals and objectives for a three- to five-year period developed first (long-range plan)? ☐

(Continued)

Exhibit 1.2. *(Continued)*

b. Are long-range goals quantified—raising an endowment, financing new facilities, or increasing staff. ☐

c. Are the prior year's results evaluated? ☐

   i. Were objectives achieved? ☐

   ii. If not, were they unreasonable? ☐

   iii. What caused variances? ☐

   iv. Were changes indicated by the ratio analyses? ☐

d. Have objectives for the coming year been established? ☐

e. Are new projects sufficiently documented? ☐

f. Are estimates of revenues and cost of programs realistic? ☐

g. Is the budget proposed by staff for approval by board (with intervening steps as the nature of organization dictates)? ☐

4. Are ancillary budgets prepared to implement the overall budget? ☐

   a. Cash flow projections? (Chapter 5) ☐

   b. Investment objectives? ☐

   c. Membership renewal tracking? ☐

   d. Capital expenditure timing? ☐

   e. Restricted fund budgets? ☐

5. Is a follow-up system for monitoring the budget in place? ☐

   a. Are financial reports timely, with actual expenses and income compared to those budgeted? ☐

   b. Are variances analyzed to determine why projects were wrong? ☐

   c. Is the budget revised for recurring changes during the year? ☐

D. Evaluating Performance with Ratio Analyses (Chapter 7)

1. Is the current ratio or working capital level (cash and other liquid assets compared to debts due in one year) at least 2:1? ☐

Exhibit 1.2. *(Continued)*

(Note that too low a ratio means short-term liquidity problems; too high sacrifices income for safety.) ☐

2. Is the acid test or quick ratio at least 11? (Cash today versus debts due in one month). ☐

3. Do contributors or members satisfy pledges on time? ☐

4. Compare this year's sources of funding to the past five years (has funding base changed?). ☐

5. Measure activity costs to overall expenses (how much of revenue devoted to exempt purposes?). ☐

6. Analyze profitability or lack of it for all income-producing activities. ☐

E. Satisfying Donor Restrictions (Chapter 5)

1. Are all restricted funds accounted for separately?

   a. Endowments. ☐

   b. Plant and equipment. ☐

   c. Restricted donations or grants. ☐

2. Does the cost of managing and reporting on a restricted fund outweigh its benefit? ☐

3. Can costs associated with restricted projects be identified? ☐

4. Are matching-fund grant records available to measure compliance? ☐

5. Is endowment income sacrificed for capital appreciation? ☐

6. What is the extent of, and reason for, interfund borrowing? ☐

F. Prudent-Investor Rules (Chapter 5)

1. Is maximum amount of interest earned on short-term cash funds? ☐

   a. Is cash flow planning utilized for liquid funds? ☐

   b. Are bills paid on a scheduled basis? ☐

(Continued)

Exhibit 1.2. *(Continued)*

    c. Are services invoiced timely allowing efficient collections? ☐

    d. Is there a membership renewal system? ☐

    e. Are non-interest-bearing accounts kept to a minimum? ☐

    f. Can tracing of restricted funds be accomplished through the accounting system rather than separate bank accounts? ☐

    g. Are higher long-term interest rates obtained on funds committed for use in over six months or a year? ☐

    h. Is short-term borrowing available if needed? ☐

2. Are investment policies prudent? ☐

    a. Is priority given to preservation of the endowment or to production of current income? ☐

    b. Are provisions made for replacement of the physical plant or facilities or adequate working capital for new projects? ☐

    c. Should property be leased or purchased? Mortgaged or not? ☐

3. Is an outside investment manager utilized? ☐

    a. Are investment yields measured using a "true" cost basis? ☐

    b. Should the organization use two different managers? ☐

    c. Are investments sufficiently diversified? ☐

    d. Should stocks be sold? Collections deaccessioned? ☐

4. Is the organization prepared for economic change?

    a. For disinflation or inflation? For business cycles? ☐

    b. How will new tax legislation affect the organization? ☐

    c. What are the funding source consequences of such changes? ☐

G. Hazards for Risk Management

  1. What measures are needed to protect assets from risk of loss? ☐

    a. Does the nonprofit organization have insurance or does it self-insure? ☐

Exhibit 1.2. *(Continued)*

b. Are deductible levels commensurate with working capital? ☐

c. Are properties maintained in good condition? ☐

d. Is adequate data available to identify lost items? ☐

e. Is property labeled and identified with organization's name? ☐

f. Are personnel required to be trained before using equipment? ☐

g. What is the condition of physical facilities in which they work? ☐

2. What types of insurance are appropriate for the organization?

a. Basic fire, theft, vandalism, and extended coverage? ☐

b. Liability? ☐

c. Workers' compensation? ☐

d. Volunteer/employee auto usage? ☐

e. Officers and directors' errors and omissions? ☐

f. Fidelity bond for employees/volunteers? ☐

H. Public Disclosure of Financial Condition (Chapter 6)

1. Are annual financials issued by independent accountant(s)? ☐

a. Is positive assurance provided by an audit appropriate? ☐

b. Would negative assurance provided by review suffice? ☐

c. Is a compilation sufficient? ☐

d. Is an audit required by funding agencies or foundation? ☐

e. Is a "single-audit" required under OMB A-133? ☐

f. Do revenue sources, level of internal accounting skills, or lack of internal control indicate a need for an audit? ☐

2. Have recommendations in the auditor's management letter been implemented? ☐

3. Are accounting/business staff and systems adequate? ☐

a. Are monthly financial reports, including budget comparisons, available in a timely manner? ☐

(Continued)

Exhibit 1.2.   *(Continued)*

---

b. Are they provided to the board? ☐

c. Would hiring a trained bookkeeper/accountant reduce outside accounting fees and/or allow timely reports? ☐

d. Should records be computerized? ☐

4. Is a system of internal control in place? ☐

a. Does the bookkeeper or custodian of funds sign checks? ☐

b. What contracts are approved by a board member? ☐

c. Is proper documentation required for expenditures? ☐

d. Are personnel policies in writing? ☐

e. Must expenditures in excess of the budget be approved? ☐

f. Are asset records adequate (serial numbers, etc.)? ☐

5. Are archival records evidencing exempt activities kept (theatre performance program, student grades, patient records)? (Chapter 8) ☐

6. Is a governmental reporting compliance calendar maintained? ☐

a. Are Forms 990, 990PF, or 990T filed timely? ☐

b. Are payroll taxes withheld, deposited timely reported? ☐

c. Must Forms 5500 be filed for benefit plans? ☐

7. Is Form 990 made available to public upon request? ☐

8. Are fund-raising or lobbying limit tax disclosures made? ☐

9. Must the nonprofit register as a charitable solicitator? ☐

CHAPTER TWO

Structuring the Organization for Fiscal Strength

Who's in charge? Who's responsible? The answers to such simple questions can mean the difference between a nonprofit's financial success and failure.

The manner in which positions are created and filled, duties are divided, and efforts are coordinated determines the degree to which an organization can carry out its mission in a fiscally sound manner. Financial management is most successful with the right mix of people all knowing what their jobs are. The board, along with the nonprofit's constituents, funders, and regulatory authorities, serve to monitor and help assure that the nonprofit carries out its mission in a fiscally sound manner. The hierarchy depends upon the form, maturity, and size of the organization, but together those in charge must:

- Plan for and measure funding needs.

- See that necessary resources are raised.

- Assure the acquired assets are dedicated to the nonprofit's mission.

- Keep financial records to prepare reports and analyses of financial activity.

- Comply with regulatory and grantor requirements.

A nonprofit organization's hierarchy is illustrated in the organizational charts similar to Exhibits 2.1a, b, and c. By showing exactly who will be in charge of what, this chart maps the relationship between the people responsible for meeting the objectives listed above. Job descriptions for each position detailing duties, responsibilities, and qualifications supplement the chart. Optimally, organizational and personnel policies are documented in a manual for all to see, understand, and follow.

Exhibit 2.1a.   State Association of Nonprofit Managers Organization Chart.

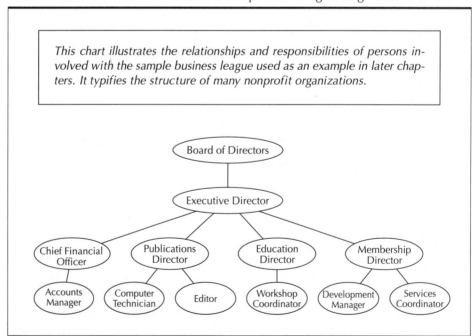

This chart illustrates the relationships and responsibilities of persons involved with the sample business league used as an example in later chapters. It typifies the structure of many nonprofit organizations.

Exhibit 2.1b. Endowed Educational Institution
Investment Management Organization.

This chart reflects only those persons involved in managing a nonprofit's investment activity. The Board of Trustees is ultimately responsible for forming policies regarding asset allocations, expected returns, risk tolerances, and other issues discussed in Section 5.7. In this example, the board delegates its responsibility to the finance committee which in turn has hired an outside investment manager to recommend and then implement such policies. The Chief Financial Officer works with the Finance Committee by providing budgetary projections of revenues required (see Sections 4.7 and 4.11), cash flow needed for operations (see Section 5.3), and follow-up periodic reports comparing budgets to actual investment results.

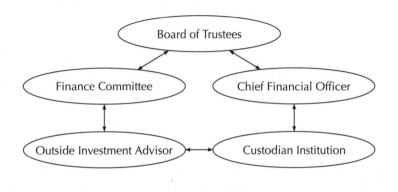

Exhibit 2.1c.   SHAPE Organizational Structure for Stabilization & Preservation.

This chart is used by SHAPE Community Center in Houston, Texas and portrays another way in which a nonprofit's management structure can be illustrated.

Board of Directors
Community volunteers with ultimate legal and financial authority/responsibility for SHAPE.

Executive Director

Management Staff
Operations; Program; Child Care Administration; Bookkeeping; Community Enterprises Managers: BETA Store, Cafe, Silkscreening Manufacturing & Sales

Operations & Programs Staff/Contractors
Includes paid staff/contractors and volunteers that perform day-to-day functions in the operation of SHAPE programs and services.

Council of Elders
Leaders of the community with wisdom and experience.

Community
Addressing the ever-changing needs of our community in both a responsive and proactive manner is the mission of SHAPE. What/who is our community in 1996? in 2006?

Advisory Council
Committee volunteers mobilized and working with the Board of Directors on (1) Short-term fundraising/financial/audit and operations matters and (2) Long-term development of strategic plan.

Fundraising/Finance/Audit Committee
Community volunteers representing private sector, public sector and children/families.

Operations Committee
Community volunteers representing private sector, public sector and children/families.

Strategic Planning Committee

2.1   ESTABLISHING THE HIERARCHY

Who's in charge and who's responsible are distinct issues. The governing body—usually the board of directors or trustees—is ultimately responsible for carrying out the nonprofit's mission and safeguarding its resources. The board, however, is entitled to delegate responsibility and the concomitant authority to a chief executive or operating officer (CEO). In other words, the CEO is in charge and manages the day-to-day affairs of the organization. Hopefully, the board can look to the CEO to lead the organization, manage programs that accomplish its mission, and represent the nonprofit organization in its community. The CEO in turn hires, works with, and supervises a chief financial officer, or CFO, and other necessary personnel.

The CFO may have one of many titles, including CFO, Vice President for Finance, Chief Financial Officer, Director of Finance, Business Manager, Controller, or even Treasurer. The CFO participates in planning and budgeting and then follows up by monitoring cash inflows and outflows, making sure financial resources are actually devoted to planned purposes, and seeing that expenditures remain in balance with available assets.

Typically a nonprofit organization is focused on its mission and places most emphasis on its programs. For good reasons, precious resources are allocated to hiring the best possible professionals—the teachers, the physicians, or the artists. Those creative individuals often lack financial training and experience. When department heads are selected for other than business skills, the CFO's financial skills may be vital to an organization's fiscal health. Reliance on the CFO also grows with the size and program scope of the nonprofit organization. The financial affairs of a statewide nonprofit organization with branches in 20 towns are necessarily more complicated than the affairs of a church with a congregation of 200 persons.

Who beyond the board, the CEO, and the CFO should be involved in financial planning depends again upon the size, breadth, and maturity of the organization. Program managers, department heads, volunteer committee chairs, and other persons actively involved in carrying out the nonprofit's activities can and, some say, should participate in the planning processes. Their input is particularly useful in budget preparation as described in Section 4.6. Outside accountants serve an important oversight role as discussed below in Section 2.5. The best financial planning team will be unique to each individual nonprofit. For guidance the planners can consider the fashion in which for-profit businesses organize themselves.[1]

2.2 THE ROLE OF THE BOARD

A nonprofit organization is typically governed by its board of directors or trustees. Although the board controls the organization, the board members do not beneficially own the organization and may not operate it to serve their own private purposes or those of their families. Board members are expected to carry out the organization's mission in the best interest of its constituents—the charitable beneficiaries or members. Upon dissolution, a nonprofit organization exempt as a charity must either give its remaining assets to, or spend them on, a charitable purpose. No charitable funds may be returned to donors or board members. A business league, a union, and other mutual societies may, under certain circumstances, rebate its accumulated surplus to members if building such a reserve was not a primary purpose of the organization. Nevertheless, the governors of a mutual society must also serve without self-interest.

The board members govern and direct the nonprofit's affairs, but are not expected to operate it. The board selects officers and agents to whom it delegates the job of managing day-to-day activities. This separation of roles is key to allowing the director's to oversee and monitor the organization's activities. In a modest-sized nonprofit with few staff members to manage the organization, some directors may necessarily serve in overlapping positions. Especially in those situations, board policies should be established to prevent board interference in operations.

(a) Standards for Directors

Depending on the legal form of organization, a nonprofit's governors may have a variety of titles, including directors, trustees, council members, or elders. Their responsibilities, termed fiduciary duties by the legal profession, have evolved through local legislation and judicial interpretations. Specific duties are set out in the Model Nonprofit Corporation Act to establish a standard of conduct to which an individual corporate director

[1] A thorough discussion of organizational structure for nonprofit organizations is beyond this book, but the bibliography contains several references that can be studied by those seeking more information on the subject.

can adhere.[2] Conducting oneself in accordance with the rules provides a director some protection if a controversy arises. The extent of such legal protection will vary from state to state and may apply differently to trustees of private trusts. The rules of conduct should serve as a guide in establishing a nonprofit's organizational structure and determining the reliance the management and funders can place in the board.

The model says a director's fiduciary duties fall into two basic categories: the duty of care and the duty of loyalty. These duties require the director or trustee, including his or her duties as a member of a committee, to exercise caution and prudence in establishing policies and making decisions regarding the organization. Attentive management is required. The director's duty of care expects one to act in good faith and fulfill his or her responsibilities by:

- Exercising independent judgment when participating in decisions of the board.

- Being informed as to data relevant to board decisions.

- Regularly attending meetings.

- Monitoring the organization's activities, assessing the efficiency of the organizational structure, and providing for both short- and long-range planning.

A director may make decisions based upon information and reports received from others whom the director reasonably regards as trustworthy. In reviewing information, the director is expected to use good common sense. Decisions should be made using what in a for-profit corporate setting is called the "Business Judgment Rule."[3] The rules allow a director to rely on information, opinions, reports, or statements, including financial statements and other financial data, if prepared or presented by:

- One or more officers or employees of the corporation whom the director reasonably believes to be reliable and competent in the matters presented;

---

[2] The American Bar Association Business Law Section published its suggested Revised Model Nonprofit Corporation Act in 1987 that has been adopted by some states. The rules applicable to a particular state may vary.

[3] *Guidebook for Directors of Nonprofit Corporations,* Nonprofit Corporations Committee, Section of Business Law, American Bar Association, Chicago, Illinois, page 27.

- Legal counsel, public accountants, or other persons as to matters the director reasonably believes are within their professional or expert competence;

- A committee of the board of which the director is not a member, as to matters within its jurisdiction, if the director reasonably believes the committee merits confidence.

The Duty of Loyalty requires a director act with trustworthiness and integrity. Honest management is required. The director's actions must be in allegiance to the organization, its mission, and the constituents to be served. A director who takes advantage of the organization's assets, for example, for purposes other than those of the organization violates the duty of loyalty. A conflict of interest policy as described in Section 2.7 can be adopted to govern a transaction that might cause a violation of this rule. A director whose private interests are in conflict must disclose that fact and absent his or herself from decisions regarding the conflicted matter. A director also has a responsibility to keep information about the organization's affairs in confidence until it is publicly disclosed.

Each nonprofit director or trustee should be familiar with the specific standards applicable to the state(s) in which the nonprofit operates. Since directors who follow the standards are provided some legal protection, prospective directors will want to be assured the nonprofit has organized itself in a fashion that will enable them to act in compliance with the standards.

(b)   A Director's Duties

A nonprofit director's role is to act on behalf of others. Whether or not called trustees, directors are in a position of trust. Their wards are the members of the general public the organization was established to serve. Their relationship to the organization is much like that of parent to child. As the nonprofit's parents, directors oversee and provide guidance based (one hopes) on their good judgment and integrity. The organization's volunteers and staff (sometimes including the directors) must be left to grow and function independently while relying upon the directors to maintain a structure within which the mission can be accomplished.

The actual tasks performed by the director depend again upon the size and scope of the nonprofit's activities. At a minimum, a director should regularly attend board meetings for the purpose of reviewing and condoning the activities that are carried out on a daily basis by the managers and staff. Meeting dates should be regular—first Mondays of the month at 5 PM, for example. Minutes of the meetings should be circulated in advance of the succeeding meeting at which their approval is requested. The applicable code of conduct for directors of nonprofit organizations found in state law defining fiduciary responsibility should always be followed.[4] Exhibit 2.2 provides a checklist for visualizing and actualizing the standards applicable to the fiduciary role and contains suggested issues for which the director is responsible.

(c) Reviewing Financial Reports

The duty of care requires that a director be informed regarding the nonprofit organization's financial affairs. Board members actively involved in the affairs of a modestly sized nonprofit organization may need to receive and review all the reports listed in Exhibit 2.3. It is prudent for board members in nonprofits of all sizes to receive and review the independent accountants' reports and the monthly status reports, items 1 and 2 on the Inventory of Financial Reports. In a larger organization with functioning finance and executive committees, the board may delegate total responsibility to the committee members to oversee financial affairs. If he or she does nothing else, each director should review the annual opinion accompanying the financial reports prepared by outside accountants. It is not sufficient, in my opinion, for the board treasurer to simply say to the board members, "Everything is OK, so you need not worry to read the auditor's report."

The financial reports are most useful when they are issued and reviewed close to the closing date of the financial information. Unfortunately, nonprofit organizations that receive reduced-fee or pro bono accounting services may not be able to expect timely service. For a calendar-year nonprofit, timely service would mean receipt of the outside accountants' reports by the directors no later than March 31. Monthly activity reports with budget comparisons should be expected by the twentieth of each succeeding month. The time frame for budget planning is discussed in Section 4.4.

Chapter 6 contains brief descriptions of an accounting system's components and explains the fashion in which financial information is accumulated and presented. Accounting terms like accrual method, restricted funds, and receivables are defined according to the new accounting standards and sample financial statements are provided. A nonprofit

---

[4] Ibid. Note 2.

Exhibit 2.2.   A Board Member's Checklist of Fiduciary Duties.

This checklist can serve as a board member's guide to meeting fiduciary re-sponsibilities. Some questions have simple yes/no answers for actions taken personally by the director. Others prompt the director to ask if others have carried out responsibilities delegated by the board.

The Duty of Care

1. Am I sufficiently informed to perform my director role with prudence and caution?

   a. Do I regularly attend board and committee meetings? ☐

   b. Have I read the charter and bylaws? ☐

   c. Did I review the mission statement, long-range plans, basis for tax exemption, and other documents? ☐

   d. Have I become informed about any significant contractual obligations or potential claims on organizational assets? ☐

   e. Are minutes of all board and committee meetings sent to members regularly in advance of meetings? ☐

   f. Are periodic financial reports, compared to approved budget amounts and received on a timely basis? ☐

   g. Are the organization's newsletters and other publications reviewed regularly to assure adherence to exempt purposes? ☐

   h. Are meetings of sufficient length and frequency to allow adequate discussion of the issues? ☐

   i. Are independent consultants with adequate knowledge engaged to provide expert advice when needed? ☐

2. Is the organizational structure adequate to assure an efficient and fiscally sound operation?

   a. Are internal financial controls in place? ☐

   b. Do independent accountants issue financial reports at least once a year? ☐

   c. Are local, state, and federal compliance rules followed?

     • Has an exempt status checklist been completed? ☐

     • Is charitable solicitation registration required? ☐

     • Are payroll tax deposits current? ☐

Exhibit 2.2. *(Continued)*

- Are ERISA/Labor Department standards followed? ☐
- Do private foundation rules apply? ☐

d. Are personnel policies written, published, and monitored at least annually by a board committee? ☐

e. Have restricted or endowment fund covenants been met? ☐

f. Is investment performance for endowment, working capital, and restricted funds monitored regularly? ☐

g. Are duties delegated sufficiently? ☐

h. Should an executive committee be formed? ☐

i. Are other board committees needed? ☐

j. Should staff serve on the board? ☐

3. Do long- and short-range financial plans exist?

a. Are financial budgets for 1 to 3 year periods approved before the fiscal year begins? ☐

b. Is ratio analysis applied to periodic financial information to detect problem areas? ☐

c. Are staff members required to develop feasibility plans for proposed projects? ☐

d. Are plans monitored after approval to assure accomplishment of both financial and organizational goals? ☐

4. Can I rely on staff and consultants?

a. Are the legal and accounting advisors independent? ☐

b. Is the quality of the service rendered high? Are they sufficiently knowledgeable about nonprofits? ☐

c. Can I satisfy the "business judgment" rule?

d. Is the executive director evaluated periodically? Does she or he conduct regular personnel reviews? ☐

e. Can volunteers be relied upon? ☐

5. Are board members involved, qualified, and dedicated?

a. Is there a good system for seeking new members? ☐

b. Are efforts made to balance skills and interests? ☐

c. Are the interests of the constituents represented? ☐

(Continued)

Exhibit 2.2. *(Continued)*

d. Is there rotation of members, or staggered terms? ☐

e. Is there new-member orientation? ☐

f. Are board members provided a written manual of organization documents, policies and procedures? ☐

The Duty of Loyalty

1. Do I have allegiance to the organization? Am I satisfied that the organization is accomplishing its mission and serving its constituents?

   a. Am I sure resources are dedicated in accordance with the charter, trust instrument, and funding agreements? ☐

   b. Are exempt purposes being carried out? ☐

   c. Are assets preserved and replenished? ☐

   d. Is there honest and efficient management? ☐

2. Do I oversee and supervise appropriately with regard to my position?

3. Do I use my position and power to advance personal interests?

   a. Am I, my business, or my family involved in a conflict of interest with the organization? ☐

   b. If any self-interested transaction occurs, is due diligence exercised to ensure that no private benefit results? ☐

   i. Did I fully inform other members of the board? ☐

   ii. Did I absent myself from discussion and voting? ☐

   iii. Is there adequate outside evaluation and appraisal of the transaction? ☐

   d. Does the nonprofit organization have a written conflict of interest policy? ☐

   e. Are there interlocking directorates or affiliated for-profit or nonprofit entities? ☐

Exhibit 2.3.   Inventory of Financial Reports.

A suggested list of financial reports needed by board members to oversee a nonprofit's financial affairs follows. The duty to review may be delegated to the finance or executive committee dependent upon the nonprofit's structure. Indicate date of review and whether or not delegated.

Type of Financial Report	Delegated	Date
1. Independent accountants' financial statements.		
• Opinion letter	(yes/no)	_____
• Statement of Net Assets	(yes/no)	_____
• Statement of Activity or Statement of Changes in Net Assets	(yes/no)	_____
• Statement of Cash Flows	(yes/no)	_____
• Notes to Financial Statements	(yes/no)	_____
• Management letter	(yes/no)	_____
2. Monthly status reports with actual compared to budget.	(yes/no)	_____
• Ratio analyses and statistical program service reports.	(yes/no)	_____
• Investment performance.	(yes/no)	_____
3. Projected budgets for future periods		
• Operational revenues and costs by function	(yes/no)	_____
• Capital expenditures	(yes/no)	_____
• Cash flow analyses	(yes/no)	_____
• Fund-raising projections	(yes/no)	_____
4. Personnel report showing number of permanent, temporary, and volunteer workers; compensation, raises, vacation accruals, benefit costs, compared to the prior year.	(yes/no)	_____
5. Insurance/risk management evaluation with associated costs.	(yes/no)	_____
6. Financial Planning and Annual Tax Compliance checklists.	(yes/no)	_____

manager or volunteer board member who lacks financial training can study Chapter 6 to enhance his or her ability to read the financial reports and participate in financial decisions they, as board members, are required to make.

2.3 FILLING BOARD POSITIONS

There is merit in the view that the board should include a lawyer, an accountant, a banker, a philanthropist, a doctor (for a hospital), a scholar (for a school), and so on. Ideally, board positions are filled with persons who, in combination, have the requisite skills to promote efficient functioning, maximization of financial resources, and successful performance of the nonprofit's worthy goals. To achieve this objective, begin by defining management positions in the areas of proficiency required for smooth operation, for example, finance, human resources, program development and management, planning, and oversight. Then, seek prospects with knowledge and experience in such areas.

(a) Finding Prospects

The nominating committee's job is to find candidates whose talents will contribute to the organization's success. Suitable candidates also exhibit a personal commitment to, or interest in, the nonprofit organization's mission. Posing a few questions will narrow the selection process:

- Will the nominee spend the time the job requires?
- Has he or she been involved as a volunteer or participant in the nonprofit's activities or in a similar project of another nonprofit?
- How long has the prospect been a member or donor?
- Are his or her friends or business associates involved?
- Will he or she enhance the respect of the community for the nonprofit?
- What technical skills will he or she bring to the organization?

The nonprofit organization should communicate its expectations clearly to prospective board members and organize itself to facilitate the involvement of new members.[5] Policies and procedures that include definitions of duties can be developed in a fashion similar to that discussed in Section 2.4 in the context of the financial management.

(b) Staff Representation on the Board

A commonly raised question is whether paid staff members can serve on a nonprofit's board of directors. There is no federal prohibition against having a paid staff member as a board member. In Texas, a director may serve in a staff capacity for compensation as long as the pay is reasonable and not in violation of his or her fiduciary responsibility. In California, on the other hand, no more than 49 percent of the board members may be staff members. Obviously, this question should be investigated under the laws of the state in which the nonprofit exists.

Whether or not it is a good idea to have staff representation on the board is another issue. Strong opinions, usually based on experience, are held on opposing sides. Those that favor staff representation argue that the voice of staff can only add to realistic decision making, especially when decisions will impact staff operations. The contrary view is that staff are not in a position to exercise the necessary oversight for an impartial decision-making process. Nonprofit organizations should, however, consider including the chief staff person on the board or, at the very least, letting him or her be present at board meetings.

(c) Compensation for Board Service

Another issue is whether board members can receive director's fees or be compensated for serving on the board. Again, local law applies. Texas, for example, permits such payment as long as the amount paid represents reasonable compensation for the work performed. Even private foundations can pay reasonable compensation to related parties for services rendered.[6]

---

[5] The Nonprofit Management Series Booklets published by Independent Sector, Washington, D.C., contain a wealth of information on this subject. Booklet 2 (out of 9) of the series is entitled *Finding, Developing, and Rewarding Good Board Members*, by Brian O'-Connell (17 pages). O'Connnell's book, *The Board Member's Book*, is also a good resource on the subject and is published by The Foundation Center, New York.

[6] Internal Revenue Code § 4941 entitled *Self-Dealing*, prohibits most financial transactions between directors and trustees and the foundation regardless of the benefit gained by the foundation.

If directors are to be paid compensation or are to be involved in any other financial transaction with the nonprofit, follow the organizational protocol for conflicts of interest. The National Charities Information Bureau recommends no fees be paid to board members except to reimburse the cost of board participation. See standards reprinted in appendix. See Section 2.7 for a discussion of the adoption of a conflict-of-interest policy.

(d) Number of Directors

To prevent deadlocks in voting, keep the number of directors to an *odd* number. In deciding on the appropriate odd number, consider the role the board members will play in governance. What skills are needed for what committees? How much supervision does the staff require? What amount of work is expected to be accomplished by board committees? Answers to these questions can help arrive at the total number of directors suitable for a particular organization. Keep in mind the bylaws might need to be changed to increase the number. Even though the organizers of a newly established nonprofit expects it can function with 7 or 9 board members, it might be advisable for the bylaws to allow a much larger number, say up to 21 to leave room for future growth.

Some organizations prefer to limit the number of board members. Many people choose not to accept the responsibility and potential liability of serving as a board member. For these reasons and others, organizations may wish to establish an advisory groups auxiliary to its board. This group usually includes persons who bring credibility to the organization through their positions in the community and specialized skills.

2.4 ROLE OF THE TREASURER AND THE CFO

As the typical nonprofit organization is conceived and begins its life, activities may be performed and managed by volunteers. Often, there are few, if any, paid staff members. In many cases, the young nonprofit cannot afford to pay independent accountants or even a bookkeeper. The work of paying the bills, preparing the financials, and reconciling the accounts may fall to the board treasurer. Nonetheless, the nonprofit should adopt policies and procedures that define the roles that will, as the organization matures, be performed by different people. Exhibit 2.4 provides

Exhibit 2.4.   Roles of the Treasurer and the Chief Financial Officer.

> *The separate roles of the board treasurer and the chief financial officer are outlined in this checklist. The distinction in the positions should be respected and written, even if the organization in its earliest stages has one person performing both roles.*

The Board Treasurer

Exercise of Fiduciary Responsibility.

- Attend meetings and actively participate in activities. ☐
- Assure development of short- and long-term policies/plans. ☐
- Monitor policies/plans with regular financials. ☐
- Review financial transactions among insiders and the nonprofit. ☐

Assurance of Financial Accountability.

- Oversee inside/outside accountants. ☐
- Establish financial committee of board, if organizational size dictates. ☐
- Monitor internal controls and procedures. ☐
- Depending on staff size and capability, the board treasurer may also:
  - Cause to be prepared or prepare regular financial reports and budgets. ☐
  - Sign checks. ☐
  - Negotiate contracts/purchases. ☐
  - Oversee compliance filings and public information. ☐
  - Manage or cause investments to be managed. ☐

Chief Financial Officer

Responsibility for Financial Data.

- Process primary financial documents (bills, payments, bank statements, donor information, etc.) as they are received into the organization. ☐
- Monitor investments, receivables, payables, inventories, and other financial matters requiring supervision. ☐

(Continued)

Exhibit 2.4. *(Continued)*

- Follow internal control procedures and accounting systems manual. ☐
- Produce accounting journals and ledgers. ☐
- Maintain filing system. ☐
- Create efficient audit trail. ☐
- Label files for record retention purposes. ☐
- Identify restricted fund transactions. ☐

Produce financial reports.

- Basic financials, including Statement of Net Assets (Balance Sheet), Statement of Activity (Support, Revenue, and Expenses), Statement of Cash Flows, Statement of Functional Expenses (by program). ☐
- Supplemental planning reports for:
  - Event income/expense, cash flow projection. ☐
  - Daily sales/attendance/contributions reports. ☐
- Maintain compliance with governmental regulations and reports.
  - Maintain payroll system and deposit taxes timely. ☐
  - File all reports due according to compliance calendar. ☐
  - Compliance with granting agency reporting/application deadlines. ☐
- Coordinate timing and work with outside auditors, both CPAs and governmental/agency.
  - Prepare workpapers and detail analyses requested. ☐
  - Respond timely with information requested. ☐
- Plan for, develop, and coordinate approval of budget(s). ☐

Facilitate Flow of Financial Information.

- Work with and train volunteers. ☐
- Work with the board treasurer. ☐
- Prepare any financial analyses requested by finance committee and board; and attend meetings when invited. ☐
- Review policies/procedures and provide recommendations to the board regarding fiscal management. ☐
- Maintain technical skills required to perform the job and seek qualified advisors when needed. ☐

a model for establishing duties appropriate to the separate roles of a Board Treasurer and a Chief Financial Officer.

2.5 INSIDE AND OUTSIDE ACCOUNTANTS

A certified public accountant (CPA) is trained to evaluate the financial condition of an entity and issue reports to explain such condition. A CPA will also evaluate the systems for maintaining financial records and securing internal control over the entity's funds. The CPA's technical skills and experience are also useful in budgeting, financial planning, computer system design, and other financial aspects of a nonprofit organization.

Although CPAs bring valuable skills to a board of directors, the AICPA code of ethics stipulates that the CPA must be independent of an entity to issue an audited opinion. An independent CPA does not serve on the board of directors or have a financial interest in the nonprofit. Other levels of financial reporting may be issued by a CPA who serves on an organization's board. However, it is advisable for all organizations to adopt a policy of retaining independent accountants for financial reports including reviews and compilations as well as audits.

(a) Financial Management Team

Ideally, the complete financial management team consists of the board finance committee headed by the treasurer, outside advisors (investment managers or bankers), the chief financial officer, the staff (the inside accountants), and the advice of the independent CPAs (the outside accountants). In reality, a nonprofit's resources or circumstances may not allow it to engage all desirable members for the creation of such a team. In such cases, the organization should identify and analyze the consequence of overlapping or combined roles.

Some combinations of duties simply cannot be performed effectively by a single member of the financial team. Consider a church treasurer who also serves as the church bookkeeper and essentially functions as the chief financial officer. In such a situation , another board member (elder) should sign checks and oversee and review the financials, although this duty would, if the team were complete, be the treasurer's.

As the functions involved in evaluating the nonprofit's financial affairs become complicated, the finance committee can be fragmented. The new parts might include a budget committee, an audit committee, and an investment committee, and others devoted to specific issues, such as new building construction or salary review.

(b) Defining *Inside* and *Outside Accountants*

Inside accountants are primarily responsible for financial reporting and planning on a daily basis. They pay the bills, collect the money, and keep the books. They plan, prepare, and monitor budgets, see that sufficient resources are available for the tax-exempt mission, and maximize the use of available resources for the benefit of the organization's constituents.

The *outside* accountants evaluate financial reports prepared by inside accountants and inform the public regarding the validity of the financials by issuing a formal opinion. The treasurer, with the help of the finance committee, coordinates the work of both inside and outside accountants. To provide a credible evaluation, the outside accountants must be truly independent, or impartial. They must be free of any vested interest in the organization. Appropriate fiscal control can only be achieved with the division of these duties. The prudent organization will not rely on a single volunteer treasurer to serve as both its inside accountant, by keeping its books, and its outside accountant, by issuing an opinion about the periodic financial statements stemming from such records.

2.6 SELECTING FINANCIAL REPORTING SERVICES

CPAs perform three levels of financial reporting service: audits, reviews, and compilations. The highest level of reliance can be placed on audits. But all three services can be used to present the nonprofit organization's financial statements. For all three services, the starting point in the CPA's evaluation process is the nonprofit organization's internally produced financials. The following discussion details what is involved in each level of service.

(a) Understanding the Auditing Process

An audit provides the highest degree of assurance an accountant can offer that the financial statements are a fair presentation of the data shown. The CPA examines the financial records for the reporting period and certifies that the information is reliable. The accountant's report includes a reminder that the financial statements are the representations of the organization's management.

In performing an audit, the CPA conducts tests and procedures designed to ascertain the accuracy of the reported financial information. By no means are all transactions audited or examined. The CPA looks at a representative sample to determine whether one can reasonably expect that the procedures and documentation maintained for those selected items are indicative for all records. The CPA considers the level of internal auditing inherent in the nonprofit's organizational structure. The internal controls are reviewed to determine whether the nonprofit's system of checks and balances and its division of duties functions to prevent misstatements or diversions of resources. See also Section 4.8 for further discussion of this matter.

The most important step in the process is to obtain outside verification of the organization's reported transactions for the year. The auditor writes to a sampling of the nonprofit's contributors and creditors, asking them to confirm the transactions by sending verification or explanation of differences directly to the CPA. Similarly, the auditor requests the nonprofit's bank(s) to confirm or deny the existence of the accounts and the accuracy of the balances stated in the organization's balance sheet. Grantees may also be contacted to verify the receipt and purpose of the grants. The responses to such requests for outside verification are to be returned directly to the CPA firm.

The objective of this confirmation process is to go beyond the nonprofit organization's own record of the transactions. Independent validation enables the CPA to offer its assurance that the reported amounts are correct. Such validation creates an important distinction in the level of reliance that can be placed on an audit as opposed to either a review or compilation. The types of opinions that may be issued by the auditor are

- *Unqualified:* An unqualified opinion says the financials clearly reflect the nonprofits financial position and operating results. It may also be referred to as a *clean* opinion.

- *Qualified:* In a qualified opinion, the CPA says "except for . . ." all is accurate. (In situations where, for example, branch offices were not audited, appraisals were not obtained for a significant asset, or an inventory count was not performed in a timely manner at year end, a qualified opinion will be required).

- *Adverse:* The financial statements do not fairly present the financial situation or there is a question as to whether the nonprofit is a going concern (that is, debts exceed assets).

- *Disclaim:* The CPA is unable to express an opinion.

(b) When to Audit

Nonprofits seek audited financial reports for a variety of reasons. Many governmental funding agencies and grantor foundations require an audited financial report. The Office of Management and Budget requires a special *Single Audit* of certain federal grants. Some national or statewide organizations require their branches or chapters to obtain audited financial statements.

Without an imposed requirement that the organization seek an audit, many organizations consider the expense involved worth the result. The persons responsible for the nonprofit's financial affairs may seek an audit to satisfy their duty of care, discussed in Section 2.2. Situations that may indicate a need for an audit, rather than a review or compilation, include:

- The nonprofit's funding sources allow for misappropriation. Donations collected by volunteers, sales of donated goods, individual ticket sales for public performances or trade shows are all examples of such funding sources.

- The sheer number of financial transactions deserves outside verification.

- Activities are conducted in a number of different locations.

- Internal control procedures are poor and need scrutiny and suggestions for improvement.

(c) Review and Compilation Processes

In performing a review, the CPA makes inquiries and evaluates the reasonableness of the financial information provided by the organization. However, no opinion is given as to the validity of the figures. The review opinion simply offers the negative assurance that the CPA found nothing wrong. Depending on the nonprofit's size and complexity, an annual review may suffice to meet the board's fiduciary duty to oversee fiscal management.

A review might, for example, be an appropriate level of CPA service for a smaller organization with modest assets whose board members monitor the financial affairs regularly. An appropriate review candidate would be a nonprofit with a good internal control system and an active CPA treasurer who reconciles the banking records and prepares monthly financials throughout the year. A review may also serve the interests of a grant-making private foundation whose endowment is held in marketable securities, managed by a professional investment advisor.

In compiling, the CPA takes information from the nonprofit's accounting records and arranges them in financial statement format. No outside verifications, inquiries, analyses, or tests occur. Compilations are usually prepared for internal purposes only or as a by-product of the preparation of a tax return. Basically, the CPA preparing a compilation functions as an internal accountant. In larger organizations, a monthly compilation might be prepared for the board in addition to the year-end review or audit.

(d) Requests for Proposals for Accounting Services

When seeking the services of an accounting firm for an audit, review, or compilation, organizations customarily request proposals from one or more firms. Exhibit 2.5 presents a model proposal letter.

2.7 CONFLICT-OF-INTEREST POLICY

The Model Nonprofit Corporation Act requires that the directors of a nonprofit corporation abide by a Duty of Loyalty. As explained more fully in Section 2.2 above, the director must act in the best interest of the organization, not in their own interest. The federal tax law specifically requires that no profits or assets of an exempt organization inure to the benefit of officers and directors or other private individuals. Private foundations are specifically prohibited from most financial transactions involving their directors and major contributors.

A fiscally prudent nonprofit organization will adopt a conflict-of-interest policy to ensure that personal benefit is not given to insiders as financial decisions are made. The policy expresses the nonprofit's ethical obligation to use resources solely for the benefit of constituents (or members). Transactions involving insiders are not necessarily prohibited, but they must be fully disclosed and subjected to scrutiny. All relationships and possible self-interest must be revealed and examined in a document similar to Exhibit 2.6.

Exhibit 2.5.   Request for Proposal for Audit.

The following letter requests a proposal from an accounting firm for an audit. Sending such letters to more than one accounting firm enables the organization to make comparisons before it makes its selection.

Community Benefit Projects
Hometown, Texas

John J. Adams, Partner
Adams, Banks, & Coffee, CPAs
1111 National Bank Building
Hometown, Texas 77777

Dear Mr. Adams,

COMMUNITY BENEFIT PROJECTS (CBP) services the people of Hometown in many ways. We help the underprivileged by conducting training classes for the unemployed, after-school programs for sports and tutoring for our youths, aid senior citizens with shut-in visits and transportation services, and greet newcomers to town with information and referrals. CBP invites you to submit a proposal to conduct audits of our financial statement and related information for the year 19xx. The audits must be in accordance with generally accepted accounting principles and meet governmental reporting requirements.

Audits: We are required to have two audits as follows:

* Audit of statement of net assets, statement of activity and functional activities, and statement of cash flows.
* Single audit of our grants required under OMB Circular A-133, *Audits of Institutions of Higher Education and Other Nonprofit Institutions,* and the U.S. General Accounting Office's *Government Auditing Standards.*

Tax Work: In addition to the annual audit, we require the following tax returns be prepared for filing in a timely manner:

* Form 990, Return of Organization Exempt from Income Tax,
* Form 990-T, Exempt Organization Business Income Tax Return.

Work Schedule: Our staff is available to provide support and preparation of the underlying schedules based upon

Exhibit 2.5. *(Continued)*

your guidelines. We would prefer that you arrange a planning meeting in December prior to our year end. We expect the books will be closed by February 12, so that you could schedule the field work after that time. The report must be completed in draft form for presentation to the finance committee on March 20. The final report must be completed by March 31, the date of our annual meeting.

Qualifications: Please provide a description of your firm's qualifications to serve a tax-exempt organization such as ours, resumes of key personnel, and a list of other nonprofit organization clients.

Fee: Your audit proposals should reflect the total fee and include the time budgets for audit and tax work reflecting the number of hours and rate per hour for assigned personnel. (Note many nonprofit organizations request reduced rates in recognition of their nonprofit status.)

Site Visit: We would welcome you to visit our offices in the coming weeks to obtain information necessary to make an accurate proposal You can call our controller, Ms. Joan Levy, to schedule an appointment.

Proposal Deadline: The proposal must be submitted by October 10. The finance committee will meet October 20 to review proposals and make a recommendation to the board of directors regarding the choice of auditors.

If you have any questions or would like further clarification of any aspect of this request for auditing services, please contact me or our senior manager, Harry Smart. We look forward to receiving your proposal.

Sincerely,

John J. Hay, CFO

Exhibit 2.6. Conflict-of-Interest Questionnaire for Board Members.

> *A questionnaire similar to the one below may be used to make directors aware of the nonprofit's policy regarding conflicts of interest. The answers provide disclosure, identify, and explore the potential for self-interest arising in financial transactions.*

Nonprofit organization (name the organization) is a tax-exempt organization which operates to benefit the general public (or the xyz profession, certain workers, or church congregants or other suitable description of exempt constituents). We intend to avoid any possible conflict between the personal interests of those that govern our organization and operate it and our constituents. Therefore, we ask each of our board members and responsible staff persons to complete and sign this conflict-of-interest policy questionaire.

Name: _____

Position in
nonprofit organization: _____

Relationships: List any businesses in which you or members of your immediate family (parents, siblings, grandparents, children) have a financial interest through employment or private ownership.

name of business   nature of relationship
_____   _____
_____   _____
_____   _____

Permitted Transactions: Circumstances may arise in which it would be financially beneficial to do business with you, your relations, or friends. Our policy allows transactions that are clearly shown to benefit our organization based upon the information indicated below and approval by a two-thirds majority of the directors, not counting the interested party(ies).

Proposed Sale or Service: Describe a proposed financial transaction:
_____
_____
_____

CONFLICT-OF-INTEREST POLICY

Exhibit 2.6. *(Continued)*

	Related Party	Bidder #1	Bidder #2
Suggest price:	_____	_____	_____
Payment Terms:	_____	_____	_____
Delivery date:	_____	_____	_____
Other terms:	_____	_____	_____

To the best of my knowledge and belief, except as disclosed above, neither I nor any person with whom I have or intend to have a personal or business relationship is engaged in any transaction or activity or has any relationship that may represent a potential competing or conflicting interest as defined in the statement of policy.

Date: _____   Signature: _____

Financing the Dream

Nonprofit organizations are based on hope, sometimes on prayer, and almost always on dreams. Optimum planning can turn dreams into realizable goals.

A nonprofit's reason for existence or its primary goals are mission-based—to cure the sick, to advance a profession, to discover new technologies, to educate the public, and to do other tasks of benefit to others. The nonprofit's financial goals are secondary to its mission and not the top priority. Financial success, though, can enhance an organization's ability to provide services. A nonprofit's managers need to ask this *chicken-and-egg* question: What comes first, the mission and programs designed to accomplish the mission or the cash to finance the program? Actually it is useful to realize that aspirations and financial resources intertwine as management works to coordinate the two. Both goals must be recognized and coordinated to identify results in both fashions. Attention to this unruly pair is the process that turns dreams into realizable goals.

3.1 BALANCING MISSION AND FINANCES

The nonprofit organization's dual goals may make its planning processes complex. Most for-profit entities can focus on their single-minded profit motive. Whereas the for-profit exists to enrich its owners, the nonprofit has the twin purpose of accomplishing its mission and meeting the financial goals necessary to do so. Financial planning for a nonprofit, therefore, must be thought of as a cycle of intertwining philosophical and financial concerns as shown in Exhibit 3.1. Evaluation and development of organizational goals and ambitions are critical, but assessment of available resources and past results is an equal part of the process. The work of keeping the pair in coordination never really stops. It is always useful to translate and study the results attained by nonprofits in terms of mission-oriented goals and financial goals.

Mission-oriented goals and financial goals may also be viewed as concurrent objectives that advance each other. The two sets of goals should interact in a complementary fashion. Each should facilitate the other.

Certainly, the trust an organization's constituents place in its programs can only enhance the likelihood of financial success. A community center that is recognized for the worth of its programs has a far easier time gaining financial support than a center with great ideas but no accomplishments. In other words, resource acquisition or fundraising is most successful when program presentations are successful. At the

Exhibit 3.1. Financial Planning Cycles.

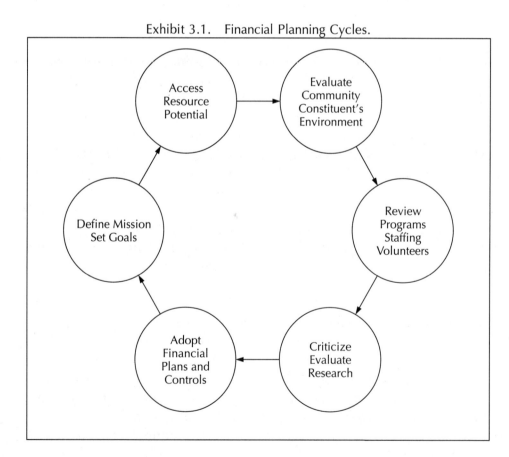

Exhibit 3.2.   The Balance Between the Mission and Financial Resources.

This chart is deliberately simple to clearly reflect the connections that exist between a mission-oriented goal and its financial counterpart. Each goal on the left is matched with a related financial solution or means to attain the necessary resources for program performance.

Goal to Accomplish Mission	Financial Resource
Feed more children to relieve the suffering of the poor.	Get donations of outdated food from grocery stores and cafes.
Double the congregation to spread the church's spiritual message.	Market the church through weekly gospel programs on public radio.
Publish more training manuals to better educate our league members.	Replace overworked staff with skilled writers to update and expand manuals.

same time, the converse is true. The best of programs may fail if a non-profit's financial management is poor. Overextended programs quickly earn a negative reputation with financial constituents. It is much harder to raise funding to cover a deficit in a struggling or discontinued program than to seek support for a prospective program.

The relationship between the mission-oriented goals and financial resources is critical. Exhibit 3.2 illustrates the connections that should be made between mission-oriented goals and its financial ones.

3.2   DEFINING THE MISSION

Prior to spending the first penny, the organization must understand its dreams and define its mission and the accompanying mission-oriented goals. Equally important, of course, is translating those goals into realizable steps using a process that can be called *quantifying the mission*. How many children would the organization hope to serve? How many papers can be presented?

Ideally, the board, the staff, and possibly major supporters convene in an annual or biannual meeting to develop a consensus on what exactly the aim of the organization will be. What needs to be accomplished as the end result of the organization's activities and efforts must be established. Many nonprofit organizations engage trained facilitators to guide these meetings. The facilitator brings impartiality to the deliberations and can help balance the many versions of the organization's dreams in the minds of the participants. A thorough discussion of the mission side of the long-range planning process is beyond the scope of this book, but a wealth of information is available on the subject.

(a)   Mission Statement

The consensus reached at the planning meeting is most often referred to as the mission statement. This statement succinctly presents the organization's reason for being. A business league's mission statement, for example, might read as follows:

> The Association of Nonprofit Managers is a league of chief operating and financial officers of nonprofit organizations formed to provide professional training, assistance, and career support, and to enhance communications among its members.

A new organization's creators write the first version of its mission statement when completing IRS Form 1023 or 1024 to seek recognition of tax-exempt status. Plans for the programs will flesh out the expressed statement of purpose, or mission. Financial projections are presented to reflect the available (or expected) financial resources. Questions such as how the programs will be supported, who will be served and where, how recipients will be charged, what assets will be used to conduct the programs, and other relevant details must be answered. These answers are considered and if necessary, the mission program will be revised as a part of an ongoing planning process.

(b)   Prioritizing Goals

Using the system suggested in Section 3.1 for identifying connections between the mission and financial resources is not always easy. But planners must assure that sufficient financial resources can be made available to accomplish the mission. Although tough choices will have to be made at times, it is always important to keep aspirations high. The process of prioritizing goals should be performed with the full extent of the mission in mind. The steps involved in achieving the mission must first be stated before they can be arranged in a logical manner. Exhibit 3.3 illustrates a chart to be used as a model for listing organizational objectives.

3.3 ASSESSING THE RESOURCES

The next step is to assess financial resources with respect to the priorities for organizational objectives. A viable organization is one that continually assesses resources. The staff is alert to coming changes and prepares for them. How well the organization serves its constituents should be foremost in the minds of planners during the annual evaluation.

Did the membership or volunteers grow in number? Did the non-profit receive public recognition for its accomplishments? Is there a need to seek new volunteers or to engage consultants to measure the organization's performance? The information gathered during the budgeting process, discussed in Chapter 4, may be used to make both micro and macro resource decisions.

(a) Making Micro Resource Decisions

Micro resource questions focus on the mission-oriented program rather than the nonprofit's fiscal health as a whole, but the best answers to micro questions will keep the connection between mission-oriented goals and financial ones in view. For example, the mission-oriented goal of doubling the number of hungry children fed by an organization may necessitate an increase in financial resources as shown in Exhibit 3.2. In such a case, the additional children are much more likely to be fed if the organization planners translate the mission-oriented goal into related financial goals, such as: hiring additional staff, buying more food, and receiving more contributions or grants.

On the other hand, when a nonprofit needs to limit, rather than increase, its use of financial resources, financial issues should first be explored in terms of the mission. The selection of the best financial solution will depend on the mission-oriented objectives that may still be achieved.

A symphony society that faces budget cuts needs to view all aspects of its choices to determine which programs best serve its mission and what may still be accomplished. The planners must ask whether the primary goal is to present formal concerts in the civic hall. Should they capture the finest rendition of a great symphony on an electronic medium for public distribution and sale? Do they want outreach into

Exhibit 3.3.   Prioritizing Organizational Objectives.

A chart such as the one below may be used to weigh organizational objectives. Each nonprofit's list of goals that it is considering as a part of the annual planning process and mission-statement update would be compiled as shown, for example, in the right column. Participants would then weigh, or prioritize, the choices by grading the objective on a scale ranging from 9 (highest) to 1 (lowest).

Priority Level 1–9	Goal	Organizational Objective
	A.	Expand number of persons served, locations where services are provided, hours or days on which service offered.
	B.	Increase type or scope of services offered to existing clientele.
	C.	Decrease scope of or eliminate services, seek another organization to perform the services or fill the need, or teach the service recipient's self sufficiency (conduct self-extinguishing projects).
	D.	Improve quality of services provided (supplement nurse practitioner with weekly physician; change hiring criteria to require higher education or experience level).
	E.	Create new projects or expand existing ones.
	F.	Phase out organization's existence by developing decentralized units to conduct now centralized programs.
	G.	Enhance visibility in community and with constituents.
	H.	Increase number of and services provided by volunteers and hire a volunteer coordinator.
	I.	Raise standards for program—for graduation, for certification, for permanent or senior membership, or for participation.

the community by performing chamber music in schools? Should they hire the most highly qualified director to teach and develop the finest musicians?

Once the planners have reexamined and redefined the symphony society's mission-oriented goals, they can begin the process of matching the mission with the best financial solutions. Exhibit 3.4 outlines various financial alternatives.

Exhibit 3.4.   Chart for Weighing Choices: Financial Solutions for Tight Budgets.

This chart may be used by a nonprofit faced with revenue reductions and/or needs to reduce spending. The financial solutions for each organization will be different. The CFO or financial committee might prepare this list of possible actions as a worksheet to guide a discussion to evaluate the choices. Each person would rate the financial steps with a V for Viable or a U for Unacceptable or the steps would also be weighted by assigning priorities as in Exhibit 3.3.

Financial Step	Rating V or U
Research public perception of accomplishments; interview recipients of services or participants to evaluate their needs/ideas.	
Establish a development department to increase contributor base.	
Raise membership prices, service fees, publication rates.	
Charge for services now offered for free.	
Eliminate programs or downsize staff.	
Merge with or absorb another organization.	
Sell off underutilized assets.	
Improve marketing, hire development specialist, publish magazine, sponsor public events, involve celebrities, and so on.	
Reallocate resources to realign strengths and weaknesses.	
Establish new measurement systems to evaluate performance.	

(b) Macro Resource Analysis

A critical look at the organization's big financial picture is also part of the planning process. An overall view of the nonprofit's macro financial condition provides an opportunity to evaluate its long-term fiscal stability. The planners first study financial reports similar to those found in Section 6.6, beginning with the Statement of Financial Position (also called Balance Sheet). Questions are asked like, "Are the unrestricted fund balances sufficient to survive a change, temporary or otherwise, in funding sources?" The financial information can be evaluated using the financial indicators and ratios discussed in Section 7.1.

Depending on the results of the financial analysis, the nonprofit would adopt specific financial steps to be taken to improve its macro, or overall, financial situation. This process can be explored by studying the fiscal attributes of a model church presented in Exhibit 3.5.

For planners who look only at the bottom line, the church's financial picture may seem healthy. The model church has $108,510 in *unrestricted net assets* (formerly called *fund balances*), on its balance sheet. The church has $390,000 of assets and only $281,490 of debt. This situation indicates that, during its life, the church has accumulated assets well in excess of the money it owes. If the church was a for-profit company, its stockholder's equity would equal $108,510.

Exhibit 3.5.   Holy Spirit Church Statement of Financial Position
(December 31, 199X).

This exhibit is designed for use in connection with the discussion of macro resource decisions and is based on financial report shown in Exhibit 6.6.

Current (liquid) Assets	$ 20,000
Operating equipment & furnishings	120,000
Buildings	250,000
Total assets	390,000
Current Liabilities	81,490
Long term Debt	200,000
Total liabilities	281,490
Unrestricted Net Assets	108,510
Total liabilities and net assets	$390,000

But a closer examination of the balance sheet reveals an entirely different picture. The church simply does not have the money to pay the bills that will soon be due. Compare the top asset line of $20,000 (which represents the assets currently available to pay bills) with the top liability line of $81,490. They show a negative current ratio of 1:4. In other words, the debts coming due in the next year amount to four times the current assets.

First glances at the bottom line of a financial statement can be misleading. The church's unrestricted net assets of more than $100,000 might appear reasonable for an organization of its size. However, after looking at the various categories of assets, one observes that the fund balance is comprised of noncash assets, that is, the church's equipment and buildings. Because these assets are used daily in conducting services, they certainly are not available for sale to pay bills. This condition leaves the church vulnerable. A delay of a few days or weeks in funding can produce such havoc as late creditor payments, missed paychecks, and/or delinquent employee tax deposits, among other financial embarrassments and failures.

Once the church planners have recognized their financial problem, they can develop macro resource goals to correct the situation. Over the course of the next few years, the church should particularly focus on *financial goals A, B, C, and D* shown in Exhibit 3.6. No doubt those four would all be given top priority on the chart used to prioritize macro resource goals. To facilitate realization of the macro goals, the church would also establish specific steps to balance its Mission and Financial Goals using the chart shown in Exhibit 3.2.

In facing its financial problem, the church would implement a formal financial planning system. First, it would prepare a budget for the coming year following the guidelines in Chapter 4. Next, it would convert the budget into a monthly cash flow projection as illustrated in Exhibits 5.3a, b. The church's financial managers would study Chapter 6 to evaluate the existing accounting system. If necessary, the system would be upgraded to ensure they will receive timely and informative financials, compared to the approved budget, each month throughout the year. Lastly, one hopes the church would begin to use ratio analyses as explained in Section 7.1 to currently evaluate and improve the current funding situation.

Exhibit 3.6.   Prioritizing Macro Resource Goals.

This chart lists the nonprofit's Macro Resource Goals. The CFO or financial committee would prepare the list of goals as a part of the annual
planning process. Each nonprofit's list would be unique but similar to the
examples shown in the right column. Planning participants would then
weigh, or prioritize, the choices by grading the objective on a scale ranging from 13 (highest) to 1 (lowest).

Priority Level 1–13		Macro Resource Goal
	A	Establish working capital base.
	B	Maintain three (or more) months operating cash balance (improve cash flow).
	C	Retire debt or reduce accounts payable.
	D	Seek endowment funding to provide investment income to offset annual fluctuations in grant funding?
	E	Buy or build permanent facilities.
	F	Establish branches statewide or citywide.
	G	Increase portion of exempt function revenues.
	H	Conduct marketing campaign (to expend membership, to educate public about mission, sell tickets, and so on).
	I	Raise salaries or increase the number of personnel.
	J	Improve employee benefits—retirement, medical, education, child care, cafeteria plan.
	K	Establish a volunteer guild.
	L	Replace major governmental funding source or be prepared if funding is cut or eliminated.
	M	Hire chief financial officer to improve financial reporting, monitoring, and planning.

Budgeting

A budget is the numerical expression of an organization's dreams that serves as a guide or measure of acceptable financial performance.

After the organization has examined its priorities and refined its mission in view of the financial resources, it is time to prepare the budget. The budget charts a direction for allocating and maximizing the use of resources and ideally identifies any financial problems that could arise in the coming year. The budget itself provides indicators for evaluating employee performance and gives the staff goals to reach and steps to achieve them.

4.1 BUDGET PLANNING ISSUES

As a financial measure of the nonprofit's goals, a budget compiles programs planned for the coming year in some detail based upon assumptions. It shows how many students the nonprofit expects to enroll next year, how much money it plans to spend to save which endangered species, or the number of members expected to become new and renewing dues-paying constituents next year. The scope and size of a nonprofit's programs and asset base dictates the complexity of its budget(s). One or more years of projected revenues and expenses might be suitable dependent upon the sophistication of the nonprofit's long range planning and its computerized accounting system. In its most complete form, a budget is a compilation of plans and objectives of management that covers all phases of operations for a specific period of time.[1] Exhibits 4.6 through 4.13 illustrate budget workpapers for a model business league, State Association of Nonprofit Managers.

It is important to distinguish between the portion of the budget based upon reality and that stemming from dreams. The budget planner needs both a healthy skepticism and optimism. Necessarily, the process involves uncertainty; decisions are made about the indeterminate future that the organization cannot control. Should the financial planners simply assume that a nonprofit's existing programs will continue? Which, if any, of the nonprofit's programs are essential? How will the organization face the unknown? Before developing the budgets, the planners must make the specific policy decisions outlined below.

(a)   Balancing

The nonprofit must decide whether the budget is to be balanced. Should the budget reflect sufficient revenues to pay expenses? An organization that needs to build up its working capital might want to project a budget imbalance of revenues over expenses (a profit). Program priorities are

---

[1] Robert Rachline and H. W. Allen Sweeny, *Handbook of Budgeting,* Third Edition, John Wiley & Sons, New York, 1993.

also balanced in an effective budget. The nonprofit's capabilities and resources are allocated or balanced to impact the maximum audience or beneficiaries. Those programs to continue and those to close are balanced. The wrenching debate over balancing the federal budget in 1995 illustrates the complexity of the task.

Most nonprofits cannot afford the luxury of an imbalanced budget and fewer still have the accumulated surpluses or financial stability to borrow money to finance a deficit year. Organizations that charge for their services may not be able readily to increase the price of programs. Nonprofits are not like the lettuce growers who seem to simply announce, "Sorry folks, the weather was bad so we are doubling the price of your leafy salad greens."

(b) Timing

Budgets need to be completed within a time frame that allows for planning in advance of the applicable period. As discussed in more detail in Section 4.4, the lead time required for grant requests and multi-year projects make it imperative that the budget process be properly timed. Realizable target dates for the completion of the planning should be established for all to follow. Some aspects of the budget process—accumulation of statistical data and client evaluations—are timeless and are ongoing tasks constantly feeding the budget system and keeping it current.

(c) Evolution

Although not a common practice, some organizations might adjust the budget throughout the year as changes are indicated. The budget establishes criteria that signal the need for change or identify the need to refine or alter the course of action. Although it may be difficult to modify once it is adopted, a budget found to be unrealistic or inaccurate can be changed. In its original or unaltered state, it continues to signal a problem even though the issue has been addressed and changes have been made to correct it. A budget updated for the new situation might better serve as a monitoring system as it is tailored to respond to unforeseen conditions. Most nonprofits choose to continue to compare current financial information with the originally approved budget and provide footnotes, as shown in Exhibit 6.6, explaining changing conditions that have caused the results to be less or better than originally expected (or hoped).

(d) Accountability

The people expected to accomplish the program(s) and financial goals expressed in the budget are identified and actively involved in the budgeting process. Responsibility is associated with those that are actually capable of realizing the goals. A budget developed, monitored, and revised in the controller's office is of little value to the program staff. Without the active awareness and participation of those actually carrying out the activities, a budget's usefulness is diminished as discussed in Section 4.4 below.

(e) Zero Basis versus Incremental

The budgeteers adopt either a zero-based system or an incremental methodology for preparing the financial guideline for the coming year. Zero-based budgeting essentially incorporates the planning process for setting organizational objectives as part of the budgeting process. Starting from a zero base, the financial planners assume no program is necessary and no money need be spent. The programs to continue will have to be proven worthy, as well as fiscally sound, following an orderly evaluation of all elements of revenue and spending. Each program is examined to justify its existence and is compared to alternative programs. Priorities are established and each cost center is challenged to prove its necessity. The worthiness of a program justified with abstract terms is tested and must be proven to be financially sound to be adopted. For this reason program managers may feel threatened by and not participate as fully in the zero-based method.

An incremental budget, on the other hand, treats existing programs and departments as preapproved, subject only to increases or decreases in financial resources allocated. Essentially the nonprofit's historical costs are the base from which budget planning starts. The focus of the budgeting process is on the changes anticipated in last year's numbers; the planning process has already been completed and program priorities established. Incremental budgeting is, therefore, often less time consuming and also felt by some to be less threatening to program managers.

(f) Forecasting

The organization must decide whether its budget is to be based upon measurable and predictable statistics or only on good guesses. Although it is useful for program officers to have a healthy dose of optimism about predicting the future results, outside opinions may prove to be more accurate. When the organization can afford the expense involved, business marketing tools, such as statistical sampling of previous donors, can be applied to forecast or predict a reasonable level of donations for the coming year. The effort to maintain peripheral data systems that capture statistical information such as renewal rates, source of renewals, results of marketing campaigns, and other historical profiles must also be considered as discussed in Section 4.8.

4.2 TYPES OF BUDGETS

Before the budget process begins, the nonprofit considers the type of budgets that are best suited to its planning and monitoring needs. The basic budget is a comprehensive look at the entire organization's overall projection of the revenues or financial support and its expected expenditures. An endless number of varieties of this basic form can be created for particular planning and assessment needs.

Specialized or supplemental budgets can provide a pinpoint focus on fragments of financial activity germane to individual programs or revenue centers. For example, a membership organization establishes goals for its various categories of members. The number of members and the amount of funds received from members can be quantified according to useful information including (a) new, renewing, and nonrenewing, (b) unsolicited versus solicited, or (c) zip code, religious preference, age, and so on as shown below in Section 4.8. Such quantification of membership serves to guide not only the business office in monitoring cash flow projections, but also the development, and possibly the program department throughout the year as membership projections are matched up with the unfolding reality. A listing of all potential budget reports might be endless, but a brief look at the possibilities includes at least the following:

- Annual, quarterly, and/or monthly projections of income and expense for the entire organization as well as each of its divisions, departments, branches, and so on.

- Revenue projections by type, such as contributors or student tuition.

- Individual project, department, branch, or other cost center projections.

- Service delivery costs by patient, by student, by member, or other client.

- Capital additions (building or equipment acquisition).

- Investment income (and/or total return).

- Cash flow (short and long).

- Fund-raising event revenue and expenses.

- Book store, pharmacy, or resale shop sales.

- Personnel projections.

4.3 ADVANTAGES AND DISADVANTAGES

The budget is a tool to allocate resources and to implement strategic plans effectively. It can be a useful tool that produces a spectrum of beneficial results. Significantly it serves as a guideline for program personnel directly involved in carrying out activities enabling them to numerically measure their accomplishments and respond to unexpected changes. Management personnel can use it to evaluate staff performance. Like any tool, the budget can produce either advantages or disadvantages, depending on the skill and diligence with which it is used. The chief advantages and benefits of effective budgeting include:

- A thoroughly planned and implemented budget enhances the likelihood a nonprofit will be financially successful.

- A budget is a tool that translates abstract goals into determinable bites or bits; it stipulates performance goals.

- The planning and preparation process leading to a budget force the organization to look at itself, to set priorities, and to narrow its choices.

- A budget facilitates coordination and cooperation between the various programs and financial departments.

- Periodic budget comparison to actual financial performance can signal trouble and allow for response to changing conditions in a timely manner.

- A budget measures financial performance in relation to the non-profit's expectations.

The chief *disadvantages or difficulties* with the budgeting process include:

- The karma or presence of controls may stifle creativity.

- There is a natural tendency to emphasize cost control due to a myriad of unknowns at the time of budget preparation.

- A budget based upon historical information alone can fail to keep up with a rapidly changing society.

- Too often nonfinancial personnel do not participate in the budgeting process resulting in operational blueprints approved without the input of program personnel.

- A budget is not easy to implement and may require extra enthusiasm among the management personnel to be accepted as useful.

4.4   WHO PARTICIPATES IN BUDGETING?

A good budget cannot assure its own success and will not take the place of responsible management. Almost everyone involved with a nonprofit may suitably participate in the budget planning. At a minimum, the organization's top administrators, program heads, and board members or trustees contribute to the final result. The budget ultimately should be a compilation of information furnished by all the responsible program and administrative personnel who have in turn factored in the input of the people with whom they work. No one person should be responsible for the budget. The organization's financial (also called accounting or business) office compiles and monitors the budget. How far into the organizational chain the leaders seek input depends upon each nonprofit's circumstances.

Ideally the budget process is participatory and involves input from all the nonprofit's program staff and volunteers devoted to accomplishing its goals. Outside funders sometimes influence the process. The budget allocation panel of a united giving campaign often coordinates their projected funding levels with the nonprofits they support. Such funders want to know if the organization plans to provide services that are already being provided by another organization in the community. They may try to influence a grant recipient to conduct programs to accomplish the funder's goals.

A budget imposed from the top down hampers the staff enthusiasm and can negatively influence realization of the expressed goals. A nonprofit may need to curtail the vociferous leader seeking more money for his pet projects. The input of the volunteer case workers, for example,

Exhibit 4.1. Who Works on the Budget When?

	WHO	**WHAT**	**WHEN**
Step 1	Accounting department.	Provide budget worksheets.	6th month of year (or before).
Step 2	Responsible program officers and admin- istrative personnel based upon input of all.	Do research; solicit and com- pile ideas, pre- pare projections.	Next two months.
Step 3	Chief financial officer.	Combine all budgets into one.	3 months before year end.
Step 4	Chief operating officer, subject to board or trustee approval.	Review and finalize budget.	2–3 months be- fore year end.

may yield a more realistic and realizable budget for a social services program. During the process, compromise and tradeoffs will naturally occur. The participation of the staff from the outset makes them more enthusiastic about alterations not initiated by them. Optimally, it may also make them more understanding or accepting of changes, including budget cuts that impact them personally (low or no raise). The participation of the board, officers, staff, and volunteers in the goal-setting process enhances the nonprofit's chances of reaching its goals. The whole budget process should motivate personnel and inspire the organization's performance. Everyone should be informed of the plan with a chart similar to the one in Exhibit 4.1.

4.5 SELLING THE BUDGET

The most effective budget is one prepared with broad and informed input from many personnel in the organization, including the chief operating and financial officers, administrative staff, and program people as discussed above. To achieve success, communication among all participants is encouraged during the whole process.

(a) Budget Policy Manual

A formal budget manual containing written procedures and guidelines governing the process, budget models, checklists, and other aids to preparation is desirable to document the process. At a minimum, the organization should prepare a budget policy statement to stipulate the following:

- *Philosophy:* How the nonprofit uses the budget is described to encourage ongoing participation in the process. Folks need to know what to expect. They want to know how the nonprofit plans to respond to variances and whether the budget evolves or changes during the year. (Section 4.1)

- *Responsible Persons:* Who does what when during the budget process is outlined. (Section 4.4)

- *Time Frame:* A schedule of the expected steps. (Section 4.6)

- *Forecast Guidelines:* Guidelines can indicate the economic assumptions to be applied, methodology to be used for making projections, independent sources of information, and circumstances under which outside professionals can be engaged to perform forecasts. (Sections 4.7 and 4.8)

- *Report Design:* A standard or suggested form for input by various programs or departments is furnished with clear instructions as to amount of detail desired, explanation of assumptions, and so on. (Section 4.11)

- *Follow-up:* The ongoing budget monitoring system and its recurring time frame is described. See periodic financial reports shown in Exhibits 6.6 and 6.7.

(b)   Communicating the Process

All involved in the budget preparation should be informed well in advance of how the process will work. They receive a copy of the budget policy manual if one is prepared. At a minimum, an office communication similar to Exhibit 4.2 is suggested.

4.6   SCHEDULING BUDGET PROCESS

In the best situation, budgeting is an ongoing process repeating itself in a cyclical manner. Also ideally, the philosophical basis for budget decisions is established in consideration of the nonprofit's long range plan. To reach this optimum budget condition, the participants described in

BUDGETING

Exhibit 4.2.   Interoffice Memo on Annual Budgeting.

TO: Program and administrative officers (suitable titles
     used, such as chief, head, manager, and so on)

FROM: Chief financial officer

RE: Annual Budgeting Schedule and Guidelines

I invite your contribution to our annual financial
planning process. Our continued success depends upon the
accomplishments of your program. This package is a follow-up
to the strategic long range planning sessions you
participated in last month. Now it is time to translate our
goals into the specific activity we expect in both a
financial and narrative fashion. Additionally we invite you
to compose a narrative description of your plans.

Worksheets reflecting the actual results of your program for
the past year and the six months to date in this year broken
down as follows are enclosed.

- Revenues
- Operating expenditures
- Capital additions

Assumptions: Projections should factor in the following
assumptions:

- Overall price increase will average 2.3%.
- Salary increase for all will equal 3%.
- Meritorious raises should not exceed 7%.
- Membership revenue should increase 10%.

Narrative: Please explain changes your department plans to
make in response to changing economic conditions, grant
funding, constituent needs, and so on. Explain any major
differences between the past and projected financials.

Time Frame: The deadline for submission is July 1 (one month
hence).

Exhibit 4.1 must allow sufficient time for the plans to be fully developed. The steps to follow include:

Step 1.	Set Goals.	Perform long range planning.
Step 2.	Establish objectives.	Identify programs and activities to accomplish goal.
Step 3.	Design programs.	Describe method of actualizing the goals.
Step 4.	Budget preparation and approval.	Quantify revenues and expenditures based upon forecasts and program services accomplishments.
Step 5.	Monitor progress.	Compile reports comparing budget to actual.

Prior to the accumulation of the financial aspect of a budget, the planning process occurs as described in Chapter 3. Goals are critiqued, evaluated, and established. Programs that can accomplish the goals are examined, compared, and studied. Past successes are considered and compared to failures or results falling short of desired goals. Finally program planning and development are complete and the financial aspects begins.

Exhibit 4.1 suggests the actual budget preparation process begins essentially six months prior to the date to which the budget applies. An organization whose fiscal year ends December 31—the calendar year—starts the process for the coming year by July, if not before. Enough time is allowed before the fiscal year starts to gather reliable forecasting information and to provide a reasonable period for an orderly approval process. Keep in mind that the board of directors ultimately approves the final product as discussed below.

(a) Changing Budget Midyear

The astute project manager is alert to outside forces that will impact fiscal performance of the organization and regularly catalogs new information that is useful in preparing the next year's budget. Networked personal computers can facilitate the accumulation of information on an ongoing basis. Some organizations may find a "living" budget that regularly changes throughout the year as circumstances change to be preferable to a fixed and unchanging budget.

The reasons the budget needs to change are endless. Forecasts often prove inaccurate for reasons of inadequate information or circumstances beyond the organization's control—an expected grant renewal is cut back or denied, a major funder defaults on a pledge, a natural disaster compounds demand for aid to the public, or the cost of newsprint doubles. Holy Spirit Church certainly did not expect the results shown in Exhibit 6.7 when it approved its original budget.

The issue when unforeseen changes occur is whether the approved budget should be altered or updated to reflect the changing conditions. Alternatively as shown for State Association of Nonprofit Managers in Exhibit 6.6, the monthly financial statements can use footnotes to explain significant variances from the approved budget. The attributes of a "living" or constantly changing budget are compared to a static budget.

Static Budget	Living Budget
Compares dreams at a point in time to reality of current situation.	Presents realistic statistics in view of changing circumstances or conditions.
No time spent on revisions.	Requires continual updating.
Wastes funds expended on program to be discontinued or found to be ineffective.	Constant maximization of resources.
Allows unreasonable expectations.	Positive context for accomplishment.

(b) Timing Dilemmas

Certain aspects of a nonprofit's financial life span years or involve years different than its fiscal year. Projects with multiyear time frames must be coordinated with the annual budget planning cycle. Consider, for example, the scheduling dilemma posed when an organization seeks funding from the state arts council that operates on a different fiscal year. Say the council funds programs for the state's fiscal year beginning on October 1 and requires grant applications no later than February 1 with awards approved by July. A calendar year nonprofit's normal budget approval date is the end of November.

The gap in time between the grant submission deadline and budget approval date in the above example requires at least a two-step process. First the grant budget is prepared for approval essentially six months in advance of its due date and a whole year before the program start date. Three months of the upcoming grant period, October to December, are included in the proposed calendar year budget. Due to the contingency, the chief financial officer or board treasurer could be authorized to alter the requests for subsequent events, if necessary, prior to actual submission the following February.

Too often in my experience grant requests are not approved as part of the normal budget cycle. Submission of a grant request essentially commits the nonprofit to carry out the program. The grant funds may not be sufficient to pay for all the costs involved, including the time and effort to apply and monitor the grant. It is prudent, therefore, for all grant requests to be subject to the same advanced approval system and be a part of the annual operating budget planning as discussed in Section 4.4.

Retiring board members or executive directors should never approve the coming year's budget as their last official act. The most effective budget is one developed and approved by the persons with a vested interest in its execution. Timing the annual change in officers or board members optimally occurs well in advance of the nonprofit's year end. For example, a calendar year budget ideally is approved in November or December with plans complete before the new year begins on January 1. To facilitate that time frame, the board members could take office in October or November to allow them time to study and approve the budget for which they will be responsible.

4.7 PREPARING FORECASTS

A nonprofit organization may face unique problems in forecasting its revenues. Those nonprofits supported by contributions and grants face the most difficult task. Voluntary donations are often based solely upon the giver's compassion or support for the organization's mission and their personal generosity. The public's concern about a particular social problem—AIDS, for example—may wane. Other intangible factors compound the degree of difficulty in making projections for a nonprofit. Unfortunately, human psychology seems to make people value those services for which they pay more. Fund-raising activities are for some a social activity that can lose its cachet—the celebrity appeal of the organization may fade.

A service-providing nonprofit, such as a school or a business league, may have a slightly easier task in forecasting future revenue. Fees for services are motivated by the payor's perceived or actual need for the services the nonprofit is offering. As long as the services are of high quality and meeting the needs of the students, the sick, or the members, the nonprofit can reasonably project repeat or renewed participation. The adage, "You value what you pay for," is a factor. In planning training seminars for the Texas Accountants and Lawyers for the Arts, we discovered that those registrants who paid a fee, even a modest $5 fee, were much more likely to show up for the class than those required to pay no fee.

A forecaster first studies current revenue and spending levels and asks if the amounts can be sustained. If unusual and nonrecurring events occurred in the past year or two, will they reoccur? Is it instead reasonable to expect an increase in revenues? What level of increase does the nonprofit expect due to some action taken in the past, such as last year's establishment of a development department? What increases might result if some new marketing scheme is added to the expense side of the budget?

Information about the nonprofit's demographics and the conditions in its community are factored into the projections. National and local reports of economic activity can be studied in the public library, local city planning office, small business administration office, university, referral agencies, and similar resources. In view of the prevailing and predicted economic conditions, the forecaster then asks how the nonprofit may be affected by those uncontrollable outside forces. The nature of the nonprofit's constituents is also evaluated. Are they getting older, more educated, healthier, and so on? If the data is unclear, the nonprofit may need to test its internal projections or have them validated by outside consultants. Uncertainty may indicate the need to perform market surveys.

(a) Donations and Memberships

Forecasting voluntary contributions and membership support is a job that becomes easier as the organization matures. The best source of data on which to predicate the future is the organization's own history. In making projections, statistical charts reflecting several years of revenue can serve as a guide. This is illustrated in Exhibits 4.5. Some nonprofits have a high level of goodwill generated after years of operation, such as a 50-year-old church or CPA society. A new or young organization may need to be more careful in weighing the past and evaluating the likely success of development plans.

(b)   Service Delivery Fees

Again, the organization's age impacts the predictability of the revenue projection. The mature organization knows the average number of students, attendees, research reports, or other services delivered in the past year and years. Presumably the need for the services and policy decisions about their delivery have been reviewed as a part of the long range planning process. The budgeteer's job may simply be one of translating those goals into a financial format. The number of persons to be served and the expected prices are coordinated with the planners.

Absent guidance from some goal-setting procedure, the person(s) compiling the budget may need to perform market analysis—evaluate the need and past effectiveness of the service(s), changing constituency base, or demand for the services. On the basis of these planning steps, the nonprofit projects the numbers to be served and price to be charged in order to arrive at the predicted service revenue.

(c)   Grants and Contracts

Predicting the renewal or approval of grants from governmental funding agencies, private foundations, and business sponsors is a difficult and troublesome task. Uncertain facts and unanswerable questions must be faced. Will some legislative body reduce or eliminate the program? Will the foundation's asset values fall, causing a reduction in money allotted to grants? (The annual payout requirement for a private foundation equals 5 percent of value of its investment assets.) Are priorities among funders changing?

Corporate sponsorship levels are usually tied to the sponsor's profit levels—a fact often unknown at budget preparation time. Renewal of a government research contract may depend upon an incomplete project or preliminary data that makes a prediction impossible at budget time. Governmental regulations concerning cost reimbursements or bidding process may affect the forecast.

Particularly where a portion of the nonprofit's operating overhead or administrative funds are paid for with grant funds, very cautious projecting is prudent. Think about the consequence when the grant that funds half of the executive director's salary is not renewed. Where a good possibility exists for nonrenewal, the uncertain forecast indicates the need for a flexible or evolving budget as discussed in Sections 4.1(c) and 4.6(b). Employment arrangements with staff members funded by a grant (and the corresponding expense budget) should be tailored to fit any contingency that the funds may cease.

(d) Investment Income

The care required in projecting investment income is determined by the portion of the organization's revenues expected to be provided by such income. For many nonprofits, the portion is modest. The higher the portion; the more significant the methodology and expertise used in making predictions. For an endowed grant-making foundation all of whose revenues come from investment returns, for example, the forecast is vital to establishing funding levels for the coming year.

To appreciate the task an organization faces in projecting investment income, recall that during the year 1994 interest rates dropped over 50 percent only to bounce back and forth in 1995. Although many nonprofits misjudged the 1994–1995 interest rate swings, few suffered program cutbacks due to their reduced level of interest income. Generally fluctuations in short term interest rates should not seriously affect an organization's overall financial picture.

The degree of forecasting difficulty rises for the nonprofit with long term investment funds. If the organization funds are administered by a professional investment manager, the manager should provide investment income projections. Otherwise, the nonprofit must do its best to predict the unpredictable while keeping a healthy level of skepticism about the unknown. The fact is no banker, governmental official, or country on earth controls the interest rates, price of equity investments, inflation or deflation rates, relative currency values, or other economic factors that will influence a particular nonprofit's return on investment in the coming year. To complicate the matter, what constitutes expendable income from investment assets is a much debated subject. The budgeted revenues may be suitably based upon concepts of total return. Where this forecast is significant, consult Sections 5.5 and 5.6 for more information useful in projecting investment income.

(e) Expenses

For most nonprofits, expenditure levels can be predicted with a fair degree of certainty partly because the nonprofit has more control over expenses than revenues. The compensation arrangements with personnel are known, for the most part. Facility costs may be relatively stable under the terms of a lease agreement or mortgage note. Historical expense reports form the basis for the expense budget subject to adjustment for the expected rate of growth or decline in prevailing prices according to the Federal Reserve Bank or other economic predictors.

One major issue in forecasting costs is identifying those that are variable in relation to revenue stream or client demand. A disaster relief agency may know how much it costs to clothe and house flood victims, but it cannot know when the storm or storms might occur. Again, historical records may be useful. For example, the government's hurricane bureau predicts how many storms will confront the Gulf of Mexico each year and where they will occur.

A contingency based upon client demand for the nonprofit's services is sometimes as difficult to predict, but the same crystal-ball judgments can be applied. It can be very important to acknowledge the uncertainty and submit a flexible budget. The prudent budget preparer seeks the best possible information to prepare and submits projections subject to change. Another way to view or face the job of forecasting costs is to identify costs according to those that are controllable versus those that are uncontrollable.

If expected costs are too high, the financial planners consider alternatives. Sometimes a nonprofit needs people with skills to supervise a project, but the suitable person's expected compensation level would skew the nonprofit's overall pay scale. In such a situation, the organization has many alternatives:

- Outsource the job to another nonprofit or company (may be able to receive some fee for selling the program's goodwill),

- Hire the skilled consultant on a part-time or hourly basis to operate the program and have him or her train a permanent person, or

- Eliminate or reduce the scope of the program or enter into a joint venture with another nonprofit to conduct the program.

Projected expenses must also be matched to the expected revenue flow. The proposed expenditure budget should be tested by preparing a cash flow report as illustrated in Exhibit 5.3a and b. Although the State Association of Nonprofit Managers' overall budget projections looked well-balanced and reasonable, a marketing campaign planned early in the year would have caused cash flow deficits. The second version of the exhibit shows how the plans were changed to match the monthly spending with the expected revenue flow.

Exhibit 4.3.   Resource Assessment Checklist.

Question	Comments
How secure are the funding sources?	_____
How many people attend or benefit from the activity?	_____
What does the activity cost per person?	_____
How much revenue does it produce?	_____
Does the activity appeal to volunteers?	_____
Is the program readily fundable with grants?	_____
Does the program produce peripheral or ancillary benefits or costs?	_____
What portion of the nonprofit's overhead is funded by the activity?	_____
How dependent are the nonprofit's grantees upon its funding?	_____
Is the activity performed by some other organization?	_____
Should the budget include a marketing campaign to broaden public support and public awareness of the program?	_____

Choosing which programs to continue is a decision made in light of their affect on incoming resources. Sometimes the program is simply one the nonprofit itself shouldn't attempt to sponsor or conduct. A variety of questions can be asked to assess the impact of program planning decisions on the nonprofit's resources as shown in Exhibit 4.3.

4.8 STATISTICAL OPERATIONAL DATA

On a regular basis, the nonprofit needs to gather statistics and information relevant to the budgeting and planning process. Each organization needs a mechanism to measure its overall and individual program effectiveness. How can it determine whether its goals are being reached? What are the results of its efforts? Successes and failures and weaknesses and strengths should be regularly evaluated and quantified. The information can form the basis for decisions, establishing priorities, and making choices. The sophistication and scope of the self-assessment process will vary by organization. To be effective, not only program performance and accomplishments of the organization itself are measured, but staff, volunteer, manager, and board performance as well.

(a)   Sample Customer Survey

To facilitate evaluations, the organization develops written documents to compile information. The response of constituents—members, donors, and service recipients—is solicited and accumulated. Some call constituents customers and recommend that customer satisfaction be emphasized. The response measurements for a nonprofit's customers will be different from a business, but they are equally important to consider.

For each situation, a suitable follow-up system should be used to implement changes indicated by the data. Why gather data if they are not studied and if changes indicated are not implemented? The steps the organization takes in reaction to constituent suggestions should also be shared or reported back to them. The type of questions to include on a customer or constituent survey are shown in Exhibit 4.4.

(b)   Useful Statistics

A myriad of data can be organized and presented in a manner that aids the nonprofit's planners to predict or forecast the future. National surveys of the compensation levels of nonprofit personnel can be consulted to see if projected levels are in line with outside trends.[2] The examples in Exhibit 4.5 should serve only to inspire creativity for designing statistical summaries germane to each particular organization.

4.9   CAPITAL ADDITIONS BUDGET

Beyond the operating budget lies the capital budget shown in Exhibit 4.12. Here plans are developed for spending funds to acquire assets, such as equipment and buildings, that will benefit the nonprofit over a period of

---

[2] The Council on Foundations publishes an annual survey of compensation levels of various positions for foundations of varying sizes. Towers Perrin of Rosslyn, Virginia compiles an annual *Management Compensation Report for Not-for-Profit Organizations.*

Exhibit 4.4.   Service Delivery Evaluation.

This survey is intended to serve as an example of the type of questionnaire a nonprofit might use to seek evaluations of its program service delivery. The survey could be completed at the time one is served or could be mailed to a sampling of participants or members.

STATE ASSOCIATION OF NONPROFIT MANAGERS

Member (Constituent) Survey

Name of Member (patient, student, donor, or such) _____

    Address   _____

    Phone   _____

    Fax, E-Mail, or Net Path   _____

Date   _____

Are you happy with SANM?   [   ] (yes)   [   ] (no)
    If not, please explain. _____

    _____

    _____

Why do you value services
    received from SANM?   _____

How could SANM be of
    better service to you
    or your organization?   _____

Would you pay more?   _____

Please tell us more!   _____

time. Because the capital spending benefits the organization in a more tangible and often longer-lasting fashion, the nonprofit may arrange to pay for the acquisition over a period of time, sometimes many years. Therefore, in capital budgeting several distinct issues are considered:

1. Will the new asset improve our performance and enable the organization to better accomplish its mission?

2. How will the acquisition be financed?

CAPITAL ADDITIONS BUDGET

Exhibit 4.5.   Typical Nonprofit Organization Membership History.

Membership Renewal Statistics

Membership Categories:	Members renewing	New members	Total for year 19xx	Nonrenewing Members	Original forecast	Prior year actual	Forecast for year 19xx
Basic	5,000	2,000	7,000	1,800	7,500	6,800	7,200
Family	2,000	500	2,500	600	2,800	2,600	2,600
Friend	500	50	550	20	500	520	540
Supporter	70	10	80	30	75	100	90

Membership Profiles

Member, patient, student, etc. Characteristics:	Forecast for year 19xx	Actual for year 19xx	Forecast for next year 19xx
TOTAL OF ALL SERVED	10,875	10,020	10,430
Gender:			
Female	6,075	5,840	6,030
Male	4,800	4,200	4,400
AGE: (use brackets suitable for the nonprofit)			
under 10 years	700	780	800
age 11–18	1,200	1,010	940
age 19–25	2,475	2,200	2,180
age 26–40	3,800	3,600	3,910
age 41–64	2,000	1,820	1,940
over 65	500	510	460
age unknown	200	100	200
	10,875	10,020	10,430

OTHER POSSIBILITIES:

ZIP CODE

ETHNIC ORIGIN

PROFESSION

CATEGORY OF MEMBER

Angels

Saints

Patrons

Disciples

(Continued)

Exhibit 4.5. *(Continued)*

Revenue Source History

	Four years ago	Three years ago	Two years ago	Last year	Average	Forecast Next year
Individual Contributions	520	640	780	1,000	735	1,200
Grants from Private Foundations	100	200	300	400	250	500
Government Grants	1,200	1,200	1,000	600	1,000	400
Program Service Revenue	40	80	200	600	230	700
Income from Endowment	30	−10	80	100	50	80
OPERATING REVENUES	1,890	2,110	2,360	2,700	2,265	2,880
ENDOWMENT or CAPITAL GIFTS	120	200	50	10	95	0
TOTAL REVENUES	2,010	2,310	2,410	2,710	2,360	2,880

Expenditure Levels

	Four years ago	Three years ago	Two years ago	Last year	Average	Forecast Next year
Direct Program Service Costs:						
Program #1	1,200	1,100	1,000	800	1,025	800
Program #2	200	300	300	300	275	320
Program #3	200	350	700	1,000	562	1,200
Management and General	200	260	280	410	287	420
Fundraising & Development	10	30	40	50	32	80
Property & Equipment Acquisitions	200	50	0	10	65	40
TOTAL EXPENDITURES	2,020	2,060	2,320	2,570	2,246	2,860

3. What will it cost to obtain and maintain the asset throughout its life?

The issues in answering question 1 are the same as described for considering an operating expense budget. Procedures and forms to use in making such purchase decisions are suggested in Section 7.3. The type of statistical data gathered to propose capital additions is illustrated in Exhibit 7.7. Issues to consider in deciding to acquire or purchase capital assets versus leasing them is illustrated in Exhibit 7.8. In the following sample budgets, the capital additions are incorporated into the overall nonprofit budget and treated much like other operating expenses.

Questions 2 and 3 add another dimension—that of financing the acquisition. Should the nonprofit buy the equipment for cash? Should it lease or buy under an installment purchase agreement? Equally important is question 3—what will the asset eventually cost in total for the time the organization uses it? Section 7.3 suggests some tools for answering these difficult questions.

4.10 MONITORING VARIANCES

Once the budget is approved for the upcoming year, a monitoring system is in order. Computers can certainly make this process easier. Even the most basic accounting software packages available over the counter today contain modules for budget reports. As a part of the routine monthly financial reporting, the actual financial transactions to date are compared to the budget, as shown in Exhibits 6.6 and 6.7 for Holy Spirit Church and for the State Association of Nonprofit Managers.

The report design should deliver the information succinctly so that variances reflecting situations that require action or changes, are clear and apparent A variance is the difference between the expected or projected outcome and what actually happened. When they occur, they must be interpreted and analyzed. Holy Spirit Church's variances certainly show that its financial condition is not as expected, and it should cause alarm. The report reflects a serious problem that the church's financial managers must face.

4.11 MODEL BUDGETS

This section contains illustrative budgets for a mock business league, State Association of Nonprofit Managers, also known by its acronym,

SANM. The design of the budget workpapers follows the format of SANM's monthly financial statements shown in Exhibit 6.6. The intention is to make it easy to prepare monthly variance reports and to facilitate understanding of the comparisons. A variety of formats, however, are successfully used by nonprofit organizations. Briefly SANM's budget workpapers shown in Exhibits 4.6 through 4.13 serve the following purpose in their budget planning process and can serve as a model for varying types of nonprofits.

(a) Proposed Overall 19x7 Budget Compared to 19x6 Actual

The overall budget comprehensively reflects all resource flow to be approved by the board and to serve as a blueprint to measure accomplishment of financial goals for the coming year. Note that the proposal is

Exhibit 4.6.   Proposed Overall Budget Compared to Actual.

STATE ASSOCIATION of NONPROFIT MANAGERS				
PROPOSED OVERALL BUDGET COMPARED to ACTUAL				
	Actual	Actual to date	Projected	Proposed
	19x5	(6 months)	19x6	19x7
REVENUES				
Chapter member dues	$238,000	$102,000	$249,700	$270,000
Members at large dues	76,000	47,000	78,600	80,000
Information services	40,000	76,000	120,000	150,000
Publication sales	180,000	89,000	204,000	230,000
Continuing education	98,000	62,000	106,000	110,000
Annual meeting	42,000	28,000	28,000	20,000
Royalty income	1,000	32,000	42,000	52,000
Interest income	3,000	600	1,000	1,000
Total revenues	678,000	436,600	829,300	913,000
EXPENSES				
Salaries & payroll taxes	310,000	178,000	363,000	360,000
Retirement & medical benefits	26,000	11,900	25,300	30,000
Professional fees	30,000	4,000	32,000	32,000
Supplies	20,000	10,900	24,000	26,400
Telephone	12,400	9,700	18,000	20,000
Postage & shipping	16,800	10,100	18,000	20,000
Building costs	43,200	14,500	36,000	38,000
Equipment repair & insurance	9,600	8,500	12,000	14,000
Printing & publications	140,000	68,400	120,000	137,000
Travel	15,000	4,200	17,000	30,000
Meetings & classes	26,000	9,600	22,000	32,000
Information services	32,000	44,000	57,000	80,000
Depreciation on equipment & furnishings	36,000	21,000	42,000	47,000
Marketing	13,000	8,700	17,000	46,600
Total expenses	730,000	403,500	803,300	913,000
Excess of revenues over expenses	($52,000)	$33,100	$26,000	$0

prepared, as suggested in Section 4.6, mid-year, or almost six months before the budget period begins. The actual financial results for the prior year and the current six months form the basis for projecting both the current year's and the upcoming year's results. The overall budget is a compilation of the information contained in SANM's seven other budget segments illustrated.

(b) Functional Revenue and Expense Budget

This report, Exhibit 4.7, compiles the detailed projections prepared by each department. Note that the six month numbers do not appear on this sheet because the column totals are calculated on the following worksheet.

Exhibit 4.7.   Functional Revenues & Expense Budget.

STATE ASSOCIATION of NONPROFIT MANAGERS						
FUNCTIONAL REVENUES & EXPENSE BUDGET						
	Projected Actual 19x6	Proposed 19x7	Member Services	Publications	Meetings & Classes	Administration
REVENUES						
Chapter member dues	$249,700	$270,000	$270,000			
Members at large dues	78,600	80,000	80,000			
Information services	120,000	150,000	150,000			
Publication sales	204,000	230,000		$230,000		
Continuing education	106,000	110,000			$110,000	
Annual meeting	28,000	20,000			20,000	
Royalty income	42,000	52,000	42,000			
Interest income	1,000	1,000				$1,000
Total revenues	829,300	913,000	542,000	230,000	130,000	1,000
EXPENSES						
Salaries & payroll taxes	363,000	360,000	128,000	82,000	32,000	118,000
Retirement & medical benefits	25,300	30,000	8,000	5,000	2,000	15,000
Professional fees	32,000	32,000	12,000		8,000	12,000
Supplies	24,000	26,400	8,800	4,400	6,600	6,600
Telephone	18,000	20,000	8,500	4,500	2,500	4,500
Postage & shipping	18,000	20,000	4,000	11,000	2,500	2,500
Building costs	36,000	38,000	6,500	12,500	6,500	12,500
Equipment repair & insurance	12,000	14,000	2,000	4,000	2,000	4,000
Printing & publications	120,000	137,000	10,000	98,000	26,000	3,000
Travel	17,000	30,000	20,000		5,000	5,000
Meetings & classes	22,000	32,000	6,000		26,000	
Information services	57,000	80,000	80,000			
Depreciation	42,000	17,000	4,600	2,800	1,600	8,000
Marketing	17,000	46,600	25,000	5,000		
Total expenses	803,300	883,000	323,400	229,200	120,700	191,100
Excess of revenues over expenses	$26,000	$30,000	$218,600	$800	$9,300	($190,100)

(c) Member Services Budget Worksheet

SANM's program officers each suggest a desired functional, or departmental, budget for the respective activities for which they are responsible, similar to the one shown in Exhibit 4.8 for the member services department. This worksheet is the type to attach to the interoffice memo (Exhibit 4.2), to invite participation of the department in the budget process. The financial information shown in the two left-hand columns—actual 19x5 and actual to date—would be completed by the business or accounting office prior to distribution. For large organizations, there could be layers of such workpapers for segments within the department or activity center.

Exhibit 4.8. Member Services Budget Worksheet.

STATE ASSOCIATION of NONPROFIT MANAGERS MEMBER SERVICES BUDGET WORKSHEET	19x5		19x6	19x7
	Actual	Actual to date (6 months)	Projected Actual this year	Proposed Next year
REVENUES				
Chapter member dues	$238,000	$132,600	$249,700	$270,000
Members at large dues	76,000	28,200	78,600	80,000
Information services	40,000	38,000	120,000	150,000
Royalty income	1,000	22,000	42,000	42,000
Total revenues	355,000	220,800	490,300	542,000
EXPENSES				
Salaries & payroll taxes	108,000	60,000	126,000	128,000
Retirement & medical benefits	6,480	2,900	6,000	8,000
Professional fees	15,000	4,200	12,000	12,000
Supplies	10,000	3,840	8,000	8,800
Telephone	12,800	5,020	8,000	8,500
Postage & shipping	3,600	2,290	4,000	4,000
Building costs	6,200	5,800	8,000	6,500
Equipment repair & insurance	1,800	1,100	2,000	2,000
Printing & publications	6,250	2,300	5,000	10,000
Travel	19,000	4,800	10,000	20,000
Meetings & classes	1,760	800	2,000	6,000
Information services	22,900	26,100	61,000	80,000
Depreciation on equipment & furnishings	12,400	7,000	14,400	4,600
Marketing	500	2,000	4,600	25,000
Total expenses	226,690	128,150	271,000	323,400
Excess of revenues over expenses	$128,310	$92,650	$219,300	$218,600

(d) Budget Increases (Decreases) Projected for 19x7

This report shown in Exhibit 4.9 calculates the actual dollar increases or decreases in the overall revenue and expense categories and shows the percentage of change. Many versions of this report, including graphs and other financial or economic information, could be designed to translate and best explain the budget for those who must approve the proposals.

(e) Personnel Budget

The expected personnel costs for the upcoming year for SANM is shown on Exhibit 4.10. This report customarily is kept confidential and

Exhibit 4.9. Budgeted Increases (Decreases) Projected for 19X7.

STATE ASSOCIATION of NONPROFIT MANAGERS				
BUDGETED INCREASES (DECREASES) PROJECTED for 19X7				
	Expected	%	Increase	Projected
	Actual	Change	(Decrease)	for 19x7
	19x6			
REVENUES				
Chapter member dues	$249,700	8%	$20,300	$270,000
Members at large dues	78,600	1%	1,400	80,000
Information services	120,000	12%	30,000	150,000
Publication sales	204,000	10%	26,000	230,000
Continuing education	106,000	2%	4,000	110,000
Annual meeting	28,000	-3%	(8,000)	20,000
Royalty income	42,000	4%	10,000	52,000
Interest income	1,000	0%	0	1,000
Total revenues	829,300	34%	83,700	913,000
EXPENSES				
Salaries & payroll taxes	363,000	-1%	(3,000)	360,000
Retirement & medical benefits	25,300	19%	4,700	30,000
Professional fees	32,000	0%	0	32,000
Supplies	24,000	10%	2,400	26,400
Telephone	18,000	11%	2,000	20,000
Postage & shipping	18,000	11%	2,000	20,000
Building costs	36,000	6%	2,000	38,000
Equipment repair & insurance	12,000	17%	2,000	14,000
Printing & publications	120,000	14%	17,000	137,000
Travel	17,000	76%	13,000	30,000
Meetings & classes	22,000	45%	10,000	32,000
Information services	57,000	40%	23,000	80,000
Depreciation on equipment & furnishings	42,000	-60%	(25,000)	17,000
Marketing	17,000	174%	29,600	46,600
Total Expenses	803,300	10%	79,700	883,000
Excess of revenues over expenses	$26,000	15%	$4,000	$30,000

Exhibit 4.10.   Personnel Budget.

STATE ASSOCIATION of NONPROFIT MANAGERS						
PERSONNEL BUDGET						
Projected Compensation for the fiscal year 19xx, compared to 19xx						
	Base	Fringe	Payroll	Actual Comp.	Budgeted	Budgeted
Position and/or Name	Compensation	Benefits	Taxes	This Year	This Year	for 19xx
FULL TIME						
Executive Director	$60,000	$7,600	$5,000	$72,600	$72,000	$78,000
Chief Financial Officer	48,000	5,400	3,800	57,200	57,000	60,000
Career Counselor/Referrals	40,000	3,000	3,200	46,200	38,000	48,000
Publications Director	40,000	3,000	3,200	46,200	46,000	48,000
Computer/Internet Guru	30,000	1,800	2,400	34,200	34,000	36,000
Assistants (4)	88,000	4,100	7,000	99,100	108,000	90,000
PART-TIME						
Editor (1/2 time)	20,000	400	1,600	22,000	25,000	20,000
Assistant	10,000		800	10,800	10,000	10,000
TOTALS	$336,000	$25,300	$27,000	$388,300	$390,000	$390,000

prepared in the accounting department in consultation with department heads rather than being broadly circulated.

(f)   Program Cost Analysis

SANM evaluates the viability of its member dues, publication prices, and class fees with the calculations shown in Exhibit 4.11. This exhibit report shows the meetings and classes revenues barely cover the direct cost of

Exhibit 4.11.   Program Cost Analysis.

STATE ASSOCIATION of NONPROFIT MANAGERS				
PROGRAM COST ANALYSIS				
	********** Program Services ************			
	Member	Publications	Meetings &	Total
	Activities		Classes	
Total Direct Program Costs	$267,000	$229,600	$122,000	$618,600
Supporting Service Costs	$92,350	$36,940	$55,410	$184,700
Total Cost of Program	$359,350	$266,540	$177,410	$803,300
# of Members	2,500			
Publications sold		23,860		
Hours of education			12,000	
Per Unit Direct Cost	$106.80	$9.62	$10.17	
Total Program Cost @ member	$143.74	$11.17	$14.78	

this activity; in other words, the revenue does not pay any portion of the association's administrative cost burden—it needs to control the cost or raise the price for meetings and classes. The per participant direct and total program costs for the service provided should enable SANM to reevaluate its class and meeting fees.

Many variations on this theme could be utilized for fund-raising event costs, student or class-hour costs, per patient costs, and so on. The concepts and methodology used in cost accounting, outlined in Section 7.2, can be consulted for guidelines on cost analysis.

(g) Other Reports and Analysis

SANM's relatively simple capital acquisitions budget is shown in Exhibit 4.12. For some organizations this report and the accompanying cost analyses, including competitive bids and other plans, can be quite extensive. The insurance coverage report in Exhibit 4.13 serves two purposes. For budgeting purposes, the premiums for the coming year are reflected. For risk analysis purposes, the types and limits of coverage are reported for review by those fiscally responsible for protecting the organization's resources as explained in Chapter 2. For a list of other financial report and statistical information that might prove useful to other nonprofits see Section 4.2.

Exhibit 4.12. Capital Acquisition Budget.

STATE ASSOCIATION of NONPROFIT MANAGERS						
CAPITAL ACQUISITION BUDGET						
	Total cost	New adds	Projected	Sales or	Total cost	Proposed
Description of asset	thru 19x5	to date 19x6	thru yr end	Dispositions	thru 19x6	Next year
Buildings	$300,000				$300,000	
Computers & statewide network	62,000	$18,000	$12,000	($12,000)	80,000	
Upgrade memory - 8 computers						6,400
New computers (3)						6,000
Office Furnishings	80,000	12,000	2,000	(4,000)	90,000	
Publication storage racks						3,000
New classroom furniture						12,000
Totals	$442,000	$30,000	$14,000	($16,000)	$470,000	$27,400

Exhibit 4.13. Insurance Coverage Report.

STATE ASSOCIATION of NONPROFIT MANAGERS				
INSURANCE COVERAGE REPORT				
	Insurance		Premium	Premium
Type of coverage	Company	Period of Coverage	This year	Next year
Property & casualty:				
Building	ABC Casualty	August - July	$3,600	$4,200
Equipment	ABC Casualty	August - July	1,400	1,800
Liability:				
Umbrella	ABC Casualty	August - July	3,000	2,800
Officer/director	ABC Casualty	August - July	1,600	1,600
Malpractice	Natl NPO Assn	Calendar - renew Dec.	2,000	2,400
Staff related:				
Worker's compensation	ABC Casualty	Calendar-report due Nov.	4,600	4,800
Health (1/2 pd by employees)	Best HMO	Month to month	14,000	12,000
Disability (pd by employees)	Natl NPO Assn	Month to month	none	
Fidelity bond	ABC Casualty	August - July	800	800
Total all insurance			$31,000	$30,400

4.12   A BUDGETING CHECKLIST

The Checklist appears next on pages 95–99.

A BUDGETING CHECKLIST

Exhibit 4.14. Short- and Long-Term Budgeting Checklist.

> *This checklist would be completed by the chief financial officer or other party responsible for organizing the budget effort and compiling the information. It could also be reviewed by the board finance committee to determine if all suitable steps in the process have been taken.*

1. **Why is a budget useful?**

   a. It outlines in financial terms the goals and policies approved by the board. ☐

   b. It is a tool for monitoring adherence to and deviations from plans throughout the year. ☐

   c. Its preparation causes the organization to focus on planning, evaluation of programs, and accomplishment of its mission. ☐

2. **Is the budgeting process timed properly?**

   a. Can proposed staff or project changes realistically be implemented before the fiscal year begins? ☐

   b. Is board membership scheduled to change prior to budget approval? (Avoid having a new board be responsible for a budget they didn't approve.) ☐

   c. If the budget is approved by members, when is the annual meeting? ☐

   d. Must major grant funding requests be submitted in advance of approval of the overall budget? If so, consider the need for a 2- or 3-year plan. ☐

3. **What type of budget is appropriate for this organization?**

   a. Is a zero-based budget needed for critical evaluation of priorities to force a serious cutback in level of expenses? ☐

   b. Are existing programs examined as closely as proposed projects? ☐

   c. Will functional or line-item budget allow proper review of program goals? ☐

   d. Is the budget based on existing operations, with incremental increases or decreases for economic conditions? ☐

(Continued)

Exhibit 4.14. *(Continued)*

4. **Who prepares the budget?**

   a. Is a budget committee needed? □

   b. Would a budget committee made up of accounting department staff, board members, and outside advisors be effective? □

   c. If each department does initial preparation, are standard formats and instructions furnished to lend consistency? □

   d. Is the final budget comprehensive, including restricted funds, endowments, capital improvements, and all financial aspects? □

5. **What are the steps in the budget preparation process?**

   a. Develop goals and objectives for a three- to five-year period first (long-range plan, dreams). □

   b. Quantify long-range goals, such as raising an endowment, financing new facilities, or increasing staff. □

   c. Evaluate last year's results.

      i. Were objectives achieved? □

      ii. If not, were they unreasonable? □

      iii. What caused variances? Were midyear revisions appropriate? □

      iv. Were changes indicated by ratio analyses? □

   d. Establish objectives for the coming year. □

   e. Prepare program justifications. □

   f. Prepare estimates of revenues and cost of programs. □

   g. Compile, evaluate, and balance the results. □

   h. The budget should be approved first by the staff, then by the board (with intervening steps as nature of organization dictates). □

   i. Amend the budget when the monitoring process shows a need for change. □

6. **Evaluate programs and services rendered.**

   a. Who are the constituents? □

   b. Is the organization reaching them? □

A BUDGETING CHECKLIST

Exhibit 4.14.   *(Continued)*

c. Should promotion be budgeted? ☐

d. Is the cost per person too high? ☐

e. Is a competing organization providing the same services? ☐

7. Evaluate the pricing of services.

a. Should charges be made? Prices increased or decreased? ☐

b. Would audience/membership/students/etc. increase with a decrease in prices, resulting in more revenue? ☐

c. Are funding sources available to cover free or reduced cost services? ☐

8. Evaluate fund-raising activities.

a. Can board members and other volunteers devote sufficient time to reach fund-raising goals? If not, should consultants or new staff be hired? ☐

b. Is an annual special giving campaign in addition to the membership campaign necessary? Would it drain membership? ☐

c. Can project sponsors or cosponsors be found? ☐

d. Should a planned giving program be established?

  i. Charitable remainder or trusts? ☐

  ii. Pooled income fund or charitable gift annuities? ☐

e. Can investment capital rather than gifts be sought for asset major acquisitions?

  i. Limited partnership? ☐

  ii. Subsidiary corporation? ☐

  iii. Joint venture? ☐

9. Evaluate expenses.

a. Could alternative approaches improve efficiency and thus reduce costs? ☐

b. Is the use of volunteers effective? ☐

c. Would "investing" in a paid development director or volunteer coordinator more than pay for itself? ☐

d. Are computers used effectively? ☐

(Continued)

Exhibit 4.14.   *(Continued)*

    i. To save money, are cheaper but time-consuming or
      inadequate programs in use? ☐

    ii. Would networking, E-mail, or Web Page pay for itself
       through saved time and mailings? ☐

  e. Are fixed and variable expenses segregated? If so,
    are they properly allocated to programs? ☐

  f. Are salary level changes factored into
   benefit costs? ☐

10. Consider outside forces.

  a. Is funding likely to be cut due to the depressed
    state of the economy nationwide or in the area? ☐

  b. Has there been a shift in population? Have plants closed?
    Are the standards of the profession changing? Is there a new
    university in town? ☐

  c. Has there been a drought, pollution increase, or stock
    market crash? ☐

  d. Are accreditation or granting requirements changing? ☐

11. Before final approval, consider these issues.

  a. Is there any doubt about the reliability of projections? ☐

  b. Do sufficient cash reserves exist to cover shortfalls/overages? ☐

    (If not, increase working capital in the budget.)

  c. Reevaluate policy goals if cuts must be made. ☐

  d. Could projects be carried out in cooperation with or
    by another organization? ☐

  e. Would charts or graphs illustrate trends and make
    decisions clearer? ☐

  f. Reconcile short-term resource needs with
   long-range growth. ☐

12. Prepare supplemental budgets to implement the overall budget.

  a. Cash flow projections. ☐

  b. Investment objectives. ☐

  c. Capital expenditure timing. ☐

  d. Restricted fund budgets. ☐

Exhibit 4.14.   *(Continued)*

---

13. Devise a follow-up system for monitoring the budget.

   a. Use timely financial reports to compare actual
      expenses and income with those budgeted. ☐

   b. Revise budget to reflect recurring changes during
      the year. ☐

CHAPTER FIVE

Asset Management

A nonprofit's planners should view its finances from a "going concern" perspective, meaning the nonprofit is alive and prepared to conduct its activities for an indefinite period of time into the future.

A nonprofit's resources, or assets, are best managed from the perspective of a *"going concern,"* that is, without assuming any limit on the organization's existence. Although financial planners strive to get the best return from invested assets, they must be sure the organization has sufficient liquid assets available to finance current operations. The goal, in brief, is to maintain the optimum balance between available assets and invested, or growing, assets. A going concern operates in a fiscally solvent fashion. Solvency in this context means the ability to pay the organization's debts in a timely manner or to meet its financial responsibilities—not to dissolve like sugar.

This chapter will consider how a nonprofit's resources flow and interact. Tools for managing that all important resource—cash—are illustrated and explained. Issues to consider in accepting and protecting restricted and permanent funds are explored in depth, along with discussion of the total return concept for measuring investment income.

5.1 MAXIMIZING RESOURCES

To be fiscally solvent and operate as a going concern, the nonprofit's managers, after the budgets are developed, focus on two more objectives:

- Smoothly financing current operations by making the most efficient use of current, or liquid, funds, and

- Maximizing available and obtainable resources to enhance return on the resources, or capital.

Conceptually the task of accomplishing these objectives can be entitled either *asset management* or *resource allocation*. All the nonprofit's resources—from its volunteers and members, to the cash in the bank, to

Exhibit 5.1a. Resource Flow for Business League.

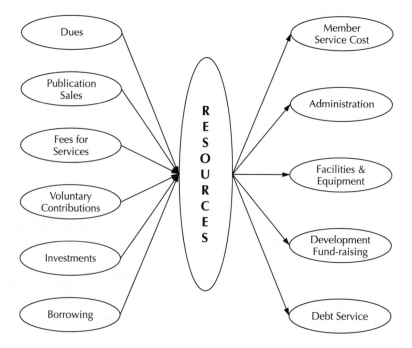

its bricks and mortar—are assets that can be fiscally managed. Such assets do not only provide a benefit and contribute to accomplishing the overall organizational goals, they also add to costs. The financial manager continually seeks to balance the forces of benefit and inherent cost. True, a planned giving campaign seeking long-term pledges of support, may be desirable; but the financial costs associated with the campaign and with monitoring and collecting the pledges must be assessed to evaluate the ultimate overall increase in available resources. Similarly, a plan to keep cash balances fully invested must take into account the salary of the person who oversees the effort in calculating the net interest return anticipated.

A nonprofit's overall resource flow is depicted in Exhibits 5.1a and b. The sources and uses of resources for a business league and an educational institution are illustrated. Although the labels may be different, the flows of resources are prototypical and may be found in a wide variety of nonprofit organizations. The resources of a church supported by its members, for example, would look very much like the business league. Similarly, a museum's resource flow would resemble that of the educational center once visitors were substituted for students, art collectors for alumni, and art exhibitions for academic programs.

Exhibit 5.1b.   Resource Flow for Academic Institution.

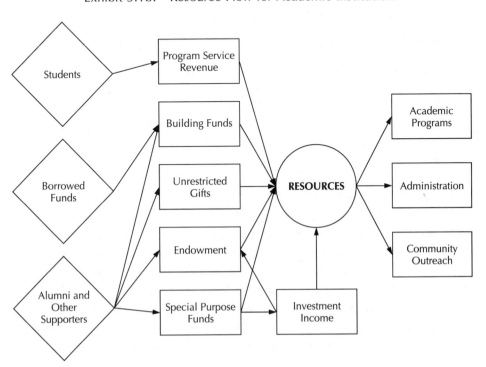

The prominent center, labeled "Resources," represents the funds available to finance operations or pay the bills. Theoretically, the flow of funds coming from the sources on the left side of the chart is sufficient to finance the outflows on the right. Some argue that the successful nonprofit focuses first on the left—the sources of funds. They would say that it is easy to spend the money; the difficult part is obtaining it. Others reason that excellent programs draw the support of a nonprofit's natural constituency and, therefore, should be the focus. One way to dissect the illustration is to ask which comes first. In other words, "Should we authorize the expenditure of funds before the funds are in the bank?" It may now be apparent that in resource management, the objective is to look at the organization holistically and to capture the benefit of its resources—from sources to programs and back again—with a balanced perspective.

5.2 GETTING RESOURCES

To further examine the resource picture, the planners consider the choices in obtaining those resources. A nonprofit's funding typically comes from one or more of the following sources:

- Contributed funds (general support and restricted gifts),
- Membership dues,
- Exempt function (related) income,
- Business venture (unrelated) income,
- Cooperating partnerships, and
- Indebtedness.

The U.S. political milieu of the late 1990's is rapidly changing the fashion in which nonprofits receive resources. Legislative proposals under consideration may create havoc and significantly alter the perimeters within which a nonprofit seeks funding. At the time this manuscript was written, it seemed possible, heaven forbid, a "flat tax" could be adopted. Although some gifts to nonprofits stem from pure generosity, the elimination of the charitable deduction would remove a traditional incentive for giving. One can only hope that the philanthropic impulses unique to Americans will survive the transformation and budget balancing acts of Congress.

GETTING RESOURCES

There is much written and a wealth of data and assistance available about fund-raising that is beyond the scope of this book. My intention in this section is to provide a bit of information to whet a financial planner's appetite by exploring resources that might be overlooked and about which there is a fairly high degree of misinformation.

(a)   Forming Alliances

As mentioned in Section 1.6 and illustrated in Section 7.4, most organizations have a valuable intangible resource—their knowhow and accomplishments. Financial planners should seek to recognize these resources and the possibilities for using them to replace evaporating government funding and for other reasons. As an example, alliances can be formed among groups of nonprofits providing similar or overlapping services. In Houston, the united giving campaign, the city government, and the major private foundations formed a consortium, in the fall of 1995, to compare notes and study the system for delivery of human services and the existing funding sources. The hope of the consortium is to identify and stretch citywide resources available to those in need. Examples of useful alliances could be extensive. To inspire the consideration of such resources, the following suggests intangible resources that might be identified:

- Can the cost of our talented programmers be leveraged by sharing their knowledge with similar organizations?
- Could the exemplary after-school program conducted on the town's northside serve as a model for centers in other locations?
- Could the award winning stage production be taken on the road?
- Could our organization cosponsor this year's seminar with similar organizations throughout the state?
- Is there a market to circulate the children's art exhibition we have approved for next year?
- Can the curators design the teaching materials in a fashion suitable for bookstores and teacher supply houses?
- Can we seek other cultural groups to join us to more fully utilize our theatre?
- Should our loosely affiliated local organizations seek a national group exemption to save each individual group the need to seek IRS approval and make annual filings?

These questions could result in plans to achieve economies to scale that enhance and maximize a nonprofit's existing resources. The attitude at the turn of the century mark can be "Why should all the arts organizations in town have individual Web pages? Why not have an *ArtSite* accessible on the internet for all?"

(b) Business Income

Most nonprofits have resources, such as their name, their mailing list, their buildings, and their knowledge and volunteers, among other assets, that can be commercially exploited for their benefit. It is very important to point out that most exempt organizations, other than private foundations, are permitted to conduct business activities for income producing purposes as long as that activity does not subsume them and become the organization's primary focus. The rules concerning business income are highly complex and represent a very good example of why people, in 1995 at least, thought the income tax system as we know it should be discarded.

Business income earned by a nonprofit must be distinguished between that earned in pursuit of its mission—called *related income*—and that earned from an activity undertaken simply to make money—called *unrelated income*. Just a few examples of related income are student tuition paid in return for education provided, fees for continuing education seminars sponsored by a business league, charges to hospital patients, and sales of books on topics germane to the organization's mission. This type of income is an expected and currently tax-free source of nonprofit revenues.

On the other hand, income from operating a public restaurant, selling advertisements in the quarterly newsletter, or providing health insurance programs are not considered to advance the mission, or to be unrelated. For federal purposes, the net profit from unrelated business activity is subject to income tax just as if the nonprofit were a for-profit company. The rules are designed to eliminate unfair competition to businesses by putting a nonprofit on the same footing as a for-profit.

The unrelated business income tax rules have been a healthy target for lobbying groups for and against them. As a result of successful lobbying by nonprofits, the rules exclude from tax a business that is operated with volunteer labor, one that sells donated goods, one that is operated irregularly (the annual bazaar), and one that produces investment income, including dividends, rents, royalties, and interest. The small business lobby continually insists these special exceptions are unfair and should be eliminated. The IRS and nonprofits argue about the rules on a regular basis, making them unclear and difficult to understand. Suffice it to say, business income can provide a good resource for the nonprofit that is willing to study the rules and possibly pay tax on the profits.[1]

(c) Planned Gifts

The term *planned gift* refers to a gift that is paid over a period of years or at some time in the future. For a variety of tax reasons, such gifts may sometimes afford the giver a considerable economic advantage over an immediate, direct gift of cash or property. A brief description of the types of planned gifts the organization might solicit follows.

1. **Split-interest trusts** are attractive giving techniques because they provide for both charitable and noncharitable beneficiaries. A charitable remainder trust pays income for a term of years to the giver or other private individuals and eventually pays the trust principal to a charity. Its economic benefit is split between the donor and the nonprofit charity. A charitable lead trust functions conversely and pays the income to charity for a period of years and ultimately gives the property to individuals. The lead trust created under Jacqueline Kennedy's will reportedly allowed her to give a substantial sum to each of her children 25 years hence tax-free. Split interest trusts may be created either during life (called intervivos) or at death (called testamentary).

2. **Retirement plan** property held in an IRA or other qualified retirement plan account is accumulated income that has never been taxed. This characteristic makes such a plan a good choice for a planned gift. When someone dies with retirement assets still in the plan, a heavy (sometimes double and possibly higher than 70 percent) tax burden is imposed. If the plan is given to charity instead, a charitable deduction allows escape from the estate tax and the charitable recipient does not pay the income tax when it receives the assets in the plan.

3. **Life insurance policies** can also be a good choice. The annual premium is an affordable gift for many benefactors and attractively provides a much greater gift upon the insured's death. Under the existing tax rules, a charitable income tax deduction is

---

[1] For a more complete discussion of these rules, see © Jody Blazek, *Tax Planning & Compliance for Tax-Exempt Organizations, 2nd ed.*, John Wiley & Sons, New York, 1993, Chapter 21. Supplemented annually.

allowed for the gift of an existing whole life insurance policy equal to the cash surrender value at the time of the gift.

For organizations interested in learning more about planned gifts, two national organizations can be contacted: National Planned Giving Council and National Society of Fund-Raising Executives. Both have chapters in major cities throughout the country.

5.3 CASH FLOW PLANNING

Often the most important resource for a nonprofit is its cash. To maintain solvency, financial viability, or plainly said, *the ability to pay its bills,* the organization must have sufficient liquid assets. Certain noncash assets, such as donations receivable, eventually contribute to liquidity and are a part of the cash-management process. Such assets are commonly called current assets on a financial statement and include those assets with potential to become liquid within a short period of time—monthly student tuition receivable, bookstore inventory, and the like. One way to conceptualize the cash management process is to think of the cycles of cash that continually flow through the organization. To maintain solvency the cash must flow smoothly and be readily available when it is time to meet the obligation to pay creditors and personnel.

(a) Understanding CPA's Cash Flow Statement

CPAs designed the cash flow statement because the financial reports we issue may reflect an excess of revenues over expenses when there is no money in the bank. This situation arises, for example, when the organization spends cash to acquire equipment. Assuming the equipment will be useful over a number of years, only part of its purchase price is expensed (depreciated) for the year of purchase but the full price was spent. A charitable pledge is reported as income in the year pledged, and it likewise may produce a noncash profit. On the other side, a nonprofit showing a deficit might have money in the bank from collecting the pledge or from selling obsolete equipment. Using the accrual method accounting, as explained in Section 6.5, may exaggerate this result. This method presents resources earned, such as a student's obligation to pay tuition monthly, as current income, even though the money is not in the bank. Similarly supplies purchased but not yet paid for are shown as an expense.

Exhibit 5.2. Statement of Cash Flows for the year 19x6.

Cash flow from operations:

Excess of revenue over (expenses)	$26,000
+ Add back non-cash depreciation:	52,000
Adjust for accrual items:	
+(-) (Increase) in accounts receivable	(9,000)
+(-) Decrease in inventory and prepayments	24,000
+(-) (Decrease) in accounts payable	(32,000)
+(-) Increase in deferred revenues	14,000
= Net cash provided from (to) operations	75,000

Cash flow from investments:

Net proceeds of sale (purchase) of securities	0
+(-) Sale of equipment	16,000
+(-) (Purchase) of equipment	(44,000)
= Net cash from (used for) investment:	(28,000)

Cash flow from financing:

+ Proceeds of new loan	0
- Payments of mortgage principal	(4,000)
= Net cash provided from (to) financing	(4,000)
Sum of net increases (decreases) in cash for year	43,000
+ Beginning cash balance	17,000
= Ending cash balance	$60,000

The statement of cash flows found in the CPA's annual financial report is designed to fully explain the differences in resource flow and cash in the bank. The cash flow report reconciles the impact on the nonprofit's resources from its current operations, its borrowing or financing activity, and lastly its investment activity. The statement calculates the sources of increase or decrease in cash to arrive at the total change in cash as shown in Exhibit 5.2.

(b) Cyclical Fluctuations

The other side of cash flow planning addresses timing cycles. Cash inflows and outflows for most nonprofits fluctuate throughout the year for many reasons other than the accounting ones illustrated in Exhibit 5.2. Churches typically receive high tithes during the Christmas season and experience lighter collection plate receipts during the summer vacation season as illustrated in Exhibit 5.4, which is based upon the financial statements of Exhibit 6.7. Schools require (or encourage by charging interest) parents to pay a full year's tuition before the school year begins. Some business leagues or unions collect member dues once a year.

For those many nonprofits funded in an uneven fashion throughout the year, cash flow planning is a must. The fluctuations in cash probably cannot be entirely controlled. Instead the planners become aware when cash shortfalls are likely to occur and prepare to bridge the gap with delayed expenditures, borrowing, or some new fund-raising projects. Postponed expenditures or acceleration of payment terms for constituent billings are typical options to solve the problem.

(c) Designing Cash Flow Budgets

Once the annual operating and capital budgets are authorized, they can be converted into a cash flow budget to verify availability of resources, to see if the nonprofit can finance the plan. The cash flow budget is prepared on a monthly basis to pinpoint possible cash shortfalls that do not appear in the annual compilation of numbers. The task is to summarize the projected sources and uses of cash for the coming year, according to the actual months of receipt and expenditure.

To do so, first estimate when collections on year-end receivables will occur. Next calculate the normal time lag, if any, between the invoicing or billing for services or pledges (the point at which the income is recorded under an accrual system) and depositing the money in the bank. Use this statistic to convert the budget into expected inflow of cash from revenue-producing activity on a monthly basis.

Correspondingly, chart the expected expenditure of cash according to the month the payment is required, as shown in Exhibits 5.3a, b, c, and d. The prediction is based on past experience and educated guesswork. Expected capital expenditures, sales of assets, borrowing, debt repayment, and other financing transactions are then factored in.

In view of any deficits revealed by the cash flow budget, consider the need to borrow or redesign the entire budget. Note that the model cash flow budget reflects a policy decision to maintain a minimum cash level. Monitoring the cash flow budget is an ongoing process. Constant vigilance is critical. Close attention is especially needed if cash flows fluctuate widely or if months of deficit funding are expected. Although it is

Exhibit 5.3a.   Business League's Cash Flow, Version 1.

STATE ASSOCIATION OF NONPROFIT MANAGERS
CASH FLOW PROJECTED for year 19x7
VERSION # 1

	January	February	March	April	May	June	July	August	September	October	November	December	Total
REVENUES													
Chapter member dues	$10,000	$40,000	$20,000	$30,000	$10,000	$5,000	$3,000	$2,000	$30,000	$40,000	$30,000	$50,000	$270,000
Members at large dues	3,000	10,000	8,000	12,000	6,000	2,000	1,000	800	1,200	5,000	11,000	30,000	90,000
Information services	14,000	14,000	12,000	12,000	12,000	10,000	10,000	8,000	16,000	14,000	14,000	14,000	150,000
Publication sales	20,000	20,000	20,000	20,000	20,000	10,000	10,000	10,000	25,000	25,000	25,000	25,000	230,000
Continuing education	8,000	8,000	20,000	8,000	8,000	2,000	2,000	2,000	22,000	8,000	16,000	6,000	110,000
Annual meeting	10,000	5,000				20,000							20,000
Royalty income		6,000	5,000	8,000					8,000				42,000
Interest income	200	200	200	200	200								1,000
Total revenues	65,200	103,200	85,200	90,200	56,200	49,000	26,000	22,800	102,200	92,000	96,000	125,000	913,000
EXPENSES													
Salaries & payroll taxes	30,000	30,000	30,000	30,000	30,000	30,000	30,000	30,000	30,000	30,000	30,000	30,000	360,000
Retirement & medical benefits	2,500	2,500	2,500	2,500	2,500	2,500	2,500	2,500	2,500	2,500	2,500	2,500	30,000
Professional fees	1,000	1,000	12,000	10,000	1,000	1,000	1,000	1,000	1,000	1,000	1,000	1,000	32,000
Supplies	2,200	2,200	2,200	2,200	2,200	2,200	2,200	2,200	2,200	2,200	2,200	2,200	26,400
Telephone	1,667	1,667	1,667	1,667	1,667	1,666	1,667	1,666	1,667	1,666	1,666	1,667	20,000
Postage & shipping	1,667	1,667	1,667	1,667	1,667	1,666	1,667	1,666	1,667	1,666	1,666	1,667	20,000
Building costs	2,000	2,000	12,000	2,000	2,000	2,000	2,000	2,000	2,000	3,000	4,000	3,000	38,000
Equipment repair & insurance	1,100	1,100	1,100	1,100	1,200	1,200	1,200	1,200	1,200	1,200	1,200	1,200	14,000
Printing & publications	12,000	8,000	12,000	9,000	12,000	9,000	11,000	9,000	20,000	9,000	10,000	16,000	137,000
Travel	1,000	1,000	6,000	1,000	3,000	3,000	1,000	1,000	3,000	3,000	3,000	4,000	30,000
Meetings & classes	500	500	18,000	500	2,500	500		1,000	2,000	2,000	1,500	3,000	32,000
Information services	4,000	15,000	15,000	9,000	5,000	4,000	4,000	4,000	5,000	5,000	5,000	5,000	80,000
Marketing	11,650	11,650										23,300	46,600
Purchase of equipment	10,000										7,400	10,000	27,400
Total Cash Outlay	81,284	78,284	114,134	70,634	64,734	58,732	58,234	57,232	72,234	62,232	71,132	104,534	893,400
Excess (deficit) of CASH	(16,084)	24,916	(28,934)	19,566	(8,534)	(9,732)	(32,234)	(34,432)	29,966	29,768	24,868	20,466	19,600
Cash at beginning of month	60,000	43,916	68,832	39,898	59,464	50,930	41,198	8,964	(25,468)	4,498	34,266	59,134	60,000
Cash at end of month	$43,916	$68,832	$39,898	$59,464	$50,930	$41,198	$8,964	$(25,468)	$4,498	$34,266	$59,134	$79,600	$79,600

Exhibit 5.3b. Business League's Cash Flow, Version 2.

STATE ASSOCIATION OF NONPROFIT MANAGERS
CASH FLOW PROJECTED for year 19x7
VERSION # 2

	January	February	March	April	May	June	July	August	September	October	November	December	Total
REVENUES													
Chapter member dues	$10,000	$40,000	$20,000	$30,000	$10,000	$5,000	$3,000	$17,000	$15,000	$40,000	$30,000	$50,000	$270,000
Members at large dues	3,000	10,000	8,000	12,000	6,000	2,000	1,000	800	1,200	5,000	11,000	30,000	90,000
Information services	14,000	14,000	12,000	12,000	12,000	10,000	10,000	12,000	12,000	14,000	14,000	14,000	150,000
Publication sales	20,000	20,000	20,000	20,000	20,000	10,000	10,000	20,000	15,000	25,000	25,000	25,000	230,000
Continuing education	8,000	8,000	20,000	8,000	8,000	2,000	2,000	2,000	22,000	8,000	16,000	6,000	110,000
Annual meeting	10,000	5,000	5,000										20,000
Royalty income		6,000		8,000		20,000			8,000				42,000
Interest income	200	200	200	200	200								1,000
Total revenues	65,200	103,200	85,200	90,200	56,200	49,000	26,000	51,800	73,200	92,000	96,000	125,000	913,000
EXPENSES													
Salaries & payroll taxes	30,000	30,000	30,000	30,000	30,000	30,000	30,000	30,000	30,000	30,000	30,000	30,000	360,000
Retirement & medical benefits	2,500	2,500	2,500	2,500	2,500	2,500	2,500	2,500	2,500	2,500	2,500	2,500	30,000
Professional fees	1,000	1,000	12,000	10,000	1,000	1,000	1,000	1,000	1,000	1,000	1,000	1,000	32,000
Supplies	2,200	2,200	2,200	2,200	2,200	2,200	2,200	2,200	2,200	2,200	2,200	2,200	26,400
Telephone	1,667	1,667	1,667	1,667	1,667	1,666	1,667	1,666	1,667	1,666	1,666	1,667	20,000
Postage & shipping	1,667	1,667	1,667	1,667	1,667	1,666	1,667	1,666	1,667	1,666	1,666	1,667	20,000
Building costs	2,000	2,000	12,000	2,000	2,000	2,000	2,000	2,000	2,000	3,000	4,000	3,000	38,000
Equipment repair & insurance	1,100	1,100	1,100	1,100	1,200	1,200	1,200	1,200	1,200	1,200	1,200	1,200	14,000
Printing & publications	12,000	8,000	12,000	9,000	12,000	9,000	11,000	9,000	20,000	9,000	10,000	16,000	137,000
Travel	1,000	1,000	6,000	1,000	3,000	3,000	1,000	1,000	3,000	3,000	3,000	4,000	30,000
Meetings & classes	500	500	18,000	500	2,500	500		1,000	2,000	2,000	1,500	3,000	32,000
Information services	4,000	8,000	8,000	8,000	8,000	8,000	8,000	8,000	5,000	5,000	5,000	5,000	80,000
Marketing		10,000								10,000	13,300	13,300	46,600
Purchase of equipment	10,000										7,400	10,000	27,400
Total Cash Outlay	69,634	69,634	107,134	69,634	67,734	62,732	62,234	61,232	72,234	72,232	84,432	94,534	893,400
Excess (deficit) of CASH	(4,434)	33,566	(21,934)	20,566	(11,534)	(13,732)	(36,234)	(9,432)	966	19,768	11,568	30,466	19,600
Cash at beginning of month	60,000	55,566	89,132	67,198	87,764	76,230	62,498	26,264	16,832	17,798	37,566	49,134	60,000
Cash at end of month	$55,566	$89,132	$67,198	$87,764	$76,230	$62,498	$26,264	$16,832	$17,798	$37,566	$49,134	$79,600	

Exhibit 5.3c.   State Assn. of Nonprofit Managers Version 1: Charted Cash Flow.

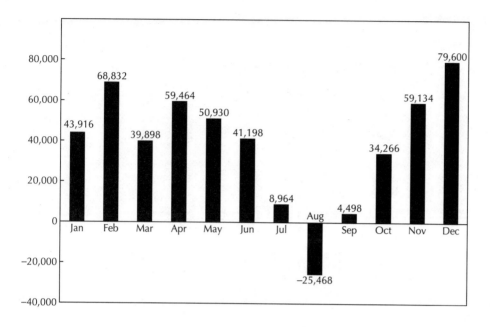

Exhibit 5.3d.   State Assn. of Nonprofit Managers Version 2: Charted Cash Flow.

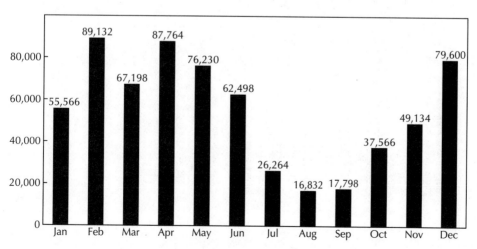

Exhibit 5.4.   Church Cash Flow.

HOLY SPIRIT CHURCH
CASH FLOW PROJECTED for year 19x6

	January	February	March	April	May	June	July	August	September	October	November	December	Total
Receipts:													
Plate collections	$3,600	$3,600	$4,600	$4,400	$3,800	$2,000	$2,000	$2,000	$5,800	$6,000	$4,200	$6,000	$48,000
Annual pledge envelops	3,000	3,500	3,500	6,000	3,500	2,000	2,000	2,000	3,500	3,500	3,500	6,000	42,000
Special gifts	600			6,500		2,000			4,000		900	10,000	24,000
After school care fees	1,000	2,000	2,000	2,000	2,000				1,000	2,000	2,000	2,000	16,000
Total receipts	8,200	9,100	10,100	18,900	9,300	6,000	4,000	4,000	14,300	11,500	10,600	24,000	130,000
Disbursements:													
Clergy & vestry	4,000	4,000	4,000	4,000	4,000	4,000	4,000	4,000	4,000	4,000	4,000	6,000	50,000
After school programs	2,800	2,600	2,600	2,600	2,600	100	100	2,600	3,000	3,000	3,000	3,000	28,000
Music & Sunday school	400	400	400	600	400	300	300	300	400	400	400	700	5,000
Building costs	2,500	2,500	2,500	2,500	2,500	2,500	2,500	2,500	2,500	2,500	2,500	2,500	30,000
Church office	1,250	1,250	1,250	1,250	1,250	1,250	1,250	1,250	1,250	1,250	1,250	1,250	15,000
Other	167	167	167	167	167	167	167	167	167	167	167	167	2,000
Total disbursements	11,117	10,917	10,917	11,117	10,917	8,317	8,317	10,817	11,317	11,317	11,317	13,617	130,000
Excess (deficit) of cash receipts over disbursements	(2,917)	(1,817)	(817)	7,783	(1,617)	(2,317)	(4,317)	(6,817)	2,983	183	(717)	10,383	0
Cash at beginning of month	6,600	3,683	1,867	1,050	8,833	7,217	4,900	583	(6,233)	(3,250)	(3,067)	(3,783)	
Cash at end of month	$3,683	$1,867	$1,050	$8,833	$7,217	$4,900	$583	($6,233)	($3,250)	($3,067)	($3,783)	$6,600	$18,400

possible to perform this task by hand monthly, cash flow budgets produced on computer spreadsheets save countless calculations. The need to closely monitor cash flow is yet another reason (in addition to those outlined later in Section 6.2) to obtain a fully integrated accounting system that can update the cash flow budget automatically as a part of the monthly financial report process.

5.4 BEYOND CASH FLOW IMBALANCES

Ideally an organization always has cash in reserve for unforeseen conditions. Imagine how important that reserve was to an arts organization in 1995 when the U.S. Congress slashed the National Endowment for the Arts budget. Contingency cash reserves can almost never be too high! A new organization particularly needs to budget for revenue surpluses in its early years until a sufficient level of cash is accumulated. To a young organization struggling to meet its payroll, building a cash reserve may seem like a luxury it can scarcely afford. Nevertheless, the fiscally prudent nonprofit plans from day one to build working capital reserves equivalent to several months, and preferably more, of operating expense.

Whenever cash flow budgets indicate excess cash reserves, plans for temporary cash investments are in order. As much money as possible can be kept in interest-bearing federally insured accounts to maximize yield on cash. The choice of temporary investment—certificates of deposit, Treasury bills, or money market accounts—should be governed by a board-adopted investment policy following the prudent investor rules discussed in Section 5.5. Once the cash reserves exceed the current year's need, the opportunity for longer term investments arises. This resource management task requires even more complex decision making—ideally, by a finance committee with the assistance of professional investment managers. Investment policies must weigh the permissible level of risk to the organization's resources in relation to expected returns.

(a) More Money in the Bank

The fiscally astute organization keeps its money in the bank as long as possible. Whether the organization is able to earn interest on the money or avoid paying interest on funds it must borrow or bills it pays late, money in the bank is obviously desirable. On the incoming cash side, when possible revenue collection procedures should accelerate the time for receiving the money. Keeping in mind that there is no reason not to act like a business in this regard, a nonprofit may charge interest on late payments and offer discounts for early payment.

Many nonprofits now accept credit cards for tuition, sales, services, and more. The accounting system should also contain suitable information and the capability to bill promptly for services rendered. Similarly, the membership renewal system should remind members promptly that it is time to send their support. Submission of quarterly cost reports required for grants payable in installments should never be late. The fund-raisers know the deadlines for submitting grant requests to potential funders well ahead of time. Unfortunately, there are too many nonprofits with cash flow problems, which are slow in sending renewal notices or grant reports that would provide the funds to pay the staff to send the notices or prepare the reports.

On the outgoing side, bills are scheduled to be paid when the terms for purchase require and not before. A regular cycle—say the first and fifteenth day of the month—can be established for bill payments. These established days are made known to the staff and creditors so that all can plan to receive their money based upon the cycle. It is amazing how much effort is saved with this simple policy in addition to interest earned on keeping the money in the bank.

(b) To Borrow or Not

When the cash flow budget indicates a deficit in cash will occur during the year, the nonprofit faces a tough decision. Does the organization attempt to borrow the funds, can it possibly find new funding, or does it reduce the projected expenditures? The answer depends upon the answers to many questions. Is the deficit temporary? Will it reverse itself in a few months? For a new organization, interim borrowing may not be an option. For a mature one expecting to refurbish an old building, there may be alternatives. The decision is made in each case based upon the particular facts and circumstances. This issue is one for which traditional business planning tools are particularly useful.

Securing a necessary loan takes good advance planning. In my experience, the nonprofit in a crisis mode only gets loans, if at all, from *angels*—patrons or funders who love the organization. But when the need for short term indebtedness is recognized as a part of the budgeting process, solutions can be found. The budget itself probably indicates that the situation will reverse itself with money expected to be received later in the year. For an organization in this situation, preparation of a business plan to make a formal application to a bank is a good exercise. If a bank cannot be persuaded to make the loan, the nonprofit goes back to the drawing board and revises its budgets and/or finds new funding sources.

A cash deficit created by proposed capital acquisitions may have a simpler and easier solution. The physical and tangible nature of a capital asset makes it suitable to serve as collateral for a loan. Therefore, it may be possible, even for a new organization, to borrow the money needed to equip the organization. The lender expects they can get their computer, truck, or whatever back if the nonprofit defaults on the periodic payments. The questions to be answered in choosing to borrow money for capital additions are outlined later in Section 7.3.

5.5 PRUDENT INVESTMENT PLANNING

Once a nonprofit organization accumulates cash assets beyond its operating needs for the coming year, it can begin to develop permanent investment plans. In managing the nonprofit's investments, the organization can be guided by the prudent investor rules compiled by the American Bar Association.[2] These standards say "a trustee is under a duty to the beneficiaries to invest and manage the funds of the trust as a prudent investor would, in light of the purposes, terms, distribution requirements, and other circumstances of the trust."[3] The business judgment rule, discussed in Section 2.2, requires essentially the same standard for nonprofit corporate directors regarding the management of endowment funds, restricted gifts or bequests, and employee benefit plans.[4]

The predecessor prudent man rule was first set forth in 1830 and directed trustees to "observe how men of prudence, discretion and intelligence manage their own affairs, not in regard to speculation, but in regard to the permanent disposition of their funds, considering the probable

[2] *Prudent Investor Rules,* Restatement of the Law of Trusts adopted by The American Law Institute at Washington, D.C., May 18, 1990, American Law Institute Publishers, St. Paul, Minn, 307 pages.
[3] Ibid, page 8.
[4] *Guidebook for Directors of Nonprofit Corporations,* George W. Overton, editor, Nonprofit Corporations Committee, Section of Business Law, American Bar Association, p. 41.

income, as well as the probable safety of the capital to be invested."[5] In explaining the rules, the guide cautions that the facts and circumstances of each investor (nonprofit organization) must be taken into account in choosing appropriate investments.

The nonprofit's financial planners must familiarize themselves with basic investment strategies and terms reflected in modern investment concepts and practices. Unless the trustees or directors individually possess expertise and time to manage the investments with care, skill, and caution, they have a duty to delegate management of such funds.[6] The fees charged by professional investment managers are often modest when viewed in relation to the possibility of enhanced yield over a period of time and professional management provided.

To evaluate a nonprofit's funds suitable to be invested in a permanent fashion, the following questions must first be carefully answered:

1. *For what length of time can the funds be invested?* The organization's liquidity needs must be projected into the future for a number of years. In choosing a suitable investment, the organization must know when or if the funds might be needed to pay future operating expenses, to build a new stadium, or to meet some other financial obligation.

2. *Can the organization afford to lose any of the money?* The answer to this question measures the level of risk the organization can take. The rate of return from interest, dividends, and/or increase in underlying value of the asset is related to the possibility that the original investment, also called principal sum, can be lost. The higher the risk of loss, the higher the expected return as explained below.

3. *How secure are the nonprofit's funding sources?* The organization must evaluate the stability of its funding sources to project the level of contingency or emergency reserves it may require. Such funds would be placed in investments with a low risk of loss of principal value.

---

[5] *Harvard College v. Amory*, 9 Pick (26 Mass) 446, 461 (1830). In 1959, the rule was changed to direct trustees "to make such investment and only such investments as a prudent man would make of his own property having in view the preservation of the estate and the amount and regularity of the income to be derived."
[6] Ibid. note 1, at page 41.

4. *Are the organization's personnel or staff capable of overseeing the invest-ments?* In the absence of a Midas touch, special talents and train-ing are required to successfully manage a fully diversified investment portfolio. As evidenced by the stock market crashes in past years, no one knows whether the stock values will go up or down. A nonprofit's financial managers must evaluate their own knowledge and experience and consider the need to engage out-side professional investment managers.

5. *How will the economic rate of inflation or deflation impact the invest-ment?* Fixed money investments, such as certificates of deposit and U.S. Treasury obligations, do not fluctuate in value according to the overall economy. Common stocks, real estate, and tangi-bles may be enhanced in value due to inflationary conditions and conversely lose value due to deflation. The nonprofit must project expected future inflation or deflation to properly diversify its investments.

(a) Facing the Unknown

A healthy dose of skepticism and an appreciation of the uncertainty that abounds in regard to investments is important. As one writer noted in describing the Federal Reserve Board's deliberations about the interest rate, "No word seems to appear more frequently in the tran-scripts than uncertainty."[7] The financial markets in which a nonprofit must choose to place its funds are influenced daily by international forces beyond its control. Who knows if the stock market will go up, if a global stock fund will sustain its yield, or if the U.S. dollar will go up against the Japanese yen?

Diversification is a very important technique designed to face the unknown. It says essentially, "Don't put all the eggs in one basket." A prudently balanced investment portfolio contains a variety of financial instruments—stocks, bonds, real estate, and so on. The mix of invest-ments assumes some go up, some go down, and in the long run the av-erages will provide a desirable stream of income. It is not necessarily conservative or prudent to maintain all the funds invested in fixed-money or interest-only bearing securities. Conserving the principal in

---

[7]Louis Uchitelle, *At the Fed It Looks Like Deja Vu, Again,* New York Times, Section 4, July 2, 1995.

its original dollar amount, inviolate and permanent into perpetuity, may not necessarily be safeguarding the fund for the donor's intentions. It should be remembered that fixed-return investments do have some inherent risk; in 1994 the value of some bonds fell over 10%.

The investment alternatives available to a nonprofit organization are the same as those available to a for-profit investor. Because the nonprofit does not pay income tax on its income, certain choices, such as municipal bonds or deferred annuities, may not be suitable. The types of investments from which the nonprofit chooses include those shown in Exhibit 5.5.

A classically diversified investment portfolio would contain some investments in each of the above categories. What portion of the total investments are held in each category depends upon the organization's risk tolerance and life phase as shown in Exhibit 5.6. Say a nonprofit organization has $1 million to permanently invest. If the board adopts a conservative approach, it would invest $250,000 in temporary cash, $350,000 in bonds, $200,000 in common stocks, $100,000 in real estate, and $100,000 in gold or commodities.

The investments within each category might be further diversified. A fixed-money portfolio, for example, would have debt instruments with staggered maturity dates and credit ratings, because fixed-return investments can also fluctuate widely in value and have some inherent risk of loss. The $350,000 in our example above might include $100,000 of 5-year bonds, $100,000 of 7-year bonds, $150,000 of 30-year bonds. Similarly a common stock portfolio would include stock of companies in different types of businesses—auto manufacturer, drug company, computer software, home building, banking, and so on.

(b) Risk versus Return

A nonprofit must carefully identify those funds that are suitable for each category of investment type. The possibility for a higher yield or overall return provided by common stock is not always worth the inherent risk of the investment. A restricted grant to be spent over a three-year period certainly should earn some interest, but probably should not be invested in technology stocks.

The relationship of risk to investment return must be understood. The reason a six-month certificate of deposit pays the lowest available interest rate is because no risk is taken. Without question, the face amount of the certificate plus a stated amount of interest will be paid (unless there is a bank collapse or other banking system crisis). As the uncertainty about

Exhibit 5.5.   Investment Alternatives.

Fixed-Money Value (principal dollar amount fixed):

    Interest Bearing checking account

    Money market account

    Certificate of deposit

    Treasury bills

    Series EE bonds

    Fixed annuities

Variable Money Value (principal value fluctuates with prevailing interest rates; but interest rate on investment usually fixed)

    Treasury notes and bonds

    Mortgage backed bonds

    Corporate bonds

    Municipal bonds

    Annuities or universal life insurance policies

Equity Investments (principal value and dividend rate varies)

    Common stock

    Preferred stock

    Convertible bonds

Real Estate

    Commercial real estate (office, store, hotel, or factory building)

    Residential real estate (single family or multi-person apartment)

    Raw land

    Agricultural land

Tangibles (the first three are also called collectibles)

    Gold or silver

    Antiques

    Art

    Minerals

    Commodities

Exhibit 5.6. Classic Investment Ratios.

	Conservative	Moderate	Risky
Cash & fixed money	25%	15%	5%
Fluctuating bonds	35	25	10
Equities	20	30	60
Real estate	10	20	20
Tangibles	10	10	5
Total Investments	100%	100%	100%

the final outcome or risk of loss increases, it is expected that the yield will increase. Correspondingly the less uncertainty, the lower the yield. The conflict between risks the organization is willing (or reasonably able) to take and the return on investment needed to pay operating expenses is the same as for individuals or for-profit companies. The pyramid in Exhibit 5.7 illustrates the concept.

(c) Investment Cycles

The categories of investment types chosen by a nonprofit organization can be based upon the phases of its financial growth cycles reflected in Exhibit 5.8. Phase 1 is the stage when the nonprofit has no cash reserves and needs to build its liquidity. During this phase, all the money would be invested in cash or near-cash securities, or those that can be converted to cash immediately without loss of principal value. Phase 2 represents the stage when the organization has begun to accumulate some working capital, maybe six months of operating expense in cash reserves, but still cannot afford to risk any loss of its principal. Phases 3 through 5 represent the three styles or investment philosophies a fully capitalized organization would follow when it is able to make permanent investments.

(d) Measuring Investment Return

For some investments the return, or income earned, is easy to calculate. Investment return is calculated by dividing the current income received

Exhibit 5.7.   Investment Risk Pyramid.

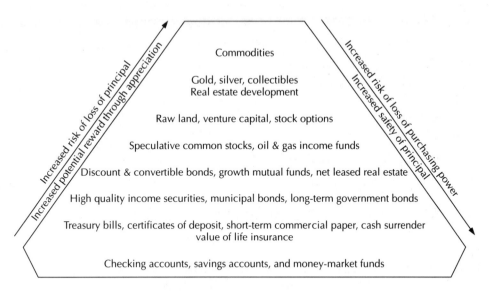

in a year—the interest paid or accrued, dividends, capital gain distributions or other profit share (for partnership), plus the increase in value of the underlying investment less any decrease in value.

Fixed-money investments, whose principal values fluctuate with the prevailing interest rates, are purchased at what is called a premium (paying $102 for a $100 bond) or discount (paying $95 for a $100 bond). When a premium is paid, the stated yield on the bond is usually higher than the prevailing rate. Conversely a bond selling at a discount likely is paying a

Exhibit 5.8.   Investment Phases.

	Short-Term Securities	Long-Term Bonds	Growth Stocks	Speculative Stocks	Real Estate	Other Types
Phase 1:						
Liquidity Accumulation	100%					
Phase 2:						
Adequate Liquidity, but no permanent funds	70	30				
Phase 3—Permanently Capitalized Organization						
Conservative Growth	30	30	30		10	
Moderate Growth	15	25	30	10	15	5
Aggressive Growth	5	15	35	20	15	10

lower percentage than the current rate. Each year the bond is held, a ratable portion of the premium or discount is added to or deducted from income to reflect the true yield as shown in example 4. Similarly, a bond originally purchased with a coupon interest rate of 8 percent does not yield 8 percent in a year when its principal value declines 2 percent; instead it yields 2 percent as reflected in example 5.

Example 1: For a one-year certificate of deposit issued at 5 percent the yield is:

$$\frac{\text{Interest}}{\text{Principal of CD}} \quad \frac{\$5,000}{100,000} \quad 5\%$$

Example 2: Common stock worth $100,000 on first day of year, paying out $2,000 of dividends and selling for $110,000 at year end.

$$\frac{\text{Dividend} + \text{Increase in Value}}{\text{Value of Year's Beginning}} \quad \frac{\$12,000\ (2,000 + 10,000)}{100,000} \quad 12\%$$

Example 3: Same as example 2 except stock declined to $98,000 in value.

$$\frac{\text{Dividend} - \text{Decrease in Value}}{\text{Value of Year's Beginning}} \quad \frac{\$\text{-}0\text{-}\ (2,000 - 2,000)}{100,000} \quad 0\%\ \text{(none)}$$

Example 4: A 5-year bond with principal sum of $100,000 bearing a 5 percent coupon is purchased for $95,000 and at year end is still worth $95,000. Note the brokerage or investment manager's report listing this bond would likely reflect that the yield is 5 percent, the face coupon amount.

$$\frac{\text{Interest Paid} + \text{Discount*}}{\text{Original Cost of Bond}} \quad \frac{\$6,000\ (5,000 + 1,000\text{*})}{\$95,000} \quad 6.3\%$$

(*The purchase discount of $5,000 is divided by five years.)

Example 5: A 5-year bond with principal sum of $100,000 bearing an 8 percent coupon is purchased for $100,000 on the day the bond is originally issued. By year end the value of the bond has decreased to $98,000 (because the current rate rose).

$$\frac{\text{Interest Paid} - \text{Decline in Value}}{\text{Original Cost of Bond}} \quad \frac{\$6,000\ (8,000 - 2,000)}{100,000} \quad 6\%$$

Example 6: For the bond in example 5, assume in the second year the value increased to $99,000. Note that for the two year period, the overall total yield might be averaged to determine the cumulative yield was 7.6 percent (6% + 9.18% divided by 2).

$$\frac{\text{Interest Paid + Increase in Value}}{\text{Beginning of Year Value}} \qquad \frac{\$9,000\ (8,000 + 1,000)}{98,000} \qquad 9.2\%$$

Professional investment managers and mutual funds governed by the Securities and Exchange Commission must conform to a unified standard for reporting investment yield.

5.6 RESTRICTED GIFTS

The nonprofit organization that pursues restricted funding does so advisedly and fully aware of the accompanying responsibilities. Once the money is received, the funder's specific designation about its use must be respected, necessitating a high level of attention to details. The financial stability afforded by such funding customarily makes the effort worthwhile for those nonprofits fortunate enough to secure it.

(a) Isolating Restricted Grants

A restricted gift is one subject to donor-imposed stipulations limiting its use. Some restrictions relate to a period of time that may expire, such as, "We pledge to give $100,000 to match any new foundation grants received in the next three years, "or" to hold until the current pastor's retirement account is fully funded." Another common type of restriction grants the funds to be spent for a particular project, for example, to buy food for children, train the unemployed, or clean up the pollution.

Perhaps the most important financial issue concerning such gifts is the responsibility to isolate the money. Under common law, the nonprofit owes a fiduciary duty to its contributors and grantors to use gifts for the purposes for which the funds are given. Accordingly, before accepting such funding, a mechanism for tracking the money must be in place. Because of this obligation, some organizations establish a separate bank account for each restricted fund. The fund accounting system discussed in Section 6.2 is designed to tag and track earmarked or restricted grants, and it should suffice to inform the financial managers on a regular basis of their obligation to have funds needed to meet the restrictions.

(b) Administrative Costs

All too often, restricted grant funds come with little or no administrative cost component. The nonprofit must consider whether or not it can afford to manage such a gift; for example, should it accept a restricted grant to distribute food to the poor if the grant only funds the purchase and provides no money for delivering the food or evaluating qualified recipients? Can it afford to fund, from its other moneys, the staff position(s) necessary to actualize the program goals? Always ask where it will get the funds to manage the grant. Another cost factor is enhanced accounting expense; the grant expenditures must be specifically accounted for. Reporting to granting agencies and foundations may require special forms and reports. As described in Section 2.6, the U.S. Governmental Office of Management and Budget has a sophisticated separate auditing process and requires a special *Single Audit* for certain federal grants.

5.7 ENDOWMENTS

An endowment is a permanent gift intended to be kept intact, perhaps forever, to produce annual income to support the organization's activities. What is referred to as the principal amount of an endowment gift is preserved or safeguarded and not itself expended for the stipulated term of years, commonly the life of the organization. Sometimes an endowment gift is invested to produce income to fund a specific project, like scholarships, or unspecified operational costs. Although such funding is a highly desirable resource, important policy issues regarding the terms of the endowment must be thoroughly discussed with the donors and agreed upon before such a gift is accepted.

The first question concerns the moment when the organization is ready to seek endowments. Potential endowment funders must perceive the organization to be sufficiently permanent or stable enough to exist a long time. Traditionally, universities, hospitals, and churches have attracted such funding. Recently cause-related organizations—some providing shelter to the disadvantaged, some dedicated to the environment, and others—have sought and received such permanent funding.

The other issues involve the terms governing the organization's use of the gift. In requesting endowment gifts, the informed nonprofit deliberates and suggests gift terms that will be to its best advantage. The issues that particularly should be agreed upon and stipulated in writing include the following, among others:

- *Endowment's life*—How many years must the endowment remain restricted? For some term of years (5, 10, or 20) or forever? Can the funds be used for another purpose in a time of crisis? If so, what type of crisis? What happens to the endowment funds should the nonprofit—or the program(s) to be funded—cease to exist? Is the endowment subject to a life income interest? (See Section 5.2c.)

- *Definition of income*—Are realized gains (defined later) treated as current income? Is the endowment principal, defined as its original sum, certain or is it the original sum plus all appreciation less declines in underlying value?

- *Nature of investments*—Do the endowment creators wish the original asset given to be retained? Can it be sold? Must it be sold in a particular fashion or offered to sale first to particular persons? If sold for cash, is there any restraint on the fashion in which the cash is reinvested?

You can quickly see from the above questions that the meaning of the term, *endowment,* is complex and multifaceted. To illustrate how the questions arise, assume that a $1 million endowment gift made payable in shares of marketable securities is accepted. Historically, the common law of endowments considered the capital gains, that is, the gains realized from sale of shares over time, as additions to the principal, the original value of the shares. Thus the principal value of the $1 million grew or shrank with market forces similar to the custom for private trusts. Only the current income (the dividends or interest) was expended currently on programs or operations. The structure of capital markets in the seventies began to favor the treatment of capital gains as current income, and the nonprofit world was faced with a dilemma.

(a) Who Gets the Appreciation?

The financial markets now expect low dividend yields equal to a small portion of the company's annual income. This "current return" is accepted to allow the corporation to reinvest most of its earnings in expansion and conglomeration. The desired result is a consequential appreciation in underlying value of the securities. Most investment managers today anticipate that annual income will be earned from a combination of dividends and interest plus gains resulting from appreciation in the value of the underlying security. The objective is to achieve what is called total return on the capital invested. What formerly was treated as an addition to the principal—the appreciation in value of the asset(s)—is now thought of as income.

The trend toward following a total return concept for a nonprofit's endowment funds was encouraged by the Ford Foundation as early as 1969 in a study entitled *The Law and the Lore of Endowment Funds.* [8] The study said, "we find no authoritative support in the law for the widely held view that the realized gains on endowment funds can never be spent. Prudence would call for the retention of sufficient gains to maintain purchasing power in the face of inflation and to guard against potential losses, but subject to the standards that prudence dictates, the expenditure of gains should lie within the discretion of the institution's directors." The study investigated whether "the directors of an educational institution are circumscribed by the law or are free to adopt the investment policy they regard as soundest for their institution, unhampered by legal impediments, prohibitions or restrictions."

(b) To Mark It to Market?

A number of parallel questions are faced by the nonprofit concerning its recordkeeping and financial reporting of its investment—endowment and otherwise. Among the issues to consider are the following:

1. Should investment assets be reported on the statement of net assets (balance sheet) at their original cost or at the current market value?

---

[8] *The Law and the Lore of Endowment Funds,* A Report to The Ford Foundation, New York, by William L. Cary and Craig B. Bright, 1969. The study was commissioned to review the law governing the endowment funds of colleges and universities with the goal of conveying new knowledge and informed commentary about charitable investments to strengthen the efforts of the institutions to improve their endowment income. The Uniform Management of Institutional Funds Act now recommends the total return concept. UMIFA has been adopted in all but 10 states and is applicable to nonprofit corporations.

2. In which fund is the total return reported?

3. How is the increase or decrease in the value of the investments reported on the Statement of Net Assets and on the Statement of Activity?

The answer to question 1 is still debated, although the CPAs have now weighed in on the side of current value. The accounting profession struggled for a long time to arrive at its recent recommendation that readily marketable equity and debt securities be reported at their current fair market price.[9] Mortgage notes, real estate investments, oil and gas interests, venture capital funds, and partnership interests can be reported at original cost or appraised value. A purchased investment is recorded originally at its cost. Donated investment assets are reported at the fair market value on date of gift. Then annually those carrying values are adjusted up or down to reflect the current market value, and the result is reported as unrealized gains and losses.

Questions 2 and 3 are interrelated and more complicated to answer. First one must ascertain whether local law or the donor stipulation say anything about the issue. The Uniform Management of Institutional Funds Act, now law in many states, sanctions the inclusion of gains (realized and unrealized) in currently spendable income alongside dividends and interest; said another way, total return is reported on the Statement of Activity (Income Statement). The Association of College and University Business Officers (NACUBO) also recommends this policy. The *AICPA Audit and Accounting Guide for Audit of Certain Nonprofit Organizations* provides that a governing board may make a portion of realized, and in some cases, unrealized, net gains available for current use.

The unexpended increase or decrease in value (appreciation) of the securities remaining in the investment portfolio are reported as temporarily restricted funds, rather than endowment funds, under Statement of Financial Accounting Standards (SFAS) # 117. Note that this issue is evolving, requiring readers to seek the most current information. There are still choices about how the financial statements reflect the total return.[10]

---

[9] Statements of Financial Accounting Standards No. 124, Accounting for Certain Investments Held by Not-for-Profit Organizations, was issued November 1995, effective for fiscal years beginning after December 15, 1995.

[10] Reporting alternatives are very well illustrated and discussed in *Financial and Accounting Guide for Not-for-Profit Organizations*, Fifth Edition, Chapter 8 and note 7.9.

(c) How Income Is Measured

According to financial analysis theories, long-term investment income may be reported for financial purposes and correspondingly budgeted as expendable income in at least four different ways. The term *realized* is used to denote capital gain or loss from transactions that actually occurred. Realized capital gain is the excess of actual sale proceeds over the amount paid for a security. *Unrealized* capital gain is the hypothetical gain calculated assuming securities still held as investments were sold on the balance sheet date. Measures of long-term income include:

- *Current return method*—Using this method, actual interest, dividends, rents, or royalties paid are treated as income (unrestricted). Any realized or unrealized gains or losses added back to or subtracted from the principal fund (restricted).

- *The overall return method*—This method classifies the current return plus realized capital gains and losses (those resulting from actual sale of the investment asset) as operating (unrestricted) income.

- *The total return method*—This method reports overall return actually received plus or minus unrealized gains and losses as unrestricted income.

- *Constant return*—Based upon an historical average amount, a fixed annual percentage of the value of the investment pool is treated as unrestricted income.

The *total return method* can be shown this way:

Total Return	=	Dividends & interest	±	Realized and unrealized gains(+) and losses (−)

(d) Endowment and Restricted Fund Checklist

As indicated by the above discussion, management and protection of restricted and endowment funds has some risks and certainly involves significant policy decisions. Again, tools are available to allow the prudent nonprofit and its directors and financial managers to exercise the fiduciary responsibility inherent in the acceptance of such funding. The checklist shown in Exhibit 5.9 is designed to be completed at least annually by the financial managers. Additionally, an adequate fund accounting system as explained in Chapter 6 must be used to monitor restricted fund flows and to assure such resources are devoted to the purposes for which they were given.

Exhibit 5.9.   Endowment and Restricted Fund Checklist.

This checklist contains questions to verify adherence to covenants and restrictions, if any, placed upon contributed funds. It suggests questions to evaluate investment policy and to check for private inurement. It is particularly designed for use by the chief financial officer and the board finance committee. Some questions have simple yes/no answers for actions taken personally and some ask if others have carried out responsibilities delegated to them.

A. Understanding General Information Endowment and Restricted Funds

To become familiar with the terms and restrictions on a nonprofit's endowment and restricted funds and the accounting procedures in place for tracking such funds, consider the following issues:

1. Does the organization have any endowment or restricted funds? ☐

2. If so, is there a master control for such funds? ☐

3. Verify maintenance of a permanent file for each endowment. ☐

4. Review the permanent files to familiarize yourself with each endowment's terms and restrictions. ☐

5. If the donor's terms are not clear, has there been a clarification made with the donor or his or her descendants; if not, has the board adopted a policy regarding the uncertainty? ☐

6. Is a fund accounting system used? ☐

7. Regarding endowment funds:

   a. Are the moneys separately invested and easily identifiable? ☐

   b. Verify annual income required to be distributed or set aside. ☐

   c. How is *income* defined? Do endowment terms allow allocation of capital gains to income? ☐

Exhibit 5.9. *(Continued)*

B. Monitoring Compliance with Restricted Grant Covenants

To assess administrative ability to track restricted funds and measure availability of funds according to grant or endowment terms.

1. Can functional accounting reports, which identify costs allocable to grants, be prepared from the financial records? ☐

2. Are detailed expense records maintained?:

   a. Staff time reports. ☐

   b. Space usage allocations. ☐

   c. Direct and indirect cost-coding system in chart of accounts. ☐

3. Encumbrance system controls authorized expenditures under grant. ☐

4. For government grants (both federal and state), are procedures of OMB Circular A-128 and A-133 followed? ☐

5. Is income recognition properly timed? ☐

6. Are funds held for future periods classified as temporarily or permanently restricted? ☐

C. Permanently restricted land, building, and equipment (LBE)

To evaluate the nonprofit's ability to monitor permanently restricted gifts in the form of land, building or equipment (LBE), ask:

1. Is this fund being reported separately from the unrestricted funds because of donor restriction or accounting practice? ☐

2. Does the LBE fund include unexpended donations? If so does their investment placement give regard to the expected timing of the building program? ☐

3. Are transfers to cover depreciation made from the current unrestricted fund? ☐

4. Is an asset inventory system used to control physical loss of assets? ☐

(Continued)

Exhibit 5.9. *(Continued)*

D. Investment Policy

To assess investment strategies in view of risks, potential for return, and professional investment management, explore such issues as the following:

1. Are yields on investment assets monitored? ☐

2. Do yields furnish a return commensurate with the risk of capital loss? ☐

3. Are funds managed by an independent professional manager? ☐

4. Is management fee commensurate with those charged in the area for similar services? ☐

5. Consider propriety of having more than one manager. ☐

6. Does diversification of investments provide protection against inflation, market forces, and other economic changes? ☐

E. Reliance on Restricted Gifts

To assess the nonprofit's dependence upon such gifts, consider the following:

1. What portion of annual operations are financed with income from endowment funds or restricted grants? ☐

2. If income decreased substantially due to market forces, would the organization's programs be jeopardized? ☐

3. Are governmental or United Way grants subject to decline in current economic climate? ☐

F. Pooled Income Funds and Split-Interest Trusts

To oversee adherence to trust provisions regarding private individual beneficiary's interest in restricted gifts, the nonprofit annually asks the following:

1. Review reports of pooled income funds and split-interest trusts. ☐

2. Are terms of gift agreement adhered to? ☐

Exhibit 5.9. *(Continued)*

3. Is current income sufficient to make agreed payments to individual beneficiaries? ☐

4. Is distinction between income and principal clear? ☐

5. Were required annual reports prepared? ☐

6. Review term endowments or charitable lead trust for termination dates. ☐

7. Are annuity and unitrust computations evaluated by outside independent accountants? ☐

G. Suitability of Raising Endowment and Restricted Funds

To evaluate the benefit from endowment and restricted funds in view of the inherent costs and the potential fund-raising alternatives, answer the following questions:

1. Based upon answers to above questions, should the organization continue to solicit endowment and restricted grants? ☐

2. Is time involved in record keeping excessive? ☐

3. Could similar levels of support be raised as unrestricted grants? ☐

4. Should existing endowment instruments be reformed to allow allocation of some or all capital gains to income? ☐

5. Are donors still living? ☐

6. Would benefit of reallocated funding deserve cost of court petition? ☐

7. Should instruments for future endowment gifts and other restricted gifts be reformed? ☐

8. Does the development department, staff, and the board adequately communicate regarding issues raised in this checklist? ☐

Nonprofit Accounting

The backbone of financial planning for a nonprofit organization is a good accounting system.

This chapter outlines the basic elements of an accounting system. When and why an accrual basis of accounting is used can be understood by comparing the preferred system to the simpler alternative, the cash method of accounting. Factors indicating when a nonprofit goes beyond maintaining its accounts on a computerized checkbook system, such as Quicken, are presented. Illustrative financial statements append the chapter to reflect the desired result of the accounting function. Information on how to design a chart of accounts with samples can facilitate that critical process. Checklists for choosing a computer accounting system, maintaining internal controls, and minimal accounting system requirements complete the tools provided.

A broad range of data, both financial and nonfinancial, is used in making financial plans for a nonprofit organization. National and local economic performance, projections of future economic conditions or population growth, surveys reflecting social preferences or the number of persons in need of services, all may be useful data relevant to the planning process as described in Sections 1.7 and 4.7. By far the most accessible and typically the most significant data is contained in the nonprofit's own accounting records and financial statements. The desired result is an accounting system that presents historical financial information in an understandable fashion that allows the organization's managers to make astute financial decisions.

6.1   WHAT IS ACCOUNTING?

The accounting profession defines *accounting* as the art of recording, classifying, and summarizing in a significant manner and in terms of money, transactions, and events that are, in part at least, of a financial character, and interpreting the results thereof.[1] The United Way of America expands the definition and suggests that a nonprofit's accounting system records and summarizes the financial activities of the organization in a manner that:[2]

- Lends itself to revealing clearly and fully the organization's financial position, sources, and amounts of revenue, and nature and extent of expenditures, including per unit cost of the benefit, where feasible, and

- Complies with all legal and technical requirements of governmental and other authoritative organizations.

Budgeting serves as a financial guideline for future financial activity; accounting captures or records the present flow of funds and presents the nonprofit's resources in a meaningful fashion for its managers and constituents. From the resulting compilation of financial history, rational decisions can be made, aspirations can be tested against performance, and if necessary budgets as well as other plans can be re-adjusted to more accurately reflect the reality faced by the nonprofit organization. The labels or titles used are those listed in the chart of accounts, as explained in Section 6.3. An accounting system for the typical nonprofit looks somewhat like that of a for-profit business, as shown in Exhibit 6.1. This section introduces the system components shared by all systems as well as the special attributes of a fund accounting system.

[1] Accounting Research and Terminology Bulletins, *Accounting Terminology Bulletin No. 1*, Final ed., American Institute of Certified Public Accountants, 1941, p. 9.
[2] *Accounting and Financial Reporting, A Guide for United Ways and Not-for-Profit Human-Service Organizations*, revised 2d ed., 1989, United Way of America, p. 9.

Exhibit 6.1. Bookkeeping and Accounting Process.

| Recording | Categorizing | Summarizing | Presenting and Reviewing | Reporting |

Copyright 1983 The Support Center.

(a) Cash Receiving Systems

The cash receiving systems document all money received through mail, cash registers, and electronic transfers. The organization might also maintain records of money due to be received in the future, or accounts receivable, as described below. Whatever the level of sophistication of the receipt system, the objective is to have a chronological listing of all moneys flowing into the nonprofit, along with an appropriate paper trail evidencing the source of the funds. The cash receiving system records are usually called the cash receipts journal, the accounts receivable ledger, and the sales journal.

Cash Receipts Journal. All nonprofits should keep one or more journals into which each cash receipt is entered, much like an individual enters deposits into a personal checkbook. A cash journal contains a chronological listing of each deposit resulting in a monthly total that is reconciled to the deposits reported on the bank statement(s). For some organizations a separate journal for cash received in a door-to-door fund-raising campaign or annual fair might also be used. Cash journals use revenue categories to classify or total receipts according to the source of each entry: contributions, sales, interest income, and so on.

Accounts Receivable Ledger. The nonprofit that sells publications, performs consulting services, treats patients, has seminars, and similar fee based programs, often provides the goods and services before it receives cash payment. Likewise members and grantors may pledge support or pay dues over a period of time. Such obligations to pay are called *accounts receivable.* A ledger is maintained that lists, either chronologically or alphabetically, the names of purchasers or givers, the amount due to be paid, and the date payment is due. For charities soliciting voluntary contributions, the receivables ledger may include a complicated database holding each contributor's history of giving. These ledgers are called *subsidiary* ledgers and contain the detailed daily posting of activity. The monthly subledger totals are recorded, or posted, into the general ledger.

Sales Journal. A nonprofit that makes over-the-counter sales through a bookstore, cafeteria, theater, and so forth may maintain a cash register-based sales journal. Again a detailed listing of all transactions is maintained. The journal typically also identifies the category of sale for purposes of making a corresponding entry into inventory accounts, reporting goods held for sale.

(b)   Cash Disbursement Systems

The steps followed in paying the bills comprise the cash disbursement system. Such a system serves two purposes: (i) moneys are tallied as checks are disbursed and (ii) a documentation systems aids in preventing misuse or theft of money. The system ideally embodies an approval system to evidence that an authorized person sanctioned the expenditure. When a budget is used, a proposed expenditure is compared to the balance of unexpended moneys in the applicable budget category before disbursal of funds. Section 7.3 explores this subject further and presents model purchasing forms. Three different systems are used as presented below beginning with the most thorough and complicated.

Purchase Orders.   Under this system, the nonprofit establishes procedures for disbursing money based upon an advanced approval system. The prospective buyer first prepares a *purchase order* to seek authorization from a designated person(s). Ideally, the proposed expense concurrently enters the accounting system to verify available funds in the current-year approved budget. Only after this two-step approval system, the items or services are purchased. Upon the goods arrival or service performance, a receiving report is prepared and the liability or obligation to pay enters the accounting system as an account payable.

Accounts Payable System.   A somewhat simpler system tracks *accounts payable,* or those bills due to be paid. The purchase first enters the accounting system when the vendor invoice or statement arrives and is approved by an authorized person. Thus the obligation to disburse funds goes into the system before the bill is paid but after the debt is incurred.

Check Paying System. Under the simplest system, the expense enters the accounting system as checks are prepared for payment directly from the invoice or statement as they are paid. The checks are registered in chronological, and (optimally) numerical order, as they were issued.

(c) Payroll Journals

The details of salaries paid, taxes withheld for employees' and the nonprofit employer's matching amounts, employee benefits, salary reduction plan subtractions, and the like are entered in a payroll journal. Thus information is accumulated for periodic tax depositing and reporting purposes. The journal may also categorize the payroll according to types of workers (full time versus part time, hourly versus monthly), by program, by location, or other suitable classification that summarizes personnel costs in some fashion useful in planning or financial reporting.

For very good reasons, some nonprofits outsource the payroll function to companies that specialize in keeping the records, preparing checks or direct employee bank deposits, and handling all of the Federal and state tax reporting. Such services facilitate confidentiality of personnel compensation. Lastly, but sometimes most importantly, the personnel and the payroll taxes get paid on time. The withheld portion of payroll taxes do not belong to the organization but to the employees. A prudent board, whose members can in some circumstances be personally liable if the taxes go unpaid, needs to assure prompt and accurate payment. Volunteer treasurers and part-time bookkeepers are not always able to devote the regular time needed to meet such deadlines.

A record of vacation, sick, or compensatory time accrued and taken, plus all qualified and nonqualified pension or other deferred compensation should also be maintained. A nonprofit reporting on an accrual basis is expected to calculate and record its liability for such employee obligations.

(d) Other Useful Ledgers and Financial Files

Depending on the size and scope of the nonprofit's activity, many other ledgers, filing systems, or databases may be necessary to maintain adequate financial information. Exhibit 6.2 provides a checklist of minimal

Exhibit 6.2. Minimal Financial Record-Keeping for a Nonprofit Organization.

> *This checklist is a list of minimal record-keeping requirements for use by a new and emerging organization and suggests types of useful detailed records.*

A. Organizational Documents

Create permanent files for the following organizational documents: ☐

1. State charter, bylaws, trust instruments, or articles of association. ☐

2. Minutes of board meetings, finance, and other board committees. ☐

3. Letters of exemption from Federal, State, and local authorities, and applications file (Form 1023 or 1024). ☐

4. Letters of intent, trust instruments, grant agreements or other documents regarding restricted funds. ☐

5. Agreements with event sponsors, fiscal agents, joint venturers, chapters, or other documents evidencing organizational obligations and entitlements. ☐

6. Employment contracts, employee benefit plans, contracts for services, policy manuals, and other personnel files. ☐

7. Leases, maintenance agreements, repair records, and other data regarding equipment and facilities. ☐

B. Banking Records

1. Check register or checkbook reflecting each transaction and the cash balance in each bank account is constantly maintained. ☐

2. Bank statements opened and bank reconciliation prepared monthly by person not maintaining accounting records, preferably a non check signer. ☐

3. Bank statements kept intact (original canceled checks remain with statement) and reconciled monthly. ☐

4. Consider need for separate accounts for restricted funds. ☐

Exhibit 6.2. *(Continued)*

C. Revenues and Exempt Function Receipts

1. Deposit checks or cash, if possible, on day of receipt. ☐

2. Enter the payer's name and describe nature of funds received, whether check or cash, on each deposit slip or create detailed report. ☐

3. Record each contribution, sale, or service rendered in detailed ledger (student rolls or member receivables). ☐

4. Maintain an alpha (by donor or client) file for copies of receipts with a deposit slip copy attached. ☐

5. For events, canisters, or volunteer solicitations, maintain Public Fund Solicitation Control checklist (Exhibit 6.8). ☐

6. Issue receipts or thank yous with donor disclosures if needed. ☐

7. Calculate, charge, and report sales tax where applicable. ☐

D. Disbursement of Funds

1. Pay bills on a regular basis, the 5th and 20th or every Friday, for example. ☐

2. Design an approval system that provides internal control. (Section 6.8). ☐

3. Maintain paid bills (invoices) in an alphabetical order, labeled with check number and date paid. ☐

4. Establish reporting system for employee/volunteer time worked, vacations, leave, expenses reimbursed, and licensing requirements. ☐

5. Keep a file for permanent assets, including copy of original invoice, serial numbers, insurance, maintenance contracts, etc. ☐

6. Keep files to document nature of activities and nonprofit purposes (copy of exhibition catalog, invitations, show announcements, patients seen, consulting provided, time expended on projects, training seminars, etc.). ☐

7. For workers hired, classify as employee or contractor and complete checklist for employee tax requirements (Exhibits 7.12 & 7.13) ☐

8. For independent contractors, obtain invoice and Form W-9 for all. ☐

9. Obtain and use sales tax exemption certificate. ☐

(Continued)

Exhibit 6.2. *(Continued)*

E. Accounting Records

1. Choose an accounting system, preferably a computerized one suitable for nonprofit's size and staff skills. (Section 6.2) ☐

2. Develop a chart of accounts. (Section 6.3) ☐

3. Establish system for documenting and recording noncash entries. ☐

4. Preferably monthly, prepare financial statements of actual financial transactions compared to budgeted figures. (Exhibit 6.6) ☐

5. Maintain report of assets and debts (also called general ledger), preferably using a computerized financial statement program. ☐

6. Prepare annual budget and compare actual results on accounting summaries to the budgeted amounts. (See Chapter 4) ☐

7. Prepare tax compliance checklist annually. (See Chapter 8) ☐

8. Develop a record retention system with advice of counsel. ☐

9. Establish throw away dates and label stored records accordingly. ☐

record-keeping requirements for use by a new and emerging organization. The types of detailed records that are useful include the following:

A General Ledger contains a record for each account listed in a chart of accounts beginning with *Cash* as shown on the master listing in Section 6.3. The detailed financial activity in each account is reflected chronologically throughout the year. When a detailed ledger, such as payroll or student tuition receivable, is separately maintained, its monthly totals are posted in the general ledger (rather than each item). At the end of each accounting period, it is traditional to prepare a *trial balance* or other summary, listing current balances for all accounts in the general ledger.

A General Journal records corrections, called adjustments, and other transactions not involving cash.

The Investment Ledger lists each separate investment held by the organization, the associated original cost or purchase price, number of shares, market premium or discount information, and so on. The expected revenue from dividend and interest might be noted alongside a comparison of the amounts actually received in a year or the prior year.

The NonCash Transaction Ledger documents noncash gifts, a description of the property or services donated, the date received, and the value, if available, as of the gift date. Assigning value to noncash gifts, such as used clothing or other goods for resale or distributions to the needy, is not easy. If the goods are resold soon after receipt, the donation value is preferably recorded as the selling price. Professional services may or may not be valued following the new rules, explained in Section 6.7. For those that are recorded, the nonprofit should obtain an invoice reflecting the normal cost for the services donated.

The Property and Equipment Ledger, also called a *fixed asset ledger,* contains a detailed listing of all tangible, intangible (copyrights or trademarks), and real properties owned by the nonprofit. At a minimum, the types of assets owned (computer, desk, truck, or building), dates purchased or received, purchase price or donated value, and depreciation information should be listed. Additionally it may record serial numbers, insurance coverage, location, or other useful information pertaining to each property item. For internal control purposes, this ledger would be used to conduct an annual check on who has what equipment and whether it is still there.

The Permanent Asset Files should be established to maintain original purchase invoices, insurance policies, guarantees or warranties, maintenance contracts, and the like. These files serve as companions to the property ledger and should always contain the original purchase invoice or contracts associated with the property as long as the asset is owned.

The Paid Bill Files contain vendor invoices cancelled or marked clearly as paid (preferably with the check number, account code, and date). There is a natural tendency to want to keep invoices for related expenditures grouped together—all the supplies, all the newsletter or meeting costs, for example. Alphabetical filing by vendor is preferable because this method provides a third sort and retrieval system for the disbursements. If it is useful to place the invoice in project files, copies should be made for that purpose. Chronological retrieval is available from the check register contained in the cash disbursements journal. Accumulated costs associated with each category of expense is found in the general ledger account.

The Personnel Files contain records associated with employees or independent contractors, arranged in individual files for each person or firm. Such files include original engagement, hiring letter or contract, wage withholding form (W-4 or SS-9), periodic reviews, awards, complaints, vacation and sick records, continuing education records, and so forth.

The Grant Files contain detail-relevant information for all grants: those to be received or paid out by the nonprofit. Beginning with the grant request, the entire history of each grant is recorded and filed. Any information required for receiving or paying the grant and any information useful for grant renewal is noted. Considering the importance of grant files and the level of detail desired, a computer database (in addition to the manual record) can be very useful. For a grant restricted to use for a particular project, the required record should detail all expenditures paid to accomplish the project. A profile of program participants, persons receiving food or training, number attending the performance, the test scores, for example, should be tracked. Such information is particularly relevant in the goal setting and budgeting process discussed in Chapters 3 and 4.

(e) Fund Accounting

A fund accounting system identifies the organization's resources according to the purpose for which it is holding the funds. The fund categories might include:

Unrestricted and available for any worthy purpose,

Unrestricted, but board-designated for a special purpose or reserve,

Restricted by the donor for some specific purposes or as an endowment, or

Dedicated to land, building, and equipment.

As discussed further in Sections 5.6 and 5.7, different funds are created within the nonprofit's accounts to segregate and report transactions attributable to restrictions placed on the funding by outside donors and grantors. Such a system enables the organization to monitor funds entrusted to it. The system accumulates information for preparing reports to evidence compliance with any legal or donor restrictions placed upon the expenditure of the funds.

A nonprofit using fund accounting designs its chart of accounts (considered in Section 6.3) to include subdivisions or sections for each fund for which it must separately account. The program or fund categories of a nonprofit will correspond to the departments or cost centers of a for-profit business.

6.2 COMPUTERIZED ACCOUNTS

The ledgers, files, and other elements of an accounting system discussed in Section 6.1 are contained in both manual, or handwritten, financial records (books) and a computerized record. Any nonprofit possessing a personal computer can and probably should computerize part or all of its accounting records. There is a dizzying array of programs available from simple checkbook/expense category programs, to customized fund accounting systems with integrated donor, member, asset, sales, or other necessary detailed ledgers. Because of this wide range of options, many find it difficult to choose an accounting program. Among the factors that complicate the decision are:

Computer skills: Do the nonprofit organization's personnel have the sophistication and skill to use the program? Why buy a program the staff cannot understand, which will likely reflect inaccuracies and prove unreliable?

Cost of specialized programs: Is a program specially designed for the nonprofit the preferred choice? Such programs have a steeper learning curve because fund accounting is applied. The cost of such programs is also often higher and may prove too costly for some organizations. The logical choice for a modest organization with a few programs may be an off-the-shelf program with the capability to departmentalize and compare actual monthly results to budgeted numbers.

Number of modules: What functions should the program be capable of performing? Integrating the detailed creditor, donor, member, and/or customer information with the accounting system is highly desirable. Both efficiency and an audit trail result when the donor's check is posted simultaneously in the donor database, as an increase in cash, and, correspondingly, entered in a revenue account as a donation received.

Time savings: Will the system minimize the work involved in repetitive payments? Payroll is a great example. The tax-calculating and reporting process becomes highly efficient using a computerized payroll system. Often the compensation is fixed so that a person may receive a check of the same amount every other week throughout an entire year. Each paycheck is net of amounts to be paid to tax authorities, to an insurance company, to a retirement plan administrator, and others. The computer can save considerable time compared to a person repetitively performing this task every payday. An organization with limited or volunteer accounting personnel should also consider engaging an outside payroll service bureau.

Computer capability: Will the computer hardware efficiently run the programs? Newer computer programs require more computer memory than most computers, made a few years ago, contain on the hard drive.

Exhibit 6.3, a checklist designed by Price Waterhouse, is an aid in the selection of suitable accounting software. The decision must be made carefully because the monetary and personnel costs involved in installing computer systems can be extensive. When the financial managers are uncertain about the choice of hardware and software, a computer consultant

Exhibit 6.3.   Selecting Suitable Accounting Software.

1. Determine the requirements that must be met by the software.

   —include those who are to produce and use the information which is to be processed in the requirements determination process

   —concentrate on critical and unusual requirements

   —consider system-generated calculations

   —define all significant reporting requirements

   —consider nature and sources of transactions

   —consider required interfaces among modules and with other systems

   —consider any limitations on computer hardware or costs

   —prioritize requirements by importance

2. Identify likely packages for detailed review.

   —use requirements list to screen potential vendors for suitability

   —focus on critical and unusual requirements

   —eliminate obviously unsuitable packages based on requirements and/or cost

   —narrow the list to two or three vendors

3. Perform a detailed evaluation of the finalist vendors.

   —prepare a detailed list of questions to ask each vendor

   —arrange to have the vendor provide a detailed demonstration of the accounting modules being considered

   —evaluate functionality and ease of use

   —obtain examples of reports produced by the system

   —obtain examples of documentation and manuals provided by the vendor

   —obtain financial information and business history of the vendor (especially if not well-known)

   —obtain at least three references from each vendor, preferably similar organizations

4. Contact vendor references.

   Develop questions to ask references, including the following:

   —perception of software strengths and weaknesses

   —software problems encountered and limitations

(Continued)

Exhibit 6.3. *(Continued)*

—ease of use, ease of implementation

—report-writing capabilities and ease

—modifications made to the software

—availability and adequacy of vendor training and documentation

—vendor support and responsiveness (e.g., local presence, telephone assistance, response time to inquires)

—satisfaction with software performance

5. Obtain and compare cost information.

Consider all potential costs and compare each candidate vendor:

—computer equipment requirements

—accounting modules

—other software (e.g., additional software required to operate the vendor's accounting software)

—cost for installation, modifications, data conversion, training, other additional costs to implement the system

—on-going maintenance costs (annual expenses for both hardware and software)

6. Make a selection.

—be willing to compromise

—consider alternatives for missing requirements

—select the software vendor with the best overall match

—base final decision on value, not just lowest cost

Source: Malvern J. Gross, Jr., Richard F. Larkin, Roger Bruttomesso, John J. McNally, *Financial and Accounting Guide for Not-for-Profit Organizations, Fifth Edition.* © 1995, John Wiley & Sons, Inc. Reprinted with permission.

should be sought. The nonprofit's independent accountants should always be asked about the choices. Many cities have management assistance programs staffed with volunteers knowledgeable about computers whose help can also be sought.

6.3 CHART OF ACCOUNTS

The chart of accounts is the master listing of the asset, liability, net asset or fund balance, revenue, and expense accounts used to record financial transactions. Exhibit 6.4 illustrates a suggested standard nonprofit chart of accounts with a description of the type of transactions recorded in each account. If you compare this chart to the IRS Annual Report of Exempt Organization, Form 990, you will note its listing of accounts mimics the order of Form 990 and is intended to encourage uniformity of reporting among all nonprofit organizations.

(a) Using National Standard

Although an organization may design its chart of accounts to suit its particular needs, the standard system used by nonprofits throughout the country can be quite useful. Certainly a nonprofit planning to seek funding from the United Way should study their standard chart and consider using the numbering system specifically provided in their accounting guide.[3] All nonprofits may find their budgetary projections and periodic financial reports understandable by more persons if the standard chart is used. Lastly for those self-preparing or seeking probono or reduced fees for their Form 990 preparation, the compliance reporting is much easier to prepare when the year-end accounting reports follow the standard chart.

(b) Functional Expense Categories

To assess flow of funds according to its programs—and to distinguish management and fund-raising costs—the nonprofit must so identify its expenditures by function or use. The label is built into the chart of accounts by appending or assigning a subcode or category. In the simplest fashion, the letters A, B, C, and so on, might be assigned to each program

[3] Ibid. note 2.

■ 151 ■

Exhibit 6.4.   Standard Chart of Accounts.

Assets and liabilities are listed in order of liquidity or maturity and may be further classified as current or non-current for financial statement purposes. Accounting theory effective in 1996 recommends all a nonprofit organization's (NPO) assets be presented as a whole rather than separated into fund columns.

Checking accounts	Separate number for each account
Temporary cash investments	Cash reserves available for current spending, also called cash equivalents.
Accounts receivable	Student, patient, member, customer amounts owed to the nonprofit, offset by amounts estimated to be uncollectable.
Pledges receivable	Contributions due to be paid to the nonprofit offset by amounts estimated to be uncollectable.
Grants receivable	Grants from foundations, governments, or common giving funds due to be paid to the nonprofit.
Other receivables	Due from employees, from purchasers of nonprofit's assets, or from program related loans to exempt constituents.
Inventories for sale	Publications, medicines, donated goods, crafts, handicapped worker products.
Prepaid expenses and deferred charges.	Deposits, advanced insurance premiums, funding campaign costs paid in advance.
Investments—Marketable Securities	Common stocks, bonds, and mutual funds.
Investments—Land, Buildings, and Equipment	Properties held for rent or for appreciation in value offset by reserves for depreciation.
Land, Building, & Equipment	Properties used by the nonprofit for its administrative offices, program facilities, or other direct exempt purpose, less accumulated annual provisions for wasting value or depreciation.

Exhibit 6.4.   *(Continued)*

| Other assets | Mineral interests, program related investments not intended to produce income, or future value of interests in an estate or trust. |

Liabilities

Accounts payable	Bills received from creditors not yet paid and amounts due to be paid not yet billed, called accrued expenses.
Grants payable	Allotments or awards the nonprofit is committed to pay.
Deferred revenues	Grants or gifts received by the nonprofit but designated for use at a future time.
Long-term debts and mortgages	Debt secured by purchased assets commonly due to be paid over a period of years plus interest.
Bonds outstanding	Loans to the nonprofit through issuance of bonds including tax-exempt municipals or church obligations.
Other liabilities	Loans advanced to nonprofit from directors or funders, deferred compensation or pension obligations.

Net Assets or Fund Balances

Unrestricted net assets	Difference between assets and liabilities available as operating funds and not dedicated to some particular purpose also called current funds, can include board-designated funds.
Temporarily restricted net assets	Funds devoted or earmarked for specific purposes; cannot be used for overall operating expenses.
Permanently restricted net assets	Endowment funds permanently invested to provide income for operations or for purposes such as scholarships, dedicated building or plant funds, or held as permanent collection.

(Continued)

Exhibit 6.4.   *(Continued)*

Revenues

Contributions and gifts	Voluntary donations from individual and business supporters, not including moneys paid in return for goods or services, includes dues of members receiving no membership benefits.
Grants or awards	Funding from foundations, common funds, or governments.
Program service revenues	Fees for services provided to patients, students, members, performance tickets, tennis or swimming pool admission, consulting contract or research revenues, publication or patent royalties, conventions or trade shows ticket sales or booth rentals.
Membership dues	Fees paid by members or affiliates to belong to the nonprofit and participate in the nonprofit's activities; also special member assessments.
Sales of goods	Books, patient drugs, donated goods, or other properties held for sale less the cost of the goods sold.
Investment income	Dividends and interest from securities and cash equivalents, capital gains or losses from such securities.
Rents and royalties	Investment property payments for rental or royalty less direct expenses associated with the property.
Fund-raising revenues	Proceeds of special events, raffles, or activities; for financial purposes may include donation portion.
Payments from affiliated nonprofits	Support from chapters or branches.

Expenses (by Function)

Grants and allocations	Payments to other nonprofits or individuals; also can include payments by chapters or branches to the parent nonprofit.

Exhibit 6.4.   *(Continued)*

Assistance to individuals	Food, shelter or other aid to individuals paid by charity, union, employee association, or business league.
Program service costs	Expenses paid to provide classes, hospital services, membership benefits, present cultural performances, send newsletter.
Management and general	Accounting, personnel, and administrative expenses, board or staff meetings, investment manager fees.
Fund-raising expense	Costs of raising money, seeking grants and gifts, also called development, solicitation, or marketing expense.

The categories of expenses listed above are called functional groupings; those below are specific, or natural, categories for expenses that are paid. The format for reporting the details varies by nonprofit type; but the following list matches the IRS Form 990, is recommended by the United Way of America, and is commonly adopted by many nonprofits. For internal accounting purposes, it is useful to adopt this standard format of functional expense designated by departments.

Expenses (by Natural Classification)

Grants & allocations
Payments to affiliates
Salaries
Employee benefits
Payroll taxes
Professional fees
Supplies
Telephone
Postage/shipping
Occupancy (Rent, utilities, maintenance of building—often separated)
Rental/maintenance equipment
Printing & publications
Travel
Conferences & meetings
Interest
Other expense

Exhibit 6.5. Functional Classification of Expenses.

Line Item or Natural Classifications	Functional Classification of Expenses					
	Program Services			Support Services		
	Program A	Program B	Program C	Mgt. & General	Fund Raising	Total
Salaries	X	X	X	X	X	X
Telephone	X	X	X	X	X	X
Supplies	X	X	X	X	X	X
Postage	X	X	X	X	X	X
Occupancy	X	X	X	X	X	X
Printing	X	X	X	X	X	X
Travel	X	X	X	X	X	X
Independent contractors	X	X	X	X	X	X
Other expenses	X	X	X	X	X	X
TOTAL COSTS	X	X	X	X	X	X

and function. Each disbursement attributable to a particular program is then assigned its natural, or generic, account code (for example, supplies or printing) plus a letter. Supplies purchased for program A are reportable two ways: as supplies and also as supplies specifically associated with program A.

Computerized bookkeeping makes this dual coding system relatively easy. Luckily, the most basic of such systems have the capability to identify and sort the accounts by departments or subcodes. Exhibit 6.5 graphically depicts what is accomplished by using functional expense codes: Note that revenues can also be identified and reported by function, as the business league financial report shows in Exhibit 6.6.

6.4   WHY A DOUBLE ENTRY?

The commonly used self-balancing system for recording financial transactions is *double-entry bookkeeping*. Each financial transaction is concurrently entered into two separate accounts as a *debit* and a *credit*, or a *plus* and a *minus*. This double-entry scheme provides a proof system by essentially adding and subtracting the same number at the same time from two different accounts. The books are said to be *out of balance* when the debits do not equal the credits. The system classifies financial transactions as those increasing or reducing net assets and those impacting the income or expense for the year.

Study the financial statement categories illustrated in Exhibits 6.6 and 6.7, and consider how a payment for the organization's rent is entered. The check is entered both as a reduction (a credit) to the cash account, and correspondingly, as an increase (a debit) in the rental expense account, showing how the money was spent. When a member's dues are deposited, the cash account is increased (debited) and the dues revenue account is credited (which paradoxically is for the revenue account an increase).

A computerized checkbook system, such as Quicken, is essentially a single entry system because the entries only impact cash in the bank

Exhibit 6.6.   Sample Accural
Basis Financials for Business League.

STATE ASSOCIATION of NONPROFIT MANAGERS
STATEMENT OF NET ASSETS

ASSETS	19X6	19X5
Cash & cash equivalents	$60,000	$17,000
Membership dues receivable	80,000	71,000
Inventory of publications	42,000	73,000
Prepayments	38,000	31,000
Total current assets	220,000	192,000
Office building	300,000	300,000
Computers & Statewide network	80,000	62,000
Furnishings and equipment	90,000	80,000
Accumulated depreciation	(168,000)	(116,000)
Net fixed assets, at cost	302,000	326,000
Total assets	522,000	518,000
Current liabilities:		
Accounts payable	52,000	84,000
Deposits and prepaid dues	42,000	28,000
Current portion of mortgage	22,000	23,000
Total current liabilities	116,000	135,000
Mortgage on building	180,000	183,000
Total liabilities	296,000	318,000
Unrestricted Assets	226,000	200,000
Total liabilities and net assets	$522,000	$518,000

(Continued)

Exhibit 6.6 *(Continued)*

STATE ASSOCIATION of NONPROFIT MANAGERS
Statement of Activity

	19x6	19x5
Revenues:		
Chapter member dues	$249,700	$238,000
Members at large dues	78,600	76,000
Information services	120,000	40,000
Publication sales	204,000	180,000
Continuing education	106,000	98,000
Annual meeting	28,000	42,000
Royalty income	42,000	1,000
Interest income	1,000	3,000
Total revenues	829,300	678,000
Expenses:		
Member services	267,000	260,000
Publications	229,600	202,000
Continuing education	122,000	96,000
Administration	184,700	172,000
Total expenses	803,300	730,000
Change in net assets	26,000	(52,000)
Net Assets, beginning of year	200,000	252,000
Net Assets, end of year	$226,000	$200,000

account. Such a one-legged system lacks the self-proving tool inherent in a double-entry system. The following chart of financial statement categories illustrates how the debits and credits interact. It is reasonable to be confused by the fact that an increase in an asset or expense account is a debit, whereas an increase in a liability or revenue account is a credit. Thinking of the entries as opposites may help. The typical double entry for each major category of account is shown below.

	An increase in this category is entered normally as a:	A decrease in this category is normally entered as a:
ASSETS: Cash, investments, equipment.	DEBIT	CREDIT
LIABILITIES: Accounts payable, mortgages, deferred revenues	CREDIT	DEBIT
REVENUES: Donations, grants, program services	CREDIT	DEBIT
EXPENSES: Salaries, rent, insurance, etc.	DEBIT	CREDIT

Exhibit 6.6 *(Continued)*

STATE ASSOCIATION of NPO MANAGERS
Statement of Functional Income & Expenses

	Member Activities	Publications	Meetings & classes	Administration	Total	Budget	Variance
Revenues:							
Chapter member dues	$249,700				$249,700	$260,000	($10,300)
Members at large dues	78,600				78,600	100,000	(21,400)
Information services	120,000				120,000	80,000	40,000
Publication sales		$204,000			204,000	200,000	4,000
Continuing education			$106,000		106,000	100,000	6,000
Annual meeting			28,000		28,000	40,000	(12,000)
Royalty income	42,000				42,000	10,000	32,000
Interest income				$5,000	5,000	2,000	3,000
Total	490,300	204,000	134,000	5,000	833,300	792,000	41,300
Expenses:							
Salaries & payroll taxes	126,000	84,200	33,800	119,000	363,000	350,000	(13,000)
Retirement & medical benefits	6,000	3,800	1,400	14,100	25,300	26,000	700
Professional fees	12,000		8,000	12,000	32,000	28,000	(4,000)
Supplies	8,000	4,000	6,000	6,000	24,000	20,000	(4,000)
Telephone	8,000	4,000	2,000	4,000	18,000	16,000	(2,000)
Postage & shipping	4,000	10,000	2,000	2,000	18,000	16,000	(2,000)
Building costs	8,000	12,000	10,000	6,000	36,000	30,000	(6,000)
Equipment repair & insurance	2,000	4,000	2,000	4,000	12,000	10,000	(2,000)
Printing & publications	5,000	92,000	20,000	3,000	120,000	130,000	10,000
Travel	10,000		5,000	2,000	17,000	16,000	(1,000)
Meetings & classes	2,000		20,000		22,000	25,000	3,000
Information services	61,000				61,000	40,000	(21,000)
Depreciation on equipment & furnishings	14,400	12,800	10,200	4,600	42,000	40,000	(2,000)
Insurance	4,600	2,800	1,600	8,000	17,000	20,000	3,000
Total	271,000	229,600	122,000	184,700	807,300	767,000	(40,300)
Change in net assets	$219,300	($25,600)	$12,000	($179,700)	$26,000	$25,000	($1,000)

Note: Information service usage fees are substantially more than projected, and correspondingly, the expenses associated with the telecommunication systems are higher.

(Continued)

6.5 CHOOSING A METHOD

An organization that records and reports financial transactions as they reach the bank account is said to use the *cash method of accounting*. If instead, revenues are recorded when the organization has an unqualified right to receive the funds, the *accrual method of accounting* is used. Analogously, the accrual basis records expenses when all events have occurred to obligate it to pay for or disburse funds instead of waiting until the check is actually disbursed. In other words, revenues and expenses are accrued without regard to the time of actual receipt or disbursal of the money.

The manner in which the two different methods function is best illustrated by examples. Under a cash basis system, office supplies ordered today and charged to the nonprofit's account are not reported as an expense until a check is written in payment of the bill. Under an accrual system, the obligation to pay for the supply order is recorded as a

Exhibit 6.6 *(Continued)*

STATE ASSOCIATION of NONPROFIT MANAGERS
Statement of Cash Flows for the year 19x6

Cash flow from operations:

Excess of revenue over (expenses)	$26,000
+ Add back non-cash depreciation:	52,000
Adjust for accrual items:	
+(-) (Increase) in accounts receivable	(9,000)
+(-) Decrease in inventory and prepayments	24,000
+(-) (Decrease) in accounts payable	(32,000)
+(-) Increase in deferred revenues	14,000
= Net cash provided from (to) operations	75,000

Cash flow from investments:

Net proceeds of sale (purchase) of securities	0
+(-) Sale of equipment	16,000
+(-) (Purchase) of equipment	(44,000)
= Net cash from (used for) investment:	(28,000)

Cash flow from financing:

+ Proceeds of new loan	0
- Payments of mortgage principal	(4,000)
= Net cash provided from (to) financing	(4,000)
Sum of net increases (decreases) in cash for year	43,000
+ Beginning cash balance	17,000
= Ending cash balance	$60,000

responsibility—an account payable—at the time the supplies are received. Some organizations using a purchase-order system enter the obligation to pay for the supplies as early as the day the purchase is approved, even though the liability does not mature until the goods are received.

Similarly, under accrual systems, a promised gift to the building fund campaign to be paid over a three-year period is recorded as income when an unconditional pledge is made. The future portion of the gift is recorded as a pledge receivable—an asset. When each installment is actually received and put into the bank, the accounting entry is posted to the receivable rather than to income (because the whole gift is recorded as income when it is pledged). A cash basis system user instead records

Exhibit 6.7.   Sample Cash Basis Financials for a Church.

HOLY SPIRIT CHURCH
Statement of Activity
(with Comparison to Prior Year and Budget) for the year 19x6

		ACTUAL	BUDGET	Variance Favorable
	19X5	19X6	19X6	(Unfavorable)
Revenues:				
Plate collections	$48,000	$46,500	$48,000	($1,500)
Annual pledge envelopes	38,000	54,000	42,000	12,000
Special gifts	12,400	16,400	24,000	(7,600)
After school care fees	16,000	18,000	16,000	2,000
Total revenue	$114,400	$134,900	$130,000	$4,900
Expenses:				
Clergy & vestry	57,000	63,000	50,000	(13,000)
After school programs	19,000	28,700	28,000	(700)
Music & Sunday school	4,200	5,600	5,000	(600)
Building costs	22,400	36,800	30,000	(6,800)
Church office	14,100	18,200	15,000	(3,200)
Other	1,990	7,900	2,000	(5,900)
Total expenses	$118,690	$160,200	$130,000	($30,200)
Change in net assets	($4,290)	($25,300)	$0	($25,300)
Net Assets, beginning of year	138,100	133,810		
Net Assets, end of year	$133,810	$108,510		

(Continued)

the installments as income and never reflects the pledged portion on its financial records.

(a)   Advantages of Cash Method

The cash method has the advantage of being simple and uncomplicated. Financial transactions are entered once when the money is deposited or paid out. Under the cash method, the nonprofit waits until the money is in hand or goes out of its hand to reflect the impact on its financial situation. There is no need to decide whether the pledge is a good and viable promise. For some organizations, little, if any, timing differences occur in the flow of their funds. They pay their bills before month end and receive payments for services provided as the benefit or

Exhibit 6.7. *(Continued)*

HOLY SPIRIT CHURCH
Statement of Net Assets for the year ended August 31, 19x6

	19X6	19X5
Cash	$6,600	$1,850
U. S. Treasury note, at cost		
approximating market	9,140	12,400
Marketable securities at		
contributed cost (market $ 5,600)	4,260	4,260
Current Assets	$20,000	$18,510
Building & land	250,000	250,000
Church fixtures, hymnals & robes (net)	88,600	86,000
Computers & office furnishings,		
net of depreciation	31,400	26,700
Total fixed assets	$370,000	$362,700
TOTAL ASSETS	$390,000	$381,210
Accounts payable	81,490	47,400
Church bonds due in ten years	200,000	200,000
Total liabilities	$281,490	$247,400
NET ASSETS	$108,510	$133,810

goods are delivered. The cash method of accounting may, in such situations, provide a relatively clear picture of finances.

It is common for a nonprofit, with regularly recurring fund flows, to maintain the internal financial records and reports throughout the year on a cash basis and to make timing or accrual adjustments only for financial reporting purposes at year end. Such a system reports regularly flowing transactions on the cash method and accrues those with major timing differences for periodic financial reporting purposes.

(b) Why Use the Accrual Method?

Many organizations have no choice in answering this question. Accrual-basis accounting is the recommended system under generally accepted accounting principals for fair presentation of financial position

Exhibit 6.7. *(Continued)*

HOLY SPIRIT CHURCH
MONTHLY REVENUES and EXPENSES, COMPARED TO BUDGET

For the Month of October, 19x6				Ten months ending Ocotber 31, 19x6		
Actual	Budget	Variance Favorable (Unfavorable)		Actual	Budget	Variance Favorable (Unfavorable)
			REVENUES			
$3,600	$4,000	($400)	Plate collections	$36,200	$40,000	($3,800)
3,400	3,500	(100)	Pledge envelopes	33,000	35,000	(2,000)
500	2,000	(1,500)	Special gifts	12,800	20,000	(7,200)
2,200	1,333	867	After school care	14,400	13,333	1,067
		0	Contributions & gifts			
$9,700	$10,833	($1,133)	Total revenue	$96,400	$108,333	($11,933)
			EXPENSES			
5,200	4,167	(1,033)	Clergy & vestry	53,000	41,667	(11,333)
2,200	2,333	133	After school care	22,316	23,333	1,017
467	417	(50)	Music/Sunday school	4,666	4,163	(503)
2,433	2,500	67	Building costs	29,700	25,000	(4,700)
1,560	1,250	(310)	Church office	15,110	12,500	(2,610)
260	167	(93)	Other	1,900	1,670	(230)
$12,120	$10,833	($1,287)	Total expense	$126,692	$108,333	($18,359)
($2,420)	$0	($2,420)	Net asset change	($30,292)	$0	($30,292)

and results of operations.[4] Organizations that seek the opinion of a CPA receive the most desirable or unqualified opinion on its financial statements if the accrual method is used.

Aside from being required to follow the accrual method, a nonprofit chooses the method because it more precisely reflects the financial situation and results of operations. The system eliminates surprises and matches revenues with the expenses that produce the revenue. Recording financial transactions as they are earned, or when the revenue due is first known (point of sale), requires additional accounting steps or transactions to be recorded (many transactions are entered twice).

The goal of an accrual system is to neutralize timing differences. As an example, consider how the income on a one-year U.S. Treasury bill flows. Interest matures and is earned on a Treasury bill daily. The accrual method prescribes such income be calculated, shown as income,

---

[4] *AICPA Audit Guide for Not-for-Profit Organizations* was proposed in April 1995 to consolidate and replace former guides on colleges and universities, voluntary health and welfare organizations and audits of certain nonprofit organizations.

and correspondingly increase the carrying value of the investment regularly (usually monthly). Under the cash method, no entry is made until the bill matures or is sold. Because the bill can actually be sold for its original face price plus the accrued interest (plus or minus market fluctuations), the accrual method shows a more accurate picture of the nonprofit's resources.

6.6 DESIGN OF THE FINANCIALS

Financial statements are designed to reflect the fiscal condition by showing the means with which an organization finances its operations. The assets are distinguished between those that are readily available to pay the bills—current assets—and the more permanent assets, like investments held to produce income and like buildings and equipment, which are physically used in the activities. The titles and presentation of net assets or fund balances tell the reader if the nonprofit's properties are subject to any special restrictions on their use. The design was significantly changed effective in 1995 to cause the reader to focus on the organization as a whole, not a fragmented assortment of funds presented in a columnar fashion. Four basic statements are contained in GAAP financial statements issued by CPAs and accompanied by explanations in footnotes.

1. Statement of financial position (may still be called balance sheet)

2. Statement of activity

3. Statement of cash flows

4. Statement of function expenses (required for voluntary health & welfare organizations; desirable for all).

The statement of net assets reflects the assets owned by and the liabilities owed by the organization on a particular day, usually at year or month end. The report reflects the plus and minus scheme of the double-entry accounting system. The assets are essentially positive and presented first, as shown in Exhibit 6.6. The basic schematic balance reflects:

ASSETS less LIABILITIES = NET ASSETS

The financial resources are shown in the order of their liquidity or ability to be converted into cash. Current assets come first and represent those properties that pay for daily operations—cash, receivables, and the like. The other assets—land and buildings, office equipment, and investments, for example—support activities, but cannot be used to pay the light bill or next week's payroll checks.

The negative side of the balance sheet contains the debts or obligations as of the balance sheet date. Debts can be shown in due-date order, and the report may also show a separate subtotal of current liabilities or those due within one year, such as the light bill due next month, the undeposited payroll taxes from last month's salaries, and the portion of the long-term mortgage due within the coming year, for example.

Lastly comes the balance, the *net assets* representing the nonprofit's accumulated excess of revenues it has received over the years less expenses it has paid out. In a for-profit organization, this difference is called stockholder's equity and referred to as net worth or book value. As explained below in Section 6.7(b), the net assets are further designated to identify restrictions on their use. Donations or grants received for a particular purpose, earmarked for a specific program, or otherwise designated by the giver are identified with titles indicating the restraints, if any, on expenditure of the resource (until they are used for that purpose).

It is useful to think of net assets as capital. Whether the nonprofit invests assets to produce income to pay for operations or uses assets directly in conducting operations, assets provide the financial capital needed to function financially. They appear in the same position on the balance sheet as stockholder's equity in a for-profit business. The nonprofit's capital is the antithesis of a for-profit's capital reserves, except for one important respect: Any profit generated from capital is accumulated to accomplish exempt purposes rather than being paid out to owners.

The statement of activity is the equivalent of a for-profit's income statement. Again, pluses (revenue) and minuses (expenses) and the difference (excess of revenue or expense) are shown. Because of the nonprofit motivation discussed in Chapter 1, the difference is not called profit or loss. The financial activities for the three major classes of net assets—permanently restricted, temporarily restricted, and unrestricted—are shown in a layered or columnar format. Voluntary health and welfare organizations are required and all are encouraged to also present a statement of functional expenses, as explained above in 6.3(b).

Lastly the generally accepted accounting principles (GAAP) report includes a statement of cash flows. This report analyzes the movement of cold, hard dollars. It explains where the money comes from to finance a deficit, to purchase new equipment, or to repay debts. See Chapter 5 for more discussion of cash flows.

6.7 MEANING OF FASB AND GAAP

Understanding the acronyms, FASB and GAAP, can help a financial manager communicate with the nonprofit's accountants. CPAs are required by their profession to follow the GAAP rules promulgated by the FASB, the Financial Accounting Standards Board. In a confusing dichotomy, the American Institute of Certified Public Accountants issues statements of position that contain recommendations that are not absolutely required to be followed.

FASB is an independent division of the Financial Accounting Foundation created by the American Institute of Certified Public Accountants in 1973. FASB's mission is to establish and improve standards of financial accounting and reporting for the guidance and education of the public, including issuers, auditors, and users of financial information. It is *the* authority in the CPA profession in defining GAAP. The standards are contained in opinions issued periodically.

(a) Listing of Pronouncements

Nonprofit organizations are subject to some of the same standards as those applicable to business organizations, plus those specific standards and guidelines for nonprofits only. Some of the major pronouncements are listed below.[5]

FASB Statement of Financial Accounting Standards No. 93, *Recognition of Depreciation by Not-for-Profit Organizations.*

FASB Statement of Financial Accounting Standards No. 116, *Accounting for Contributions Received and Contributions Made.*

FASB Statement of Financial Accounting Standards No. 117, *Financial Statements of Not-for-Profit Organizations.*

FASB Statement of Financial Accounting Standards No. 124, *Accounting for Certain Investments Held by Not-for-Profit Organizations.*

AICPA Audit Guide for Not-for-Profit Organizations was proposed in April 1995[6] to consolidate and replace former guides on Colleges

---

[5] Issued by the Financial Standards Board and the American Society of Certified Public Accountants.
[6] Final comments were due in August 1995 and the AICPA expected to release a final guide in 1996.

and Universities, Voluntary Health and Welfare Organizations and Audits of Certain Nonprofit Organizations.

AICPA Statement of Position 87-2, *Accounting for Joint Costs of Informational Materials and Activities of Not-for-Profit Organizations That Include a Fund-Raising Appeal.*

AICPA Statement of Position 90-9, *The Auditor's Consideration of the Internal Control Structure Used in Administering Federal Financial Assistance Programs.*

AICPA Statement of Position 92-9, *Audits of Not-for-Profit Organizations Receiving Federal Awards.*

AICPA Statement of Position 94-3, *Reporting of Related Entities by Not-for-Profit Organizations.*

Several industry groups have recommended reporting methods for their constituencies. The National Health Council, National Voluntary Health and Social Welfare Organizations, Inc., and the United Way of America in 1975 issued their *Standards of Accounting and Financial Reporting for Voluntary Health and Welfare Organizations.* The National Association of College and University Business Officers (NACUBO) and The American Hospital Association have similarly prescribed standards of reporting for colleges and universities and hospitals, respectfully.

Government grant recipients are additionally subject to special rules of the Federal Office of Management and Budget and state and local funding agencies. Federal grantees receiving more than $300,000 a year (formerly $25,000) must have at least a biannual *A-133 or single audit* (annual for nonprofit organizations having an annual financial audit).[7] A single audit tests financial transactions to be sure the nonprofit has expended the grant moneys for the purpose for which they were granted; total expense is reported alongside the amount of each grant awarded.

The auditor also reviews compliance with nonfinancial federal grant requirements, such as maintaining a drug-free workplace and complying with civil rights requirements. The auditors report findings about compliance, noncompliance, weaknesses in systems, or other reportable

---

[7] Office of Management and Budget (OMB), Circular A-133, Audits of Institutions of Higher Education and Other Nonprofit Institutions and Circular A-128, Audits of State and Local Governments.

conditions. The rules for conducting these audits published in the so called Yellow Book[8] and in the AICPA industry standards.

(b) Synopsis of SFAS Nos. 116 & 117

Effective for all nonprofits in 1996, FASB significantly changed the manner in which contributions received and paid are reported and restricted moneys are identified on financial statements. In summary, the highlights include the following:

Charitable Pledges: Charitable pledges received are included in revenue when the pledge is made or promised, rather than when paid in cash or other assets, if there is "sufficient evidence in the form of verifiable documentation that a promise was made and received."

Unrestricted Gifts: Unrestricted gifts received without explicit stipulation by the donor or "circumstances surrounding the receipt of the contribution that make clear the donor's implicit restriction on use," are reported as unrestricted. An organization's governing body or officers cannot cause funds to be reported as restricted, although they can temporarily restrict or designate funds.

Contributed Services: Contributed services are to be recognized if the services received meet one of the two conditions listed below. Note that this policy continues the FASB's former policy prohibiting the recognition of any value associated with fund-raising and guild-type volunteers.

1. The services create or enhance nonfinancial (meaning equipment, buildings, theater sets, or other fixed) assets rather than cash or investments, or

2. The services require specialized skills, are provided by individuals possessing those skills, and would typically need to be purchased if not provided by donations. Services requiring specialized skills are, among others, those provided by accountants, architects, carpenters, computer technologists, doctors,

---

[8] U.S. General Accounting Office, *Government Auditing Standards, 1994 Revision,* U.S. Government Bookstore, Room 188, Federal Building, Pittsburgh, Pennsylvania and available for purchase in government bookstores in most U.S. cities.

electricians, lawyers, nurses, plumbers, scientists, teachers, and other professionals and craftspeople.

Contributed Facility Use: The fair-rental value of facilities the nonprofit would otherwise have to rent are recorded for donated facilities. Likewise the difference between the fair value and a reduced rental rate is reportable income. The other side of this entry is rental expense.

Permanently Restricted Net Assets: These include the amount of those gifts or contributions subject to perpetual or everlasting conditions imposed by the donor on their use. The donor restrictions are those that cannot be removed by the organization's board or advisors and do not expire with the passage of time. Gifts for creation of an endowment or construction of a building may be permanently restricted. Such gifts are sometimes referred to as not being currently expendable.

Temporarily Restricted Assets: These are assets whose use by the organization is limited by donor-imposed stipulations that either expire by the passage of time or can be fulfilled and removed by actions of the organization. A good example of such restricted funds would be grant moneys earmarked for a program to take place in the coming year. As of the financial statement date, the remaining commitment or obligation to spend money for the program would be shown as temporarily restricted fund balance. Formerly such gifts were not shown as revenue in the year received but instead were shown as liabilities entitled "deferred revenues."

Unrestricted Net Assets: This is the category for all other resources of the nonprofit freely available for use in accomplishing the organization's purposes and subject only to the control of the organization's board or officers.

Statement of Activity: This shows the results of operations for the all organizational funds and programs and is essentially what a for-profit business report would call an income statement. This is a statement of revenues and expenses, as it was sometimes called in the past. To help donors, creditors, and others assess an organization's service efforts, accounting standards suggest the statement of activity should report expenses functionally. In other words, the total cost of major program services is to be reported along with separate amounts for supporting services (management, fund-raising, and membership development expenses). Additionally health and welfare organizations must present total expenses in both functional and natural categories—personnel, occupancy, interest, grants to others, and so on as shown in Exhibits 6.5 and 6.6. Other nonprofits are also encouraged, but not required, to provide this extra report.

Current Earnings: Current earnings on all funds, including those permanently restricted, are to be reported on the statement of activity. Revenues subject to restrictions, such as capital gains on endowment funds, are separately identified but still reported as current earnings.

Contributions or Grants Paid Out: Contributions or grants paid out by the organization are to be recognized as an expense in the year the promise to pay is made, whether or not the cash or other asset is actually disbursed. Matching, conditional, or otherwise contingent promises to pay are booked at the time the uncertainty is removed because the condition is satisfied.

(c) Practical Aspects of Implementing FASB

A nonprofit must examine its written documentation concerning solicitation of donations, dues, grants, and other revenues with a view to the new rules. They change the reporting of financial transactions spanning more than one reporting year. Two examples of such incomplete financial transactions would be (1) a pledge to give $1,000 made by a supporter during the year but no cash is received, or (2) a three-year program grant is awarded during the year. The way in which these incomplete transactions are reported is influenced by the paper evidencing them. Each nonprofit must review and possibly redesign such documents to achieve the intended result. Pledge cards and other documents evidencing gifts made by supporters may need to be redesigned to contain the unambiguous language as explained below.

Pledges: In some states, charitable pledges are not legally binding obligations. This uncertainty, combined with the difficulty of calculating a reserve for uncollectable pledges, caused many nonprofits in the past to recognize gifts or dues as revenue when the actual cash came in the door. The fund-raising, or development department, kept track of pledges received in response to solicitations. Only when a payment was actually received would the accounting department record a contribution into the financial reporting system. Now unconditional promises to give must be recognized as income. The following definitions must be kept in mind in designing solicitations that provide unambiguous responses:

- *Promise to Give:* A written or oral agreement to contribute cash or other assets to another entity. The promise may be conditional or unconditional.

- *Conditional Promise to Give:* A promise to give that depends on the occurrence of a specified future and uncertain event to bind the promisor. Such a pledge is not reported as income until cash is collected.

- *Unconditional Promise to Give:* A promise to give that depends only on the passage of time or demand by the promisee for performance. This pledge is reported as current income with a corresponding asset shown on the balance sheet.

Prepaid Revenues: Before 1995, a payment towards programs to be conducted in the future was deferred, or not shown as income, until the program actually took place and the funds were specifically expended. The unspent funds were shown as a debt of the nonprofit. The new rules require the converse—reporting or "recognizing" all contributions as they are received without regard to the period in which the money is actually to be spent. On the balance sheet such a gift is earmarked and labelled as temporarily restricted funds.

Donated Services and Facilities: The test for reporting these donations is whether the services or space would have otherwise been purchased had it not been donated. In other words, was the work or facility indispensable to the nonprofit's programs or administration? If so, its fair value is shown on the financials as a gift with a corresponding expense. If the nonprofit is required to have audited financial statements, the value of a donated audit is recorded. When a full color event invitation, instead of the usual black and white one, is created with donated services, no excess cost would be recorded. Such distinctions are not always easy to make. A policy statement, with suggested forms for documenting such gifts, should be written in view of the very specific guidelines described in Section 6.7(b) above. At a minimum, each contributor of such services, as well as donated goods, should be asked to provide an invoice or other statement of the value of their gift.

6.8 INTERNAL CONTROLS

Internal Controls protect the nonprofit's resources from intentional or unintentional misappropriation. A good internal control system works because it sheds light on problems. The keystone of a good internal control system is separation of duties; some procedures are based upon the cliché, "Two brains are better than one." Such a system is a framework providing checks and balances. If the person who receives and deposits the moneys is also the person who keeps the books, the possibility for hiding a theft is enhanced and the chance of discovering a mistake is reduced. The objective is to separate the assets themselves from the recording or accounting for them.

Internal controls foster operational efficiencies as the roles people play are defined. Duties are delegated and responsibilities are spread among staff members subject to oversight by the management. The planning processes described in Chapters 3 (Goals) and 4 (Budgeting) are also an integral part of the process. This section focuses on the systems specially designed to assure that moneys are properly received and expended and that the flow of funds is documented in the financial records. Outside auditors review the controls in planning the extent of the work they must perform to offer an opinion on financial statements. In other words, the nonprofit with good internal controls may pay less for its annual audit because its system does some of the work. The way the accounting profession sees the function of internal controls is:

> Although the internal control structure may include a wide variety of objectives and related policies and procedures, only some of these may be relevant to an audit of the entity's financial statements. Generally the policies and procedures that are relevant to an audit pertain to the entity's ability to record, process, summarize, and report financial data consistent with the assertions embodied in the financial statements.[9]

Thus an internal control system dictates the manner in which financial transactions are approved and completed by providing procedures to be followed. It can be thought of as a discipline system for organizational affairs. The rules and procedures might sound somewhat like the Ten Commandments.

> Thou shalt not hire a contract laborer without completing personnel department forms determining whether he or she is an employee.

The rules are designed to prevent both the innocent or unintended misuse of funds, as well as deliberate misappropriation for any unauthorized use,

[9] American Institute of Certified Public Accountants (AICPA) *Statement on Auditing Standards 55, Consideration of the Internal Control Structure in a Financial Audit,* New York, 1988, p. 4.

and particularly for some person's own use. Examples of problems that can occur in the absence of internal controls include:

Falsification of the organization's financial records and resulting reports used for monitoring,

Defalcations, such as conversion (embezzlement or theft) of the organization's receipts or inventory,

Actions taken in organization's name without authority to do so,

Unauthorized spending in excess of budgeted amounts, or

Totally unauthorized spending (e.g., well-meaning volunteer fund-raising event chair who has no budget).

Exhibit 6.8 contains a checklist of procedures for establishing and maintaining a system of internal controls. Although the principles of separation of duties apply to all organizations, the checklist should be redesigned or tailored to suit the needs of each individual organization. No one system is suitable for all organizations. The many variables that determine the necessary steps include the size of the staff, nature of the activities, and the sources of funding. In addition, Exhibit 6.9 explores appropriate controls for public fund solicitations.

Exhibit 6.8.   Internal Controls for Nonprofits.

This checklist of internal control procedures presents the possibilities for minimizing errors and deliberate misrepresentations in accounting records, statements and summaries. Space is provided for financial planners to note where each control is currently used and to record relevant observations.

TASK	YES	NO	COMMENTS
A. Financial Reporting			
1. Monthly financial statements are prepared.	____	____	_____
2. Operational, cash flow, and capital budgets prepared and compared monthly to actual results	____	____	_____
3. Departmentalized chart of account is used.	____	____	_____
4. Adequate accounting system is in place with proper ledgers.	____	____	_____
5. Are reporting and documentation procedures written?	____	____	_____
B. Cash Receipts			
1. Mail is opened in the presence of two persons (where staffing allows), with a receiving report prepared concurrently.	____	____	_____
2. Checks are stamped immediately with proper endorsement.	____	____	_____
3. Receipt system is in place to control cash from events or sales. (complete PUBLIC FUND SOLICITATION Checklist).	____	____	_____
4. If feasible, moneys handled by bonded employees, not volunteers.	____	____	_____
5. Daily deposits are made to the bank. (Where possible, a direct bank deposit system is used.)	____	____	_____
6. Receiving reports are reconciled to monthly bank statements by someone other than mail openers	____	____	_____

Exhibit 6.8.   *(Continued)*

7. Noncash gifts receipted under
   FASB #116.

   Donated described with value
   assigned, if available.

   Professional service invoice with
   value obtained.

   Goods subject to inventory
   control system.

   Written policy for accepting
   gifts followed?

C. Disbursement of Funds

1. Disbursements made with checks
   based on documentation.

2. Checks are prenumbered and
   accounted for monthly.

3. Voided checks are defaced
   and retained.

4. No checks are signed in advance or
   made payable to cash.

5. Check signer is not the bookkeeper,
   check preparer, or person
   responsible for authorizing
   disbursement.

   Two signatures required for
   amounts > ($500, 1,000, etc.).

   Board member is a signatory if
   staff size is limited.

   Should check protector be used?

7. Bank statements are reconciled by
   someone other than a check
   preparer or signer.

8. One person handles petty cash;
   receipts required for pay out.

(Continued)

Exhibit 6.8. *(Continued)*

D. Documentation

1. Supporting documentation, invoices, or statements are required for each expenditure and receipt of funds. ____ ____ _____

   Time sheets for personal services—employees and volunteers. ____ ____ _____

   Travel/meal/car usage/reimbursables voucher. ____ ____ _____

   Receiving reports prepared for ordered goods. ____ ____ _____

   Vendor invoices matched to receiving reports. ____ ____ _____

   Petty cash voucher for impress fund. ____ ____ _____

   Cash receiving report coded by type of income. ____ ____ _____

   Vendor/contributor/member/student return slip. ____ ____ _____

   Daily cash register reports. ____ ____ _____

2. Project manager or nonaccounting personnel approve expense. ____ ____ _____

3. Purchase orders are used. ____ ____ _____

4. Vendor statement reconciled to invoices with details of prices, quantity received, discounts, returns, and prior payments. ____ ____ _____

5. There are several layers of approval for major expenditures. ____ ____ _____

6. Invoices labeled (canceled) with check number and date paid. ____ ____ _____

7. Personnel records document that:

   Time sheets, hirings, and firings approved by responsible parties. ____ ____ _____

   Vacation, sick leave, and overtime accruals authorized. ____ ____ _____

   Pay increases made only according to proper authorization. ____ ____ _____

   Payroll taxes deposited on time. ____ ____ _____

Exhibit 6.8.   *(Continued)*

Federal Cobra, Civil Rights, Disability, and other codes followed.

_____ _____ _____

Employer Tax Requirements checklist completed?

_____ _____ _____

E. Safeguarding Assets

Cash

1. Cash management system is in place to maximize interest earned.

_____ _____ _____

2. Federal Deposit Insurance Corporation deposit limits exceeded.

_____ _____ _____

3. Certificates of deposit or money market accounts used for long-term cash funds.

_____ _____ _____

4. Personal cash or other assets of staff are not mingled with nonprofit's.

_____ _____ _____

5. Petty-cash fund replenishment requests are properly approved.

_____ _____ _____

Receivables

1. Accounts receivable are monitored and reconciled to source.

_____ _____ _____

Work orders/sales/member service & dues invoices numbered.

_____ _____ _____

Customer/donor/student ledgers balanced monthly.

_____ _____ _____

Monthly statements sent for unpaid balances.

_____ _____ _____

Uncollectable account write-offs and discounts approved by responsible employee not in business office.

_____ _____ _____

Duties are segregated between credit authorization and collection.

_____ _____ _____

2. Figures periodically verified independently from nonaccounting records.

_____ _____ _____

(Continued)

Exhibit 6.8.   *(Continued)*

Student tuition rolls are compared to registrar's office records.   ____ ____ _____

Number of hours times tuition per hour equals student payment.   ____ ____ _____

Dues receipts are traced to membership department lists.   ____ ____ _____

Hospital patient revenues are vouched to insurance reports.   ____ ____ _____

3. Interest or other charge made for late payment.   ____ ____ _____

4. Charitable pledges or grants receivable timetables are kept.   ____ ____ _____

Aged amounts receivable are established and monitored.   ____ ____ _____

Periodic reports are issued in time for installments to be received.   ____ ____ _____

Grant requests are submitted by their deadline.   ____ ____ _____

5. Are terms of income and remainder trusts monitored?   ____ ____ _____

Inventory

1. Detailed records are maintained for inventory stocks.   ____ ____ _____

2. Records are physically controlled by someone not in accounting.   ____ ____ _____

3. Counting is done periodically to proof balances.   ____ ____ _____

4. Inventory levels and product choices monitored with view to amount invested and marketing considerations.   ____ ____ _____

Property and Equipment

1. Detailed records are maintained for property assets.   ____ ____ _____

Serial numbers listed separately.   ____ ____ _____

Guarantees and service contracts controlled.   ____ ____ _____

Exhibit 6.8.   *(Continued)*

Purchase invoice copies kept in
permanent files.   ____ ____ _____

Detailed ledger of assets maintained. ____ ____ _____

2. Assets are purchased only pursuant
to a capital budget.   ____ ____ _____

3. Competitive bidding is conducted
for major purchases.   ____ ____ _____

4. Borrowing to purchase must be
approved by the board.   ____ ____ _____

5. A retirement policy assures a fair price
for old assets sold, traded, or junked. ____ ____ _____

Board approval required for
dispositions > (say, $5,000). ____ ____ _____

Outside appraisal is obtained for
buildings or major equipment. ____ ____ _____

6. Insurance coverage is adequate.
(What is not insured?)   ____ ____ _____

7. Periodic physical inventory is taken. ____ ____ _____

8. Acquisitions costing < (say $500)
are expensed.   ____ ____ _____

9. Reasonable depreciation reserve
is provided?   ____ ____ _____

Investments

1. Detailed subsidiary ledger is
maintained.   ____ ____ _____

Acquisition/sales reports are vouched
to cash recorded.   ____ ____ _____

Custodian receipts or brokerage
statements are reconciled to ledger. ____ ____ _____

Dividend and interest payment dates
are monitored for receipts. ____ ____ _____

2. Investments are managed by
knowledgeable person(s). ____ ____ _____

Investment return measured and
compared to projections. ____ ____ _____

Management fees are reasonable. ____ ____ _____

(Continued)

Exhibit 6.8. *(Continued)*

Cash income being generated is sufficient for operations. ____ ____ _____

Board investment or finance committee monitors investments. ____ ____ _____

Diversification and inherent risk of investment reviewed. ____ ____ _____

3. Endowment fund principal and income are segregated. ____ ____ _____

4. Safe custody is maintained. (Are securities in street name?) ____ ____ _____

Liabilities

1. Accounts payable system is in use. ____ ____ _____

Vendor invoices are recorded in an open invoice file. ____ ____ _____

Statements are vouched for invoices as paid. ____ ____ _____

Detailed accounts payable regularly reconciled to general ledger. ____ ____ _____

Lease terms are monitored. ____ ____ _____

2. Grant funds reserved for specific purposes and future periods identified. ____ ____ _____

Gift letters reviewed for restrictions. ____ ____ _____

Expenditures analyzed to vouch adherence to restricted grant covenants. ____ ____ _____

Procedure for return of unexpended funds in place. ____ ____ _____

Are standards of OMB Circulars, including A-122 (Cost Principles for NPOs) and A-133 (Single Audit) followed for government grants? ____ ____ _____

3. Interfund borrowing allowed only in limited circumstances and thoroughly documented for advances and repayments. ____ ____ _____

Emergency-situations policy. ____ ____ _____

Board authorization. ____ ____ _____

Formal record of loan and terms for repayment. ____ ____ _____

Exhibit 6.8. *(Continued)*

4. Payments on notes payable made
   in a timely fashion. _____ _____ _____

5. Debt covenants monitored. _____ _____ _____

Exempt Functions

1. Program. _____ _____ _____

2. Grant application process is efficient. _____ _____ _____

   Grantee forms complete and approved
   before funds are disbursed. _____ _____ _____

   Follow-up grantee reports required
   before additional payments are made. _____ _____ _____

3. Are fees for services, tuition, dues,
   subscription rates, and the like
   published in catalogs,
   bulletins, notices? _____ _____ _____

4. Program activity archives maintained. _____ _____ _____

   Weekly church bulletins filed
   chronologically. _____ _____ _____

   Visiting nurse diary with patient
   names and dates. _____ _____ _____

   Student handbooks or
   curriculum catalog. _____ _____ _____

   Research reports and publications. _____ _____ _____

   Attendance records for programs. _____ _____ _____

   Other evidence of exempt activities. _____ _____ _____

5. Tax exempt status is intact. Complete
   tax compliance checklist. _____ _____ _____

Exhibit 6.9.   Public Fund Solicitation Controls.

A. Door-to-Door Collections

1. Is campaign organized with chief, block captains, schedule for location and dates, and clear written materials instructions? ☐

2. Are receipts prenumbered with instructions for completion? ☐

3. For currency collections, is amount verified to prenumbered receipts at the time solicitor turns in money? ☐

4. Are solicitors informed about the nonprofit's mission? ☐

5. Do solicitors have proof of nonprofit's authorization to represent it? ☐

6. Are solicitor reports tallied and deposited daily? ☐

B. Festivals and Events

1. Is all money collected through ticket sales with tickets used to secure admission and purchase goods? ☐

2. Is monetary value or admission price printed on tickets? ☐

3. Are ticket numbers recorded as issued to solicitors of advanced sales? ☐

4. Is deadline and system for turning in advanced sale money written and deadlines provided? ☐

5. Are tickets collected at booths reconciled with number of items sold or food consumed? ☐

6. Is there a centralized payment booth with a cash register for entering ticket sales at the event? ☐

7. Are daily receipts tallied and deposited daily? ☐

8. Are unsold tickets reconciled to collection reports? ☐

C. Cash Canisters

1. Does nonprofit keep list of canister locations and person responsible for them? ☐

2. Are canisters replaced on regular schedule? ☐

3. Are canisters emptied in presence of two persons? ☐

4. Is currency report prepared and money deposited day of pickup? ☐

5. If risk of theft is high, can canisters be made more secure? ☐

Exhibit 6.9. *(Continued)*

D. Direct Mail Campaigns

1. Are two persons jointly controlling incoming mail receipts? ☐

2. Is a daily receipt report prepared and approved by both persons? ☐

3. Is report compared to bank statements by someone else? ☐

4. Should a bank lock-box service be used? ☐

CHAPTER SEVEN

Special Financial Tools

Specialized financial tools can allow a nonprofit to be more fiscally astute and to make informed decisions on issues with multiple, complex answers.

This chapter expands the tools useful to a financial planner. Specialized financial analyses and procedures can provide needed answers not evident from the financial reports described in Chapters 4 and 6. Using ratio analysis to critique performance sheds a different light on resource flows and allows evaluation of revenue sources. Cost accounting allows the nonprofit to calculate its expenses by programs. Money spent is reclassified according to function categories—counseling, vaccinations, and food services—in addition to generic type, such as supplies, salary, and rentals.

Comparing the numbers for leasing versus buying can be made a little easier if one asks the appropriate questions suggested later. In this time of reduced government funding, affiliating with other nonprofits to leverage resources can be critical to a program's or even an organization's survival. Section 7.4 suggests questions to ask and terms to consider in negotiating such partnerships. Classifying so called contract or part-time people as nonsalaried workers is a tempting choice many non-profits make. A fiscally prudent organization will complete the employment tax compliance checklists in Section 7.5 to assure it has no hidden tax liabilities from these decisions.

7.1 FINANCIAL INDICATORS TO CRITIQUE PERFORMANCE

Ratio analysis permits financial planners to identify trends, recognize strengths, and pinpoint weaknesses that may not be readily apparent. As an addition to the financial statements and budgets, ratios provide a different look at a nonprofit's fiscal health. Exhibit 7.1 illustrates some commonly used ratios and comments on issues that the results might raise.

The overall fiscal condition of an organization can be measured with capital structure ratios. The current, or acid-test, ratios are widely used by banks and financial advisors to assess an entity's financial health. By comparing the ratio of available cash to the liabilities or debts to be paid, the outlook for continued operation is revealed. The higher the cash flow is in relation to total debt or expense, the better. The ratio of debt to net assets also indicates the degree of the nonprofit's ability to take on additional debt or to self-finance a new project. The ratio of existing debt to current assets also indicates the existing degree of leverage, or ability to afford more debt. The lower the ratio, the better.

An endless array of operational indicators can be useful. Comparing the relative types of income received over a five-year period can reflect trends that could be meaningful. Knowing how much it costs to serve a patient is necessary to evaluate whether the price of services is appropriate, and so on.

(a) Economies of Scale

The concept here says certain costs do not increase in relation to an increase in the number of persons served or the number of units sold. The payroll department with three persons might only need to add one more person to handle a payroll for twice as big a staff. Printing bills reflect dramatic economies of that sort. The price for 1,000 sheets of letterhead is typically less than 50 percent than the price of 500. Calculating and keeping records necessary to achieve economies to scale can enhance financial results.

FINANCIAL INDICATORS TO CRITIQUE PERFORMANCE

Exhibit 7.1.   Using Ratio Analysis to Test Fiscal Health.

> This exhibit presents ratio analyses for testing an organization's fiscal situation. Financial conditions are measured with ratio calculations based partly on the sample financial statements found in Exhibits 6.6 and 6.7. Issues posed by the results are discussed.

Overall Fiscal Health

Current Ratio

	Holy Spirit Church	ratio	Assn of NPO Managers	ratio
expendable current assets*	$20,000	1	220,000	1.9
current liabilities**	80,000	4	116,000	1

* Unrestricted cash and assets convertible to cash.
** Debts payable within one year.

ISSUES: The current ratio compares the organization's resources available to pay the bills during the coming year. Classically, it is thought the current ratio of assets to liabilities should be at least 2:1. A ratio lower than 2:1 means short-term liquidity problems. The church obviously has a serious problem with its 1:4 ratio. The Association of Nonprofit Managers, with its 1.9:1 ratio, can comfortably pay the bills and have some cash left over. What if the ratio was above 2:1? Too high a ratio sacrifices income for safety. The difference between current assets and current liabilities is also called working capital. When working capital is adequate, a nonprofit may be in a position to make long-term investments as discussed in Section 5.5. This formula can also be calculated and compared for restricted and unrestricted fund current ratios.

Acid-Test Ratio

	Holy Spirit Church	ratio	Assn of NPO Managers	ratio
Cash or assests due in one month***	$20,000	1	$110,000	1.5
Total expenses within same period	40,000	2	74,000	1

*** Or three months.

ISSUES: The acid, or quick-ratio tests to see if the organization can pay its bills this month or this quarter. Ask this question: "Is the acid test or *quick ratio* at least 1 to 1? If the ratio is below 1:1, the planners asks, "Can the organization survive the month if receipt of funding is delayed?" The church

(Continued)

Exhibit 7.1. *(Continued)*

finance committee may hope it had been asking these questions sooner as it faces what is now a serious financial situation—debts equaling two times its assets available to pay the debt.

Overall Liquidity Ratio

	Holy Spirit Church	Assn of NPO Managers
Expendable fund balances	$20,000	$220,000
Total monthly expenses	10,833	67,000
Number of months	1.8	3.3

ISSUES: The overall liquidity ratio measures how long the organization could survive if it receives no new money. The Association of Nonprofit Managers has enough money available to pay its normal bills for a bit more than three months. The church only has 1.8 months of money. See Sections 3.3 and 5.3 for cash and resource planning ideas to evaluate the situation. For an organization with an endowment or other permanent funds, a similar calculation would be made to compare the permanently restricted, or unexpendable funds, to the total annual expenses.

Operational Indicators

Revenue Collection Results

		Good	Bad
1.	Average month end balance—Unpaid pledges	$50,000	$150,000
	Annual member dues or donations received	500,000	500,000
2.	Amount of pledges written off	$12,000	$80,000
	Annual member dues or donations received	500,000	500,000
3.	Number of members not renewing	26	140
	Total number of members	380	380

ISSUES: These ratios show how effectively the nonprofit collects promises of support it receives. Whether the result is good or bad actually must be determined by the particular facts in each situation. Ratio 1 essentially shows the time lag between the time the member makes a pledge and the organization actually collects the money. Ratio 2 reflects the bad debt experience and can be looked at as a percentage. The good ratio shows 2.4 percent of the pledges were not collected as compared to the bad ratio of 16 percent. In 3, a good renewal rate of 6.9 percent is shown and a bad rate of 38 percent.

Exhibit 7.1. *(Continued)*

A nonprofit's life blood comes from the collection of pledges from members and donors. An annual checkup of the sort shown in these ratios can be very helpful to spot "high blood pressure." Bad results should prompt the organization to take steps to heal the problem, such as:

- Analyze pledge collection policies and payment terms,
- Consider using computers or obtaining better software to speed the process,
- Change the nature of funding requests (mail versus phone),
- Use commercial credit cards,
- Following up with a paid staff instead of volunteers, or
- Hire a professional fund-raising consultant.

Revenue Source Comparison

Version 1	Year 1	Year 2	Year 3	Year 4	Year 5
Members dues and donations	100,000	120,000	110,000	90,000	80,000
Total revenue and support	300,000	300,000	320,000	340,000	350,000
ratio	33.3%	40%	34.4%	26.5%	22.9%

This ratio analyzes the percentage of the organization's support received from member dues and donations over a five-year period to see if this funding has changed significantly. This example reflects a 10 percent decline over five years and could signal a serious problem unless the organization has deliberately focused to increase other sources.

Revenue Source Comparison

Version 2 (using Exhibit 6.6)	Association of Nonprofit Managers	
	Prior year	Current year
Chapter member dues	$238,000	$249,700
Members at large dues	76,000	78,600
Information services sales	40,000	120,000
Publication sales	180,000	204,000
Continuing education	98,000	106,000
Annual Meeting	42,000	28,000
Royalty Income	1,000	42,000
Interest income	3,000	1,000
Total income	$678,000	$829,300

ISSUES: How does the current year's revenue portion for a particular revenue source compare with last year's? Is the change planned or expected? Should any action be taken in response or to analyze the reason for the change?

(Continued)

Exhibit 7.1.   *(Continued)*

Cost Ratios

Version 1	Year 1	Year 2	Year 3	Year 4	Year 5
Dollars spent on:					
Direct program costs	$280,000	$300,000	$320,000	$304,000	$300,000
Management and general	100,000	110,000	120,000	140,000	150,000
Fund raising	10,000	20,000	40,000	50,000	55,000
Total	$390,000	$430,000	$480,000	$494,000	$505,000
Percentage ratio:					
Direct program costs	71.8	69.8	66.7	61.5	59.4
Management and general	25.6	25.6	25.0	28.3	29.7
Fund raising	2.6	4.7	8.3	10.1	10.9
Total	100%	100%	100%	100%	100%

ISSUES: On Form 990 and on a GAAP financial statement, the nonprofit's costs must be presented in the three categories shown above for this ratio—program or exempt function costs, general and administrative (G&A) expenses, and fund-raising costs. It is, therefore, extremely important for a nonprofit to monitor this measurement annually. Funders prefer to pay for program expenditures. Some measure the worth of a proposed grantee according to the portion of the total expenditures devoted to programs. Some will not fund an organization whose combined G&A and fund-raising costs exceed 25 percent of the total. The organization shown in this example has, in five years, gone from spending 71.9 percent of its budget on programs down to 59.4 percent. This situation may be troublesome and should again be monitored annually.

Cost Ratios

Version 2	Total Cost	Percentage
Project 1	$180,000	18.4%
Project 2	304,000	31.1
Project 3	242,000	24.7
Project 4	189,000	19.3
Project 5	64,000	6.5
Totals	979,000	100%

Exhibit 7.1. *(Continued)*

Cost Ratios **More Versions**	Number	Ratio
Average daily cost per patient (student, etc.) / Average charges (income) per patient	$129 / 140	108.5%
General & administrative hospital cost (not counted in patient daily cost) / Number of patients serve in a year	$250,000 / 1,922	$130 each
Cost per participant fund-raising dinner / Average event ticket price	$44 / 75	1.7 times
Administrative costs plus value of volunteers / Number of attendees at benefit	$60,000 / 1,200	$50 each
Total membership costs / Number of members	$267,000 / 856	$312 each
Cost of newsletter or other member services / Annual membership fee	$22 / $200	11%
Fund-raising costs / Total annual support	$28,000 / $200,000	14%

ISSUES: These cost ratio variations provide a tool for the nonprofit (1) see what portion of its funds it is spending on a particular project and (2) to test profitability or lack of it for income-producing activities. Some of the ratios work in concert. The ratios can be useful in understanding and correcting financial difficulties. The numbers can be translated into fund-raising goals, into revenue increase targets, or a variety of other indicators.

The first hospital ratio looks positive with 108.5 percent of direct patient costs being charged to patients. The second, though, shows an additional $130 per patient per year is spent on administration. Similarly, one might think benefit tickets sold at 1.7 times the direct cost of the event is acceptable until the fourth ratio shows the administrative cost is actually $50 per person in addition. When the intention is to balance costs with revenues, these ratios provide a useful tool. Some states regulate the percentage fee paid to fund-raising consultants.

The member dues calculations might be used to analyze the need to raise prices or to report to members how much of their dues is spent on the types of services provided. Fund-raising costs ratios must often be considered in relation to other data. What is the normal ratio for the type of nonprofit? Has the fund-raising program just begun with too little time to bring results? Was a direct-mail campaign started just this year? Funders are interested in these ratios as discussed in Section 7.2(a) below.

(Continued)

Exhibit 7.1. *(Continued)*

Other Useful Ratios

Inventory Turnover: This ratio is calculated by dividing the total sales of the year by the inventory on hand at year end. If the answer is one-fifth, it is said the inventory turned five times. The average number of days items were unsold would be one-fifth of 365, or 73 days, or about two months.

Each day that inventory, or items bought to be resold, remain unsold theoretically costs the organization money. If the goods had not been purchased, the money could be earning interest in the bank. Thus it is important that inventory "turn" or remain as few days as possible in the hands of the seller. A low inventory turnover might also indicate poor buying decisions—the goods are in inventory because no one wants to buy them.

(b) Break-even Analysis

This calculation is somewhat like scaled economies. The point is to calculate at what point a program or project pays for itself. Say a hospital wants to equip a new laboratory that is expects will cost $1,000,000 annually; also assume the prevailing market test price is $200. The break-even point for the lab is 5,000 patients, or the number it takes to bring in the expected costs. The 5,001th patient begins to bring in some profit.

(c) Performance Statistics

A nonprofit should be constantly aware of the number of persons it serves, how much they each pay, and the changing mix of such constituents. Student enrollment, church parishioners, persons receiving legal assistance, and similar details can be tracked and studied. Performance measurements related to constituents can also be useful—test scores, number of publications sold, awards received, diseases cured, attendees at performances and their reactions, and so on.

7.2 COST ACCOUNTING

Cost accounting identifies the money spent in connection with each program, product, or other specific purpose. Economies to scale, better pricing, and more realistic expectations can result for the nonprofit that keeps track of how the money is spent. It is the cost accounting system that allows the organization to prepare the functional expense reports shown in Section 6.3(b).

By using a cost accounting system, revenues and costs are captured in generic categories (salaries or rent) and also by function (program 1, 2, or administration). When expenses are attributable to more than one function, the United Way says,

> Organizations are required to develop techniques that will provide verifiable bases upon which expenses may be related to program or supporting service functions. The functional classification of expenses permits an agency to tell the reader of the financial statements not only the nature of its expenses, but also the purpose for which they were made.[1]

More informed financial decisions are possible when functional expenses are captured in a cost accounting system. Other advantages stemming from the effort, to name a few, include:

- Charges for services can be evaluated for reasonableness.

- Indirect cost reimbursement grants can be accurately negotiated.

- Realistic overall cost of programs can be quantified to facilitate planning and, sometimes most importantly, to prepare grant funding requests, or to calculate member dues assessments.

- Deductions for unrelated business income tax purposes can be maximized.

(a) Techniques for Capturing Costs

An extra layer of details is needed to effectively use a cost accounting system. To allocate the salary of a staff person that works, for example, on three different programs, a time-keeping system is required. Suggestions for gathering the necessary data include the following:

Staff Salary Allocation System.   Records to quantify the time employees spend on task(s) performed each day should be prepared. The possibilities are endless. Each staff member can maintain a computer database or fills out a time sheet. The reports should be completed often—while the

---

[1] *Standards of Accounting and Financial Reporting for Voluntary Health and Welfare Organizations,* Revised 1988—Third Edition, National Health Council, Inc., National Assembly of National Voluntary Health and Social Welfare Organization, Inc., United Way of America. (Called The Black Book).

memory is fresh—to assure accuracy, preferably weekly. Personnel performing repetitive tasks may only need to prepare a one-week report each month; one month each year might be sufficient. Based upon employee reports, percentages of time spent on various functions can be tabulated and used for cost allocations.

Office or Program Space Utilization Charts. Physical building space rented or owned is customarily allocated according to its usage. Floor plans can be used to tabulate the square footage of the space allocable to each activity center. In some cases, the allocation is based upon the time reports of the staff using the spaces. One way to allocate space used dually (by more than one program or activity) is to allocate space costs according to the number of hours or days the space is used for the respective purposes.

Direct Program or Activity Costs. Once the chart of account is designed to facilitate cost accounting by function as illustrated in Section 6.3, expenditures are coded as the bills are paid by cost center if possible. A purchase order should indicate the cost center code as shown in Section 7.3(b). Separate departmental accounts can be established with vendors to facilitate identity of purchases. Photocopy machines can be programmed to contain cost codes. Long distance call providers, for a small monthly fee, provide a coding system to identify calls on the monthly billings.

Joint Projects Allocations. Allocations of joint costs must be made on a reasonable and fair basis recognizing the cause-and-effect relationship between the cost incurred and where it is allocated.[2] A joint project is one that embodies two or more programs or purposes. The classic example is a brochure containing both public health information (stop smoking or vaccinate your children) and a solicitation for contributions to support the dissemination of the information. At least four allocation methods provide an acceptable method for making the cost allocation as follows:

[2] Dennis P. Tishlian, *Reasonable Joint Cost Allocations in Nonprofits,* Journal of Accountancy, AICPA, November, 1992, page 66. Also see *AICPA Audit and Accounting Guide, Audits of Certain Nonprofit Organizations,* including *Statement of Position (SOP) 78-10,* as amended by SOP 87-2, *Accounting for Joint Costs of Informational Materials and Activities of Not-for-Profit Organizations That Include a Fund-Raising Appeal,* issued by the Accounting Standards Division of the American Institute of Certified Public Accountants. AICPA audit guides for hospitals, colleges, and universities and voluntary health and welfare organizations are also available.

- Activity-based (identifying the inches of brochure devoted to health information and those containing the solicitation),

- Equal cost (when two projects share the cost, divide by two),

- Ratio of the total based upon stand-alone cost (what it would cost if that department had to hire and buy independently), and

- Cost saving (costs allocated in proportion to efficiency).

Supporting, Administrative, or Other Management Costs. For many reasons, it is important that administrative costs be properly classified. Funders like to see their money spent on programs, not overhead. The Better Business Bureau (BBB) and The National Charities Information Bureau rate nonprofits according to the percentage of support and fund-raising costs in relation to total costs. What percentage of supporting costs is excessive is arguable; but the BBB says any amount above 25 percent is too much—the smaller the better.

Large nonprofits may have clearly identified administrative costs— a personnel department, a business office, and other independently functioning support staffs. In many nonprofits, support staff personnel are also involved in programs. Where the scope of such involvement can be measured, support function costs may be allocated partly to programs. Staff salaries are most often allocable. Say, for example, the executive director is also the editor preparing articles for the quarterly journal. If a record of the time spent is maintained, his or her salary and associated costs could be attributed partly to the publication.

(b) Cost Allocation Methods

Costs can be allocated using a variety of factors as listed below. The challenge is to identify the factor(s) that most suitably calculate relative costs associated with any particular program or activity. Once a method is chosen, it is advisable to use it consistently for some years so that comparable data is accumulated. The IRS manual instructs examining agents that any reasonable method resulting in identifying the relationship of the expenses to revenue produced is acceptable.[3] In an unrelated business income tax case, one court said there is no particular approved method that must be followed. The IRS says they prefer a system that

---

[3] *Exempt Organizations Examination Guidelines Handbook,* Internal Revenue Manual, Section 720(7).

allocates costs to all activities, similar to a GAAP functional expense statement. The various methods and factors to consider follow.

Actual time records should be maintained to evidence the portion of time staff and volunteers actually spend conducting various functions. In the absence of time records, or instead of them, an allocation based upon relative gross income produced by each program might be used.

Direct and indirect expenses must be distinguished. Direct expenses are those that increase proportionately with the usage of a facility or the volume of activity and are also called *variable*. The number of persons attending an event influences the number of ushers or security guards and represent a *direct* cost of the event. In other words, the cost would not have been incurred *but for* the particular scheduled performance. *Indirect costs* are those incurred without regard to usage or frequency of participation, and are also called the *fixed expenses*. Building acquisition costs, for example, do not vary with usage.

The *fraction denominator* used in the formula for calculating cost allocations can impact the result significantly. Take, for example, a college football stadium with the following statistics concerning its usage.

		Divide by days used	Divide by days in year
no. of days used by the college	52	70%	14%
no. of days rented to others	22	30	6
total days used	74		
no. of days idle	291		80
Total days in year	365	100%	100%

The gross-to-gross method of cost allocation is used to calculate the cost of goods sold when costs bear a relationship to the revenue produced from exempt and nonexempt factors. A proration based on the number of participants can also be used. This type of formula is used in calculating allocations for social clubs and publications charging different prices to members and nonmembers.

7.3 PURCHASING PROCEDURES

In the long run, a written plan or procedure for spending saves money. Acquiring goods and services for a nonprofit involves both monetary and nonmonetary considerations. How complicated the purchasing procedures need to be depends upon such factors as the size of the organization, the sheer number of transactions, the number of persons authorizing the purchases, the internal control system, and so on. Buying a copy machine for a three-person office that makes 4,000 copies a month might be relatively simply. Setting up a computerized communication network for an organization with 100 employees is more challenging.

(a) Approval Systems

An efficient purchasing system contains at least three elements:

1. Approved vendors,

2. Authorization policy, and

3. Uniform documentation system.

For many reasons it is more efficient to establish purchasing relationships with particular, or approved, vendors. Relying on approved vendors should result in better services, compatibility of equipment and supplies used throughout the organization, possibly more favorable credit terms, optimum prices, and realization of economies to scale. Considerable time may be saved because fewer checks are written for the many items purchased from approved vendors rather than an array of vendors. Staff and volunteer time is not wasted on duplicative shopping efforts.

Likewise, to maintain internal controls and respect budget constraints, purchases should only be made based upon proper authorization. Specific persons to approve purchases and monitor the expenditures in relation to the budget should be designated, before any substantial commitment to purchase can be made. An adequate purchasing system establishes a hierarchy that requires the least possible red tape for recurring and modest purchases. The chart shown in Exhibit 7.2 would serve to communicate the policies to staff and volunteers and to govern commitments of funds.

(b) How Much Paper Work?

Documentation should be designed to evidence that the purchasing procedures are followed by all persons spending the nonprofit's money. Again the documents needed varies, but the forms illustrated in Exhibits 7.3–7.6, for petty cash, check request, and capital expenditures, are a minimum. A large organization with far-flung purchasers would require

Exhibit 7.2.   Hometown Education Center: Purchase Procedure Reference Chart.

Amount of Purchase	Approved Vendor Used?	Quotes Required	Written Bid Required	Special Approval Needed	Required prior to Purchase
< $100	No	No	No	No	Petty cash req.
$100–500	Yes	No	No	No	Check request
$100–500	No	No	No	Yes	Check request
$500–5000	Yes	Yes	No	No	Purchase order
$500–5000	No	Yes	Yes	Yes*	Purchase order
over $5000	Yes or No	Yes	Yes	Yes*	Purchase order
Capital item	Yes or No	Yes	Yes	Yes* *by CFO	Feasibility study + purchase order

Exhibit 7.3.   Hometown Education Center: Petty Cash Reimbursement Request.

Name _____   Amount $ _____
(Petty Cash Custodian)   (Equals Sum
                                                                                                        of Receipts)

Expense Category	Program or Designated Fund	Description	Amount

_____   _____
Signature of Custodian   Approved by

PURCHASING PROCEDURES

Exhibit 7.4. Hometown Education Center: Petty Cash Log.

Date	Name of Person Receiving Cash	Amount Advanced	Receipts Returned	Total of Receipts	Change Returned

Exhibit 7.5. Hometown Education Center: Petty Cash Request.

Name _____ Amount $ _____
　　　　　　　(Person receiving cash)　　　　　　　　　　(Equals Sum of Receipts)

Describe Reason for Cash Advance	Amount	Receipt Yes or No

Signature of Custodian　　　　　　　Approved by

SPECIAL FINANCIAL TOOLS

Exhibit 7.6.   Hometown Education Center: Purchase Order # _____ .

Vendor: _____   Ship to   Hometown Community Center
         _____   1234 Main Street
         _____   Hometown Texas 77777

Quantity	Description	Program Function Code	Received	Unit Price	Total Price

   Totals

Special Instructions: Authorized by:

  Deliver no later than _____ (date)   _____

  Contact person: _____ (name). Cost center: _____

_____ Verify quantities received with purchase order and packing slip upon arrival.
(initial)
_____ Packing slip or invoice then forwarded to business office.
(initial)

purchase orders, might allow credit cards, and would design a bidding-process form. In all nonprofits, the purchasing system should be coordinated with the conflict of interest policy described in Section 2.7.

(c) Measuring Lifetime Cost

Capital acquisitions, particularly major purchases, involve considerable costs in addition to the basic initial price. The affiliated costs for equipment might include theft insurance, maintenance and supplies, personnel time and expense for training, and additional occupancy costs for the space required for the equipment. In addition to the check request or purchase order form suggested above, the long-term cost of the item can be calculated as shown in the worksheet shown in Exhibit 7.7.

(d) To Lease or to Buy

A related financial consideration in acquiring new equipment or other long-term property is whether to lease or buy the property. The question is essentially a financing issue. Is it better to buy today for cash, to buy with a down payment plus borrowed funds, or is it better to lease? As with investment decisions, it is important to realize there is no absolute and precise answer. Interest rates are going to fluctuate, so the benefit of keeping the money in the bank is only a guess. The potential need for repairs is impossible to predict. New technologies may or may not be developed that will render the equipment obsolete.

Despite the uncertainty, the alternatives can be evaluated with the best information available. Exhibit 7.8 outlines some of the factors to consider.

SPECIAL FINANCIAL TOOLS

Exhibit 7.7.   Hometown Education Center: Major Purchase Planning Matrix.

Description of   _____

Equipment Needed   _____

Justify the Need: _____

_____

Quantify its Original Cost:

     Purchase price $_____

     Shipping   _____

     Software, tools, accessories   _____

     Installation fees/programming   _____

     Training costs (hours $\times$ wage $\times$ 1.3) _____

     Other   _____

     Total PURCHASE COST $_____

     Annual cost (divide purchase by
         years estimated to be of
         usefulness to NPO $_____

ADD Recurring ANNUAL COSTS: _____

     Financing costs (or loss of income) _____

     Insurance   _____

     Maintenance   _____

     Training   _____

EXPECTED ANNUAL COST
     for EQUIPMENT $_____

Prepared by   _____
             (signature)   (date)

Exhibit 7.8. Deciding Whether to Lease or Buy.

> *There are potential advantages with both leasing and buying. No absolute an-
> swer to the question exists because facts are indeterminate. Six factors to con-
> sider and compare are outlined in this checklist.*

Advantages of Leasing

- Leasing allows freedom to move easily if more space is needed or if
  another location is found more desirable, or to change equipment if it
  becomes obsolete or inadequate.

- Leasing has limited financial risk. It may be less costly (particularly
  where there is rent control), it requires less commitment of time,
  resources, maintenance, and it does not tie up capital.

- The market may be at its peak. Leasing buys the time to judge
  whether prices will fall in the future.

- The nonprofit may be able to lease with an option to purchase, which
  leaves it free from commitment but retains the opportunity to buy.

Advantages of Buying

- The permanency of owning a good property can give the
  organization stability.

- If prices are rising, buying locks in lower cost.

- Alterations and choices of space utilization are not restricted.

Space and Size Considerations

1. Prepare a needs assessment for people, projects, storage,
   and other uses. How much space or equipment must be
   provided for? _____

2. Ask how far into future plans can be made with
   reasonable certainty. _____

Price Considerations

1. The prices of comparable property, whether the contemplated
   purchase is for a building, a computer, or a car, should be
   obtained (based upon square feet, capacity, quality, or
   other relevant factors). Independent appraisals might be
   appropriate. _____

2. The condition of property must be considered. _____

   a. Are major repairs needed? _____

   b. Are security and other services adequate? _____

(Continued)

Exhibit 7.8.   *(Continued)*

---

   c. How good is the location in relation to the
      nonprofit's constituents?   _____

3. The cost of occupying the property must be
   included in purchase price.

   a. Will the nonprofit need to remodel, rewire,
      paint, relocate?   _____

   b. Can skilled workers be found to perform the job?   _____

4. Consider the possibility of renting out excessive
   space or capacity.   _____

The Nonprofit's Financial Position

1. What are the consequences of using cash reserves?   _____

   a. What is the minimum amount of cash the nonprofit
      can afford to commit without jeopardizing operations?   _____

   b. Prepare cash flow projections for several years,
      including debt service and annual maintenance
      and occupancy costs.   _____

2. Can existing capital be allocated to major purchase?   _____

3. What other expenses would be reduced or eliminated?   _____

Local/State Sanctions

1. Can an occupancy permit be obtained for the purpose
   for which the nonprofit plans to use the property?   _____

2. Are there restrictive deed covenants?   _____

3. How much will it cost to satisfy building code ordinances?   _____

4. Will property tax exemptions be available?   _____

7.4 AFFILIATIONS AND AGENCY AGREEMENTS

For a number of reasons, a nonprofit organization may wish to join forces with another organization, a business, a volunteer guild, a student club, or an artist, for example. Such affiliations occur frequently in many different forms, including the joint operation of a mutually beneficial project (computer database), a fund-raising or special event sponsorship, or a fiscal agency in which the nonprofit serves to maintain the bank account (student or special grant). A number of issues need to be explored between the parties in forming such an affiliation. At least the following questions should be answered:

1. Who's money is it?
   - Will the NPO serve as fiscal agent meaning it will receive moneys as pass-through gifts that will not be its property?
   - On who's financial statements will the financial activity be reported?
   - If a charity is involved, to whom is the charitable gift made for income tax deduction and donor disclosure purposes?

2. Who bears the risk of loss?
   - With whose money will a bank account be opened and in whose name?
   - In whose name will purchases be made or obligations entered into to rent a facility, engage a performer, or print a flyer?
   - If workers are hired, who's responsible for tax reporting?

3. What other terms should be agreed to?
   - How long will the agreement lasts?
   - Who is in control of what?
   - Who's staff and other assets will be actively involved?
   - Are prior approvals required for announcements or other use of the nonprofit's name?

To protect its interests and provide operational guidelines, the nonprofit should document such arrangements with written agreements.[4]

---

[4] Gregory L. Colvin has written an excellent booklet entitled, *Fiscal Sponsorship, 6 Ways to Do It Right*, published by Study Center Press, San Francisco, CA. 82 pages. The legal relationships among the parties are carefully illustrated and explored using six different models.

The alliance may be permanent and deserve a formal prenuptial or partnership agreement. On the other hand, it may be a one-time special event or project for which a simple letter reciting the understandings and setting forth the budget is sufficient. The parties to the association must describe the nature of the association and define the responsibilities of all involved. Exhibits 7.9 and 7.10 are models provided as examples, not as a legal document to be executed. They can serve, just as the preceding checklist is intended to, as a starting point for consideration in developing the facts and circumstances to document a nonprofit's particular affiliation agreement.

Exhibit 7.9. Sample Fund-Raising Event Sponsorship Agreement.

Name of **Benefited Charity**_____

Name of **Event Sponsor** _____

Description of purpose for which the funds raised will be expended.

_____

_____

_____

Description of Event _____

_____

_____

_____

Financial Information:

Gross **revenue** expected to be raised (attach details)

# of people × ____ (price per ticket)   _____
In-kind contributions of food, facilities, etc.   _____

Total

Expenditures (attach details)   − _____

Projected net profit $ _____

Exhibit 7.9.   *(Continued)*

_____ (Event Sponsor) hereby authorized by _____ (Benefited Charity) to sponsor a fund-raising event on its behalf on _____ (date) at _____ (place). Expenditures in connection with this event are authorized by sponsor in accordance with a budget mutually agreed upon prior to event's announcement. Sponsor agrees it is responsible for any expenditures in excess of revenues, if any, incurred in presenting the event.

Sponsor warrants that all proceeds of the event, less mutually agreed upon costs, belong to the Benefited Charity. Sponsor will control event funds by using enclosed PUBLIC FUND SOLICITATION CONTROLS Checklist (Exhibit 6.9). A bank account in the name of the Benefited Charity will be established for deposit and disbursement of funds. Checks will be made payable to the Benefited Charity and deposited on a daily basis during the fund-raising period. Detailed records of the financial transactions, in accordance with the attached RECORD-KEEPING REQUIREMENTS, will be maintained by Sponsor's business office.

Use of Name: Sponsor agrees, in advance, to seek _____ (Benefited Charity)'s approval for all written announcements, press releases, tickets, and any other materials reflecting charity's name.

Termination: This agreement will cease once a full detailed accounting of revenues and expenses, along with copies of receipts and other required documentation, have been furnished to the benefited charity.

Agreed to on this _____ day of _____, 199X.

_____   _____
for the Benefited Charity   for the Sponsor

Exhibit 7.10.   Sample Fiscal Sponsorship Agreement.

1. Parties to the Agreement. Hometown Artists Fund (HAF) is a public tax-exempt § 501(c)(3) organization established to serve as sponsor for artist's projects in the Hometown area.

New Artist Project (NAP) is an unincorporated association created by Joan Fatcat and Alex Painter to honor emerging artists with exhibitions and to document their works with catalogs and similar educational materials. As its first project NAP plans to curate an exhibition and catalog of the art work of Frank Creative in the spring, 199x, at the Museum for New Art, Hometown, USA.

2. Financial Information. NAP will seek donations from individuals, businesses, and foundations to provide financial support for the exhibition. A bank account has been opened for the project. NAP will satisfy the attached Record-keeping Requirements (Exhibit 7.11) for moneys raised and expended in HAF's name and furnish a quarterly report of the financial activity. HAF will annually file Forms 990 reporting its overall activity to the Internal Revenue, furnish donor receipts, and take whatever other steps are necessary to keep its qualification as a charitable tax-exempt organization current and in good standing.

A preliminary budget for the project estimates $_____ will be raised in donations and $_____ will be expended to survey the work and prepare a catalog of Creative's work. The Museum of New Art has made an oral commitment to pay all of the costs of the exhibition. NAP hereby agrees not to commit HAF to any expenditures in excess of the moneys raised through voluntary contributions. A reasonably detailed accounting will be maintained by NAP to assure the spending is within the amount of funds available. The creators of NAP, not HAF, will be responsible for any cost overruns incurred. A budget for expenditures will be furnished for approval by HAF's board prior to NAP entering into any binding commitments to expend funds.

3. Rights and Ownership. NAP will be operated as a project of HAF. HAF will delegate to NAP's managers the authority to carry out the activity as described in the project proposal and within the approved budget. The managers of NAP will work without compensation but will engage one or more writers or curators to compose the catalog and design the exhibition. Those artists will be hired as independent contractors and will retain no ownership interest in the work product. HAF will be given a limited license for reproduction and exhibition of Frank Creative's art work. Mr. Creative will receive a fee as reflected in the budget for his work. Additionally HAF will request he receive a royalty (of up to 10%) interest in the catalog sales, if possible, in its negotiations with publishers.

Plans for the catalog are preliminary and specific ownership rights and responsibilities in that regard remain to be agreed upon. HAF's role is to assure that the catalog is used exclusively for educational purposes and that it receives the widest possible distribution and preferably as a publication of a university press.

Exhibit 7.10.   *(Continued)*

4. Administrative Fee. HAF is managed by its creators, Molly Smart, CPA., and Joe Lucky, Attorney-at-Law. They respect and admire Frank Creative and wish to support NAP, whose managers are also unpaid volunteers. Thus no administrative fee will be paid from NAP funds for handling the project through 199x. It is presumed the managers of NAP will maintain the required fiscal records and keep the project expenditures within budget so as not to expose HAF to risk of creditor claims or manager travail.

5. Duration of Agreement. This agreement shall last until the exempt purposes for which NAP is raising funds are accomplished or until NAP establishes itself as independently qualified as an exempt charitable organization. Agreed to this day of _____ in _____, 199x.

_____   _____
for Hometown Artists Fund   for New Artist Project

Exhibit 7.11. Sponsor or Agency Record-Keeping Requirements.

BANKING RECORDS	Done by
• Open bank account in name of XYZ, a project of Hometown Artist Fund.	_____
• Keep a checkbook (computerized if possible) recording each transaction and the daily cash balance.	_____
• Prepare bank account reconciliation monthly.	_____
• Keep checks with statements intact (copy items if needed).	_____

REVENUES RECEIPTS
- Deposit checks or cash as soon as possible after receipt. _____
- Keep copy of each check received and any daily cash tally. _____
- Identify nature of payment received (donation, cost reimbursement, etc.). _____
- Receipt or thank each contributor using standard HAF form. _____
- Maintain an alpha (by donor) file for receipts. _____

DISBURSEMENT OF FUNDS
- Identify each invoice or bill paid with check number, date paid, and budget category description. _____
- Maintain bills and invoices in an alpha order by merchant. _____
- Keep files to document nature of activities, such as copy of exhibition invitations, manuscripts, photos, and so on. _____
- At least quarterly, prepare summary of income and expenses by categories in grant proposal. _____

If workers are to be hired, ask for checklist to classify as contractors versus employees. **Employees can only be hired directly by HAF.** Obtain invoice and Form W-9 for all independent contractors. _____

7.5 WHO'S AN EMPLOYEE?

Nonprofit organizations who have employees must satisfy Internal Revenue Service withholding and filing requirements outlined below, as well as other regulatory agencies including the department of labor, workers' compensation statutes, Employee Retirement Insurance Security Act (ERISA) rules, and state employment taxes. Most wages are subject to tax withholding except those paid to certain ministers, members of religious orders, student workers, and fellowship or grant recipients. Exhibit 7.12 reviews the primary tax issues to be considered. The most severe penalties in the tax code are imposed upon failure to pay withheld employment taxes, because such money does not belong to the organization but instead to the employees. Of equal importance to nonprofit managers, the IRS may consider them personally liable for unpaid payroll taxes.

Exhibit 7.13 compares the attributes of employees—those for whom a nonprofit is responsible for withholding and paying taxes—versus independent contractors. There is no specific mathematical test applied to

Exhibit 7.12. Employer Tax Checklist.

> *This checklist compiles local and federal tax filing requirements and outlines types of compensation arrangements for which reporting may be required as well as other employment law issues.*

1. Does the entity have a policy for distinguishing between employees and independent contractors? ☐

   a. Complete Employee versus Independent Contractor Checklist. ☐

   b. Does the entity have a contract with independent contractors? (Exhibit 7.14) ☐

   c. Have vendors' Social Security numbers been secured with a signed Form W-9? ☐

   d. Are vendor invoices obtained from independent contractors to prove their professionalism? ☐

2. Are meals, cars, tuition, or housing allowances furnished to employees? If so, determine taxable portion, if any. ☐

3. Does the pension plan adhere to ERISA rules? ☐

4. Is Form 5500, 5500C, or 5500R required for the pension plan? ☐

5. Are the terms of any qualified or nonqualified deferred compensation plan adhered to? ☐

6. Do COBRA rules entitle former employees to continued medical benefit coverage? ☐

7. Is workers' compensation coverage required? ☐

(Continued)

Exhibit 7.12. *(Continued)*

8. Verify adherence to federal requirements. Study IRS Circular E, *Employer's Tax Guide,* for filing requirements, chart of wages subject to or exempt from taxes. Verify correctness of:

   a. Income tax withholding. ☐

   b. Social Security tax. ☐

   c. Federal unemployment tax. ☐

   d. State and local income taxes. ☐

9. Verify timely filing of the following IRS reports:

   a. Form 941, employer's quarterly federal tax return. ☐

   b. W-2 Forms for all employees. ☐

   c. W-3 Form with copy of W-2s. ☐

   d. W-4 placed in each employee's file. ☐

   e. Form 1099-MISC for all independent contractors. ☐

   f. Form W-9 placed in each contractor's file. ☐

   g. Form W-2G, Prizes and Awards. ☐

   h. Form W-2P, Statement for Recipients of Pensions. ☐

   i. Form 940, federal unemployment (not filed by 501(c)(3)s). ☐

10. Verify timely deposit of federal employment taxes. ☐

11. Are state employment commission or tax requirements satisfied? ☐

   a. Are periodic returns filed and tax paid on time? ☐

   b. If new employer, file status report to obtain account number. ☐

Exhibit 7.13.   Employee versus Independent Contractor Status:
A Comparison Checklist.

This checklist lists the six primary characteristics distinguishing an employee (E) from an independent contractor (IC). The letter E identifies the predominate characteristic of an employee and IC describes the characteristics of an independent contractor. For each pair of factors, choose best description and check either E or IC. Upon completion, the factor with larger number of checks should be the correct classification of the worker.

| | | Check One | |
| | | Employee (E) | Independent Contractor (IC) |
Factor	Attributes		
INSTRUCTION and TRAINING	E required to comply with instructions as to when, where, and how work is performed, and training is provided either by formal program or work supervision.		
	IC free to perform work according to own professional standards, use their own methods, and receive no training from purchasers of their services.		
PAYMENT TERMS	E is paid by the hour, week, or month on a regular, indefinite, and continuous basis. E's business expenses are paid. Fringe benefits are usually provided.		
	IC is often paid by the engagement with fee calculated without regard to time spent. IC not paid for excess time to perform task nor given vacation or sick leave. IC pays expenses.		
NATURE OF ENGAGE-MENT	E's Employer has the right to discharge an E; control is exerted with threat of dismissal. E has the right to quit without incurring liability.		
	IC may suffer damages if work is not performed as contracted. Payment still due if IC is fired.		

(Continued)

Exhibit 7.13. *(Continued)*

RELATION TO ENTITY	**E**'s services are an integral part to the ongoing success and continuation of entity. Services are rendered personally by E. E works only for and has loyalty to and does not compete with employer. E is bonded and provided workers' compensation.		
	IC consults on per-job, limited, or special-project basis. IC can hire and pay assistants to perform the work. IC's service is available to others on a regular basis. IC works under a company name.		
WORK PLACE & HOUR	**E** works on business premises or is physically directed and supervised by employer. Hours of work established by employer.		
	IC may work at own place of business and usually sets own time for performing work.		
INVESTMENT	**E** is dependent upon employer for tools, facilities, and usually makes no investment in the job. E bears no risk of loss for financial costs of entity.		
	IC buys own tools, hires workers, pays licensing fees, and is responsible for costs of engagement. Bears financial risk of losing money.		

Internal Revenue Ruling 87-41 provides the above characteristics. The checklist contains all of the 20 factors set out by the IRS hopefully organized in a fashion that makes the determination easier. A nonprofit that is uncertain and wants IRS sanction for their decision is invited by the IRS to submit a completed Form SS-8, entitled Information for Use in Determining Whether a Worker Is an Employee for Federal Employment Taxes and Income Tax Withholding, *to obtain the IRS opinion on the matter. Form SS-8 can also be used as a self-examination tool.*

Exhibit 7.14. Minimal Independent Contractor Agreement.

> *Agreements should be prepared in consultation with a nonprofit's legal counsel. This model is intended only as an illustration.*

Name of

Organization _____

Contractor: _____

Price:

      Fixed fee   _____

      Hourly rate $.   per-hour times ____ hours =   _____

      Reimbursable expenses:

      _____   _____

      _____   _____

Payments will be made monthly, based upon invoices submitted by you, along with receipts and other documentation for reimbursable expenses described above.

For consideration, you agree to perform the following work:

_____

_____

_____

In consideration of payment by _____, you warrant that you are an independent contractor, not an employee, agent, or representative of the company. You are responsible for all federal and state payroll taxes and insurance. You—on behalf of yourself, your assigns, and estate—waive and release any and all claims or rights whatsoever you may have against us. This agreement may be terminated by either party at any time, except that you will be paid for any unpaid services properly chargeable to us prior to termination. In acknowledgment of our understandings, we have both signed below.

By: _____   By: _____

Date:_____   Date: _____

make the determination, although more than one-half on either side is a strong indication. The facts and circumstances of each payee/payor relationship are analyzed. As a rule, classifying a worker as an employee is seldom challenged; it is finding justification for treating one as independent that is troublesome. For those treated as a contractor, a prudent nonprofit can enter into a contract of the type illustrated in Exhibit 7.14.

Making a distinction between employees and independent workers is important for two reasons. The costs associated with providing benefits and matching taxes for employees range between 10 to 30 percent of direct payroll costs; so classifying a worker as an employee is a costly decision. This factor tempts some nonprofits to treat workers as contractors, not subject to tax withholding and employee benefits. The wrong decision, however, can be costly. When the IRS finds that a worker should have been treated as an employee, they assess payroll taxes even though the organization withheld nothing from the worker's compensation. In 1995, several major universities learned this painful lesson as they were assessed millions of dollars for taxes on teaching assistants.

Obtaining and Maintaining Tax-Exempt Status

Although for-profits do not often give away food or house the poor, they do operate schools, hospitals, galleries, and other institutions serving the public good. If the work of for-profits and nonprofits can be the same, why do only nonprofits get special tax treatment?

A nonprofit organization's financial planners need to know not only why it qualifies for tax exemptions, but also the breadth of activity such status allows. Nonprofits are fascinating because they are full of paradoxes and surprises. In this chapter, the unique nomenclature defining those organizations entitled to Federal tax-exempt status is explored, and some of the contradictions are explained. The subject is complex, and tax rules are vague and grey with few generally applicable rules; the answers are typically based on the facts of each particular organization, meaning the answers are not always clear. The thorough review of the tax issues can be found in the second edition of my book entitled *Tax Planning and Compliance for Tax-Exempt Organizations* that contains 712 pages; the text is updated annually, with a supplemental text now totally over 250 pages.

The complexity of this subject is also illustrated by the fact that the Internal Revenue Code (IRC) does not contain the word nonprofit—it refers only to exempt organizations. The term nonprofit, or not-for-profit, describes the type of organizations legally created in most states, and is widely used to identify tax-exempt organizations. The terms are commonly used interchangeably.

8.1 CHARACTERISTICS OF TAX-EXEMPT ORGANIZATIONS

A nonprofit organization is not necessarily a tax-exempt organization. Exempt organizations are by necessity nonprofits and are established under state laws as nonprofit, or not-for-profit organizations, which leads to a certain amount of confusion. A tax-exempt nonprofit organization (an EO or simply an exempt) is distinguished from a nonexempt nonprofit by its ownership structure, the nature of its activities, its sources of revenue to finance operations, and what happens to its assets upon dissolution. As discussed in Chapter 1, the term *nonprofit* is sometimes a contradictory term. To grow and be financially successful, a nonprofit can and often must generate profits, and sometimes it must pay income tax on investment or business income unrelated to its underlying exempt purposes.

(a) Theoretical Basis for Exemption

Federal and state governments view nonprofits as relieving their burdens. Thus, many nonprofits are exempt from the levies that finance government, including income, sales, ad valorem, and other local property taxes. Tax exemption recognizes that such nonprofits essentially perform functions the government would otherwise have to perform. United States tax laws were traditionally designed to encourage private philanthropy. Other exempt organizations, such as social clubs or labor unions, are exempt because they are organized for the mutually beneficial purposes of their members, rather than the individual member's private financial gain. Another way to express this concept is such groups are permitted tax exemption precisely because they are nonprofits.

The thread running through the various types of exempt organizations is the lack of private ownership and self directed profit motive in their programs. A tax-exempt organization is a nonprofit entity operated without self-interest and with no intention to produce income or profit distributable to its members, directors, or officers. Most nonprofits are afforded special tax and legal status precisely because of the unselfish motivation behind their formation.

(b) Categories of Exemption

Although nonprofit organizations are often perceived as charitable, the federal Internal Revenue Code (IRC) § 501 exempts 28 specific types of nonprofit organizations, plus pension plans (IRC § 401), from income tax. States themselves, labor unions, business leagues, social clubs, and employee benefit associations are included on the list. Each exemption category has its own distinct set of criteria for qualification. Form 1023 or 1024 can be reviewed to gain an understanding of the basic criteria applied in determining that a particular nonprofit organization qualified as a tax-exempt entity. A brief abstract of the five major categories of exemption in the federal tax code follows.

§ 501(c)(3) organizations are known as charities and include those nonprofits that qualify for the charitable contribution deduction for income tax purposes. A (c)(3) organization must under the terms of its charter permanently dedicate its assets to its charitable purposes. Upon dissolution, any assets remaining must be paid over to another charity and cannot be returned to its funders. A charity cannot electioneer or attempt to influence the choice of persons running for public office. On a very limited scale, a charity can lobby or attempt to influence elected officials once they are in office. The code specifically says nonprofits who exclusively pursue the following purposes can qualify for this category of tax exemption:

1. Religious

2. Charitable

3. Scientific

4. Testing for public safety

5. Literary

6. Educational

7. Fostering national or international amateur sports competition, and

8. Preventing cruelty to children or animals.

This category includes churches, schools, hospitals, united giving campaigns, private foundations, and a myriad of organizations providing services and benefits to members of the charitable class—or the constituents for whom the charity operates. For some categories of exemption, the class members must be underprivileged or needy—the hungry, poor, or homeless low-income families. Educational and literary organizations, on the other hand, may conceivably only serve those who can afford to pay for attending their functions—symphony societies and private schools, for example.

Each type of charitable organization has its own particular set of criteria. For example, most nonprofits that support youth activities, such as a local little league team, can qualify as type 1, or charitable. To qualify as a Type 7, a national amateur sports competition sponsor is prohibited from selling sports gear and is subject to other specific rules intended to distinguish it from commercial counterparts. Charitable hospitals are not (as of June 1996) required by the IRS to provide health care for those who cannot pay, as long as they can show that they promote community's health needs. What distinguishes a church from other religious organizations is similarly governed by a specific set of published criteria. To understand the rules pertaining to a particular nonprofit, it is important to again keep in mind that many nonprofits provide the same services as for-profit businesses—hospitals, scientific-research organizations, book stores, theaters, and so on. Distinguishing such organizations that serve the general public from its commercial counterpart providing the same services for the economic gain of its owners is sometimes difficult.

§ 501(c)(4) organizations include two very different types of nonprofits.

1. Civic leagues

2. Local associations of employees.

Civic leagues are nonprofits that promote the common good and general welfare of the people of a community by implementing programs designed to have an impact on community, state, or national policy making. A (c)(4) organization can spend an unlimited amount of its funds on legislative lobbying as distinguished from a (c)(3) who may only spend a limited amount. Organizations established to defend the environment, to protect human and civil rights, to lessen neighborhood tension, to eliminate prejudices and discrimination in a pro-action fashion would seek exemption under (c)(4).

§ *501(c)(5)* permits exempt status for labor unions and agricultural groups. The statute requires that such groups serve three purposes:

1. Betterment of conditions of those engaged in such pursuits,

2. Improvement of the grade of their products, and

3. Development of a high degree of efficiency in their respective occupations.

Labor organizations are defined by the tax regulations to include an "association of workmen who have combined to protect or promote the interests of the members by bargaining collectively with their employers to secure better working conditions, wages and similar benefits." Unions also are permitted to conduct peripheral activities intended to advance the workers, such as providing strike benefits, mutual sickness and death plans, seminars and training programs, and job-placement counseling. Unions can participate in election campaigns and lobby without specific limits, as long as the union basically operates to benefit its members' interests.

Agricultural organizations are dedicated to developing techniques for efficient product and betterment of conditions for those engaged in agriculture or horticulture, or the "art and science of cultivating the ground, preparing soil, planting seed, rearing, feeding, and managing livestock." Such groups operate to benefit their members as a whole, rather than as individuals. For example, an agricultural group can conduct seed-certification programs to maintain an industry standard, but it could not (except as an unrelated business activity) sell seeds to individual farmers.

§ *501(c)(6)* provides exemption for business leagues, chambers of commerce, boards of trade, and professional football leagues. A business league is permitted exemption because it is a nonprofit association of persons having a common business interests. The league does not itself conduct a regular business or perform services for or provide benefits to its members. Instead a business league seeks to improve conditions and maintain standards for one or more lines of business. A common business interest exists for lawyers who form the American Bar Association, physicians and the medical society, accountants and the CPA societies, contractors and their association, for example. The American Automobile Association is not a business league, because its members have no common business interest; any individual motorist can join to serve his or her personal needs. Similarly a computer users group open to all persons using a particular type of computer operating system, without regard to their business interests, was found not to qualify for exemption under this category.

§ 501(c)(7) grants exempt status to social clubs. Theoretically the social club exemption permits persons to join together on a mutual basis for pleasure and recreation without tax consequence. Clubs that seek exemption, however, are subject to very stringent rules governing the limited extent to which a club can provide services to nonmembers. A social club's investment income on property accumulated as reserves is taxed, although any profits from member activities is exempt.

(c) Tax Deductibility

For reasons not always apparent, all nonprofits are not equal for tax deduction purposes and not all "donations" are deductible. For charitable nonprofits, labor unions, and certain business leagues, the deductibility of dues and donations granted to such organizations further evidence the government's willingness to forego money in favor of such organizations. Deductibility provides a major fund-raising tool for the nonprofits until and unless the Congress adopts a new tax system similar to the "flat tax" proposed in 1995.

8.2 UNDERSTANDING THE NONPROFIT'S LEGAL FORM

The requirements for nonprofit status vary from state to state and few generalizations apply. Exempt charitable institutions are called public benefit corporations in some states. Business leagues, social clubs, burial groups, and other membership organizations are sometimes called mutual benefit corporations. Rather than being organized to generate profits for owners or investors, nonprofits generate profits for their broadly based public or membership constituents.

The choice of organizational form is influenced by laws of the states in which the nonprofit will operate. The federal tax-exemption rules overlap and sometimes contradict. For example, the model nonprofit corporation charter acceptable to the state of Texas is deficient for federal tax-exemption purposes, in several respects. The choice of legal form for certain categories of federal tax-exemption is also limited. A title-holding company, for example, must be a corporation to qualify for federal exemption. Social clubs, civic associations, and business leagues may have unique organizational structures. Nonprofits functioning as a branch of a national organization may be required to adhere to the form of organization prescribed by the central and controlling entity. The common choices are corporation, trust, or unincorporated association. The need to coordinate local and federal law may make the initial choice of organizational form difficult. Retaining an attorney experienced in nonprofit matters is advisable.

(a) Corporation

Because corporate status is the most flexible, it is usually the form of choice in most states. The American Bar Association and, more recently, the Association of Attorneys General, have developed uniform procedures and rules that have been adopted by many states and can be used as a guideline.

Creating a corporation as a separate entity provides a corporate veil that shields the individuals controlling the nonprofit from liabilities incurred by the organization (unless they are negligent or otherwise remiss in their duties). Some states have adopted immunity laws augmenting protection against liability for directors and officers. In Texas, the Charitable Immunity and Liability Act of 1987 applies to charitable trusts and nonprofit organizations conducting charitable programs. This statute protects a charity's officers, directors, trustees, and volunteers, regardless of the form of organization, thus obviating one of the advantages in establishing a corporation. In California, apparently only not-for-profit corporations are provided such immunity.

A nonprofit corporation can be formed with or without members. Unless the charter provides otherwise, some states presume the existence of members. The primary role of members is to elect the board of directors who, in turn, govern the organization. In a privately funded organization, the members may be family representatives whose job it is to retain control by naming the directors, or, the founder of a charity can be named the sole member. In most public benefit corporations and certainly in churches, members serve to broaden the base of financial support and to involve the community in the organization's activities. In such cases, there may be hundreds or thousands of individual contributors (investors in the financial planning sense) who, as a group, control the organization because they elect the directors. Most mutual benefit societies, clubs, and the like are also controlled by their dues-paying members. When the democracy afforded by member control is not desirable, the nonprofit's charter can provide for a self-perpetuating board or a board appointed by another organization or other persons (the town mayor, the governor, the school superintendent, for example). Calling the supporters of a nonmembership nonprofit "members" can cause confusion.

Bylaws are adopted to provide rules of governance, such as the number of directors, duration of their terms, and procedures for electing and removing them. Bylaws typically also address the frequency of meetings, notice of meeting protocol, type and duties of officers, delegation of authority to committees, extent of member responsibility, and indemnity from liability for the directors. The manner in which the bylaws and the charter can be amended is prescribed. An advantage of the corporate form—as compared to a trust—is the ability to easily mold and change policies as the organization evolves. Usually, the currently serving board has authority to make changes to both the bylaws and the charter.

(b) Trust

Individually or family-funded charitable organizations are often organized in trust form, either by testamentary bequest under a will or by creation of an *inter vivos* (among the living) trust. Unlike a corporation, a trust can be totally inflexible, with no provisions for change in purpose or trustees. Thus, a donor with specific wishes may prefer this potentially unalterable form for a substantial testamentary bequest. Another advantage of a trust is that some states require no registration. There is some argument that charitable trusts can violate the rule against perpetuities. To avoid this potential obstacle, a trust may contain a provision allowing the trustee(s) to convert the trust into a nonprofit corporation, with identical purposes and organizational restraints, if the trust form becomes disadvantageous.

Nonprofit organization immunity statutes do not apply to trusts in some states, and more stringent fiduciary standards are often imposed upon trustees than on corporate directors. As a rule, trustees are thought to be more exposed to potential liability for their actions than are corporate directors. The tax rates on unrelated business income are lower for a corporation than for a trust.

(c) Unincorporated Association

An unincorporated association is said to be self-establishing. Two or more persons adopt an organizing instrument, usually called a constitution or articles of association, outlining the same basic information found in a corporate charter or trust instrument. For a short-term nonprofit project that does not intend to seek tax exemption, this form may be suitable. It is also used for a local branch of a statewide or national organization holding a group exemption. The central organization provides subordinates with a uniform set of documents and procedures to adopt. An unincorporated group faces substantial pitfalls. The primary concern is lack of protection from legal liability for officers and directors. Also banks and creditors may be reluctant to establish business relationships without personal guarantees by the officers or directors.

8.3 TESTING SUITABILITY FOR TAX-EXEMPTION

Before embarking on financial planning for an exempt nonprofit, the reasons why the nonprofit is exempt should be clearly understood. Proposed projects or changes in operations, particularly those involving creative methods of raising money, should be tested to assure their suitability for a tax-exempt organization. The basic questions to be addressed are the same questions one asks before creating a new organization. Although the rules are sometimes ambiguous, certain requirements are applied precisely. Five major questions can be asked to determine whether a proposed program, or by reference a new organization, is suitable for qualification for tax-exempt status.

(a) Why a New Nonprofit?

The first question to ask is whether a new organization is really necessary? Could the project, instead, be carried out under the auspices of an existing nonprofit? Several factors can indicate that a new organization is not necessary. If the purposes to be accomplished are short-term or essentially in pursuit of a one-time project with no prospect for ongoing funding, the expense and effort involved in setting up a new, independent, nonprofit may not be economically feasible. Similarly the costs of launching the project within an existing organization may not be recoupable.

A good question to ask is whether the project could be operated as a branch of an existing nonprofit under an agency agreement, as discussed in Section 7.4. Maybe a local branch of a national organization holding a group exemption can be established. Consider if there would be a costly duplication of administrative effort, or if the cost of obtaining and maintaining independent exemption would be excessive in relation to the total budget. It might make sense to find a fiscal sponsor, form an alliance with an existing group, or find a more financially viable manner in which to accomplish the objective.

(b)   What Category of Exemption?

If the proposed organization passes the first test, it is time to choose the category of exemption best suited to the goals and purposes of the project. The § 501(c)(3) charitable exemption rules are very specific, somewhat rigid, and can limit some activities. As explained above in Section 8.1(b), a (c)(3) organization cannot, for example, participate in a political campaign and may only conduct limited legislative and grassroots lobbying. A (c)(4) civic league can spend all its money on lobbying, and it can have some electioneering efforts. If no profits are expected to be generated and no tax deductibility is desired, tax-exempt status might not be necessary and the organizers might simply create a for-profit company.

   If a project is not suitable for charitable exemption, the other categories of exemption should be studied. Some projects can conceivably qualify for more than one category. There are garden clubs classified as charities under § 501(c)(3), civic welfare societies under § 501(c)(4), and social clubs under § 501(c)(7). An association of business persons, such as the Rotary Club or the Lions Club, most often qualifies as a business league. If the activities of the group involve educational and/or charitable efforts, (c)(3) status, rather than (c)(6) status, might be sought. A breakfast group composed of representatives of many different types of businesses may not qualify under § 501(c)(6), but might instead easily qualify as a § 501(c)(7) social club. The tax deductibility of member dues and taxability of income influences the desired choice of category.

(c)   How Is Money to Be Raised?

To be financially viable, a nonprofit organization needs sufficient capitalization similar to a for-profit organization; but cannot sell shares of stock as discussed in Section 1.4(a). Before the final decision to establish a new organization is made, the nonprofit's future needs for capital and its ability to raise money must be projected. The reliability of funding sources should be evaluated to assure sustainable spending levels.

   Nonprofits are normally expected to be supported by voluntary contributions, member dues, and charges for services rendered or goods provided to accomplish an exempt purpose, such as school tuition or ballet tickets. Moneys raised through services rendered or goods sold in competition with businesses, such as insurance or legal services, may be taxed as unrelated business income. Although unrelated revenue activities are not prohibited, exempt status can be revoked if such activity becomes excessive in relation to the exempt focus of the nonprofit as explained in Section 5.2(b).

A charitable nonprofit that receives the majority of its funding from a particular family or other small group of persons or that is supported by its endowment income may qualify for exemption as a § 501(c)(3) organization. Such a privately funded charity, however, is designated as a "private foundation," and is subject to a separate set of rules designed to prevent the use of the organization's for the creator's selfish purposes. All financial transactions, other than voluntary gifts to the private foundation, between the organization and its creators are prohibited by self-dealing rules. At least 5 percent of the average monthly fair market value of the foundation's investment assets must be paid out annually in charitable grants and projects. Other specific rules apply to penalize insiders who make jeopardizing investments with the foundation's money or who pay out funds for noncharitable purposes.

(d) Will Insiders Benefit?

The last and sometimes most important issue is whether the organization's creators desire economic benefits from the formation or ongoing operation of the organization. Is there any personal greed involved? Will the organization be operated to serve the self-interested purposes of its creators? The one-way-street characteristic of nonprofits is crucial to ongoing qualification for tax exemption as discussed in Section 1.4(a). If the founders desire incentive compensation based on funds raised, or wish to gain from profits generated, a nonprofit organization may not be an appropriate solution. Reasonable compensation for services actually and genuinely rendered, however, can be paid.

For a variety of reasons, it is sometimes desirable to convert a for-profit business into a nonprofit one. In the health and human service field, for example, funding is often available from both for-profit and nonprofit sources. An organization's direction may change or funds may become available only for tax-exempt organizations or vice versa. When a nonprofit is created to take over the assets and operations of a for-profit entity, the buy-out terms will be carefully scrutinized. Too high a price,

Exhibit 8.1.   Suitability Checklist for Tax-Exempt Status.

This checklist asks questions intended to tell those considering the formation of a new tax-exempt nonprofit organization whether the effort is financially viable.

Is a new organization necessary, or could the project be carried out as a branch of an existing organization?

- Life of the project is short term or indefinite. ☐

- It is a one-time project with no prospect for ongoing funding. ☐

- Project could operate under auspices of another exempt organization. ☐

- Duplication of administrative effort is too costly. ☐

- Cost of obtaining and maintaining independent nonprofit is excessive in relation to total budget. ☐

- Group exemption is available through a national nonprofit. ☐

Which 501(c) category of exemption is appropriate to the goals and purposes of the project?

- Are the activities in pursuit of an exempt purpose? ☐

- No involvement in political campaigns for (c)(3)s. ☐

- Legislative and grassroots lobbying activities may be limited. ☐

- Private foundation strictures on activities may apply. ☐

- Compare business versus social aspects of future activities. ☐

Are the sources of revenue suitable for a nonprofit organization?

- Sales of goods produced by members. ☐

- Services to be rendered in competition with nonexempt businesses, such as legal services or insurance. ☐

- Over half of revenues to come from unrelated businesses operated in competition with for-profit companies. ☐

- Will support come from particular family so as to require classification as a private foundation. ☐

Do the creators desire economic benefits from the operation of the organization?

- What are the possibilities for private inurement? ☐

- Do the creators wish to be paid incentive compensation based upon funds raised or profitability of the organization? ☐

Exhibit 8.1. *(Continued)*

- Are transactions with related parties anticipated? ☐

- Is this an insider bailout? Are assets being purchased or debts being assumed? ☐

- Will services or activities be available to a limited group of persons or members instead of a public class? ☐

- Who will use or benefit from the existence of the organization's physical facilities or other assets? ☐

Upon dissolution, where will the nonprofit's assets go?

- Do the organizational documents permanently dedicate the resources to its exempt purposes? ☐

- If the nonprofit is a (c)(3), will remaining assets be paid over to a similarly exempt nonprofit when it ceases to exist? ☐

- For a league or club, will the funds be rebated to members? ☐

ongoing payments having the appearance of dividends, and assumptions of liability that take the creators off the hook are among the issues faced in this situation.

(e) Where Will Assets Go?

The resources of an exempt organization must be permanently dedicated to its exempt purposes. When it ceases to exist, the assets remaining upon dissolution must essentially be used for the same exempt purposes for which the organization was initially granted tax exemption. Charities exempt under 501(c)(3) can only distribute funds to another (c)(3) organization, and their charters must require this. Again, the one-way-street concept is applicable. The creators must understand and intend from inception that they will gain no personal economic benefit from the organization's operations and benefits. Exhibit 8.1 summarizes the issues to be considered in forming a new exempt organization.

8.4 MAINTAINING RECOGNITION OF EXEMPT STATUS

To be officially recognized by the IRS as an exempt organization, the nonprofit submits an Application for Recognition of Exemption, Form 1023 or 1024, with the IRS Exempt Organization Key District Office. With the form, the prospective exempt paints a picture of its future self as if it were fully operational. Using both words and numbers to describe proposed activities and funding sources, the applicant submits a wealth of information to allow the IRS to judge whether the proposed activities and financing methods qualify it to be exempt from federal income tax on its net income and gain other special privileges. Recognition of exemption by the IRS typically is an automatic basis for exemption from a variety of state and local taxes.

The tax rules, upon which the IRS decides qualification, are gray and they are not necessarily made clear by the IRS regulations and rulings or by court decisions. As with most federal tax matters, the Internal Revenue Code expresses general concepts subject to endless interpretations. The categories of exempt nonprofits have expanded considerably since the Tariff Act of 1894 established a single category that included charitable, religious, educational, fraternal, and certain building and loan, savings, and insurance organizations. Since that time, the number of categories has expanded to include the 28 distinct types. The distinctions among the categories are not always clear or logical. For example, only scholars of legislative history can explain why agricultural organizations and labor unions are coupled together. Why are agricultural groups not considered business leagues? Why are agricultural auxiliaries classified as business leagues? Why was a separate category carved out for real estate title-holding companies with multiple parents, instead of placing them in the original 501(c)(2) for single-parent organizations?

To qualify for exemption, a nonprofit must be organized exclusively for exempt purposes within the specific terms described in the Code, and it must operate primarily for such purposes. *Exclusively* does not mean 100 percent, and *primarily* can mean a little more than 50 percent. The facts and circumstances are examined in each case because the regulations provide very few specific numerical tests. When used, a numerical test is most often applied to gross revenues, but it can also be applied to net profits, direct costs, contributions in kind, and the like. In each case, the IRS examines the exact facts to determine whether exemption is in order.

(a) Role of Internal Revenue Service

A special division of the IRS giveth and taketh away a nonprofit's tax-exempt status. The determination division is planned to be centralized in Cincinnati, Ohio. The personnel are typically well-trained specialists with a number of years of experience, they are usually highly cooperative, and they view their role differently than the prototypical IRS agent. This division reviews applications for exemption and anoints properly organized and operated nonprofits as exempt organizations often before the nonprofit actually has any financial activity. Throughout the nonprofit's life, the exempt organization division receives and evaluates Forms 990 and, when it deems necessary (in the past, a rare occasion), examines the organization to ascertain that continued tax exemption is allowed. Changes in the nonprofit's purpose or scope of activity, public charity status, accounting methods, fiscal year, or similar issues necessitate a voluntary report back to the exempt organization division to obtain sanction or approval for the change.

Only Section 501(c)(3) organizations are technically required to seek a determination by the IRS to qualify as exempt and are only treated as exempt if Form 1023 is filed. For all other categories of nonprofits, being established and operated according to the characteristics described in the tax code is technically sufficient. Those nonprofits, business leagues, and unions, for example, often seek IRS determination to secure proof of their status for local authorities, members, and in some cases, the IRS itself, and to insure against penalties and interest due on their income if they do not qualify. The process by which application is made is thoroughly discussed and illustrated in my tax book.[1]

The administrative burden and expense of the determination process and annual compliance are at least equal to the annual filing burden of for-profit-motivated firms. Professional assistance from accountants and lawyers familiar with nonprofit matters will ease the process. If funds are limited, a qualified volunteer can be sought. In many states, pro bono assistance is available through CPA societies, bar associations, and other volunteer groups such as the Texas Accountants and Lawyers for the Arts.

(b)   Forms 990

Annual information returns—Form 990, 990EZ, 990T, or 990PF—are filed by exempt nonprofits as an annual report to the Internal Revenue Service. Detailed balance sheets, income statements, lists of directors and officers and their compensation, and descriptions of activities are submitted, along with a report of any changes in the organization's form of organization, bylaws, purposes, activities, revenue sources, or so on occurring during the particular year. The returns contain descriptions of the organization's exempt activity along with financial information, and are open to public inspection upon request. Because of abuses by some exempts, there was ongoing pressure during 1994 and 1995 to make the Forms 990 more accessible to the general public. The IRS expects the reports will be filed electronically in the near future. One can speculate access to 990s on the Internet may not be far behind. To assure an organization is dotting its Is and crossing the Ts, an annual tax-compliance checklist for both (c)(3)s and non-(c)(3)s, is shown in Exhibit 8.2.

Forms 990 serve several purposes and should be prepared with care. In addition to the initial filing with the IRS, Forms 990 are also filed in many states. Some funders request and review as a part of their grant-approval process. Anyone who asks is entitled to view a copy of Form 990 in the nonprofit's offices. Three years of 990s and Form 1023 or 1024 must be available for public inspection upon request.

---

[1] © Jody Blazek, 1994. *Tax Planning & Compliance for Tax-Exempt Organizations,* 2nd ed., John Wiley & Sons, New York, 1993.

Exhibit 8.2.   Tax-Compliance Checklists.

ANNUAL TAX-COMPLIANCE CHECKLIST § 501(c)(3)S

NAME _____   Prepared by _____

Organizational Issues

Federal tax exemption

New organization: Has Form 1023 been filed
within 15 (or 27) months after organizational date?   _____

Young organization (1–5 yrs): If advanced ruling
received, has IRS report been filed 90 days of ending
date? [§ 18.7]   _____

All organizations: Review Form 1023 and determination
letter for exempt purposes originally represented to the
IRS and to verify category of exemption. Satisfy your
current activities in keeping with expressed purposes.   _____

State and local taxes

Obtain a copy of state tax exemption(s) letter or
prepare application for exemption(s). [§ 18.9]   _____

Does the organization use the proper form to
claim exemption?   _____

Must the EO collect sales tax on goods or services sold?
Are timely returns filed? Is tax deposited on time?   _____

Does the organization pay real or personal property tax?   _____

Would use of property qualify it for exemption?   _____

For property classed as exempt, is it devoted to exempt
use or has it been converted to commercial use?   _____

Charter and bylaws

Were there any changes to the charter or bylaws this year?   _____

If so, submit copy as attachment to Form 990.   _____

Were there any substantial changes in structure or purpose
that require reporting to the IRS?   _____

© Jody Blazek, 1996. Reprinted from 1996 Annual Supplement to *Tax Planning & Compliance for Tax-Exempt Organizations,* 2nd Ed., John Wiley & Sons, New York, 1993, 712 pps. (Book sections referenced in [   ]).

(Continued)

Exhibit 8.2. *(Continued)*

Change reported on Form 990? [§ 27.9]
New 1023 required? [Exhibit 28.1]

Review the minutes of director's meetings. Do they
reflect the exempt purpose of the EO's activities?   _____

Operational Issues

Private Inurement or Benefit

Does the EO provide benefits to persons that control,
manage, or fund it? [§ 20.6]   _____

Is the amount of compensation paid to officers,
directors, and staff or price paid for goods or services
reasonable? [§ 20.4]   _____

Are loans made to officers or directors? [§ 20.7]   _____

Does the organization benefit a charitable class or a
limited number of persons? [§ 2.2(a)]   _____

Does the organization sell services or goods produced
by its staff or members? [§ 2.2(e)]   _____

Exempt activities

Do activities further the purposes for which EO was
determined to be exempt (as described in Form 1023
or subsequently reported to IRS)?   _____

Are files maintained to document or provide an archive
of the nature of activities? For example: copy of exhibition
invitations, class schedules, grants paid?   _____

Does the organization lobby? If so, has it filed Form
5768? Does it meet the limitations? [§ 23]   _____

Has the organization participated in any political
campaigns? Review newsletters re mention of
candidates/issues.   _____

Does EO have unrelated business income? If so, complete
Form 990-T and UBI checklist. [§ 21]   _____

Does the EO make payments for personal services.
If so, complete *Employee vs. Ind. Contractor Status*
[Exhibit 7.13].   _____

Exhibit 8.2. *(Continued)*

Does the EO have a policy for distinguishing between employees and contractors? _____

Does EO comply with Federal and state payroll withholding and reporting requirements? [Exhibit 7.12] _____

Are payroll taxes deposited in a timely fashion? _____

Has the IRS ever examined the organization? Review reports for compliance with any changes. _____

Complete the "publicly supported" or "private foundation" checklist. _____

For hospitals, review IRS Audit Guidelines. _____

For college or university, review IRS Audit Guidelines. _____

Filing Requirements

FORM 990EZ: (c)(3)s with gross receipts < $100,000 and assets < $250,000, includes Sch. A. _____

FORM 990: (c)(3)s with gross receipts > $100,000 or assets > $250,000 file long form plus Sch. A. _____

FORM 990-PF: Private foundations (PFs) converting to public file regardless of support levels. _____

If the EO is exempt from filing, consider filing. _____

Address is kept current for IRS announcements, Pub. 78 listing is maintained, and statutory time starts _____

Was an extension of time requested? [Form 2758] _____

If the return is being filed late, has penalty abatement been requested? [§ 18.2(e)] _____

Does the EO need to change its fiscal year or its accounting method for tax purposes? With proper planning, can the change be made automatically? _____

Property Contributions

Has the organization received gifts of property (other than listed securities) for which Form 8283 is required? _____

Must sales of $5,000+ donated property made within two years from date of gift be reported on Form 8282? _____

(Continued)

■ 235 ■

Exhibit 8.2. *(Continued)*

Validity of Financial Information

Has a compilation, review, or audit checklist been
completed to insure proper financial reporting and
adherence to accounting principles?   _____

Tax-Compliance Checklist: Unrelated Business Income

Does the EO sell goods or services in an activity that
does not relate to or further its exempt purposes?   _____

Does the "related business" have a commercial taint?
If so, complete *Commerciality Test* on Checklist 21-1.   _____

Is the business activity substantial (as measured by gross
revenue or staff time devoted to it) in relation to the
organization's exempt activity? [§ 21.3]   _____

Does the organization do any of the following?

    Sell advertisements in its publications? [§ 21.8(d)
    and Exhibit 21.2 for calculation of taxable portion.   _____

    Accept corporate sponsorships? [§ 21.9e)]   _____

    Rent personal or real property? [§ 21.13(c)]   _____

    Earn any income from indebted property, margin
    accounts, or loans? [§ 21.17]   _____

    Sell its mailing list? [21.10(b)]   _____

    Operate a bookstore, restaurant, or parking lot for
    member convenience? If so are any sales made to
    unrelated parties causing the fragmentation rule to
    apply? [§ 21.4(c)]   _____

    Furnish or sell services? [§ 21.8(b)]   _____

Carry out any of the above activities through a separate, but
controlled, business corporation or partnership? [§ 22.4] _____

Do any of these exceptions or modifications apply?

    The activity is not regularly carried on . [§ 21.6]   _____

    Substantially all (85 percent) work in carrying out the
    trade or business is performed by volunteers.[§ 21.9(a)] _____

    The facility is operated for the convenience of persons
    participating in the organization's activities. [§ 21.11] _____

    Items sold are either donated, educational, or directly
    related to the exempt function. [§ 21.9(b)]   _____

Exhibit 8.2. *(Continued)*

Items are "low-cost" premiums sold for significantly
more than their value. [§ 21.10(a)]   _____

The income is of a passive nature (e.g., dividends,
interest, or royalties). [§ 21.12]   _____

Calculating the Tax

Do accounting records reflect allocation for expenses?   _____

Time records for staff. [§ 21.14]   _____

Square footage of spaces used.   _____

Allocation of membership dues to publications.   _____

Was Form 990-T filed in prior years?   _____

Is IRS alerted 990-T is required because Form 990,
page 5, Part VII, column B contains a number? [§ 27.10]   _____

Does the gross income exceed $1,000? If loss realized,
990-T required and useful to establish net operating
loss carryover or carryback and start statute of limitation
time period.   _____

Should estimated tax payments be made 990-T tax?   _____

Are federal tax deposit coupons (Form 8109) available?   _____

If 990-T is required, complete *Checklist for
Preparation of Form 990-T* [Appendix 27-8 in supplement]   _____

Publicly Supported Organizations

Can the EO meet its public support tests under § 509(a)(1)
or § 509(a)(2)? Complete a support test worksheet
[Exhibits 11.4 or 11.5]. Note Schedule A does not
reveal passage of test.   _____

If the organization claims to be a supporting organization,
can satisfaction of the "responsiveness" or "control and
supervision" tests be documented? [§ 11.5]   _____

Are deadlines for filing a report scheduled before the
60-month termination date?   _____

Is fund-raising conducted in a state that requires reports?
Does a state charitable solicitation act apply?   _____

Do fund-raising solicitations reflect fair market value
(FMV) of benefits offered to donors in return for gifts?
For +$75 payments, is disclosure of deductible portion
complete? [§ 24.7(c)]   _____

(Continued)

Exhibit 8.2.   *(Continued)*

Is the method for calculation for FMV of benefits provided to donors reasonable and documented? [§ 24.2]   _____

Has EO disclosed Forms 990 and 1023 to members of public requesting to see them? [§ 27.2]   _____

Does the EO have excess lobbying expense [§ 23.6] or political expenditures [§ 23.2(e)] subject to excise tax?   _____

Reconsider the need to elect § 501(h) for lobbying activities, in view of § 4912.   _____

Are expense allocations and shared expenses with related 501(c)(4), (c)(5), or (c)(6)s documented? [§ 22.4(c)]   _____

Private Foundation (PF) Tax Checklist

§ 4940 Excise Tax on Income

Does the PF have any nontaxable investment income? [§ 13.2 & § 13.3]   _____

Does the PF have records to support expense allocation among investment, administrative, and exempt activities?   _____

Is the allocation consistent with prior years? [§ 13.4]   _____

Is the tax basis of assets (donee's basis for gifts received) maintained separately from the book basis? [§ 13.3(a)]   _____

Should estate income distributions be delayed? [§ 13.2(f)]   _____

Does the PF have substantially appreciated property it could distribute to grantees (rather than cash) to reduce excise tax on capital gain from sale of the property? [§ 13.3(c)]   _____

Should the PF make extra qualifying distributions to reduce its excise tax to 1%? [§ 13.1(a)]   _____

Are quarterly payments of tax due for 990-T or 990-PF?   _____

Must large corporation method for estimating be used?   _____

Are federal tax-deposit coupons (Form 8109) available?   _____

§ 4941—Self Dealing

Did the PF pay money to disqualified persons? If, so:

Was the payment for reasonable compensation? [§ 14.4]   _____

Did the PF reimburse exempt function expenses? [§ 14.8]   _____

Exhibit 8.2.   *(Continued)*

Was interest-free loan being repaid? [§ 14.1]   _____

Did the < $5,000 transaction occur during "normal
course" of retail business? [§ 14.3]

Were benefit tickets accepted for grant? [§ 14.5(d)]   _____

Does the PF pay for memberships? [§ 14.5(c)]   _____

Does the PF indirectly do business with a DP? [§ 14.9]   _____

For bequeathed property, should distributions from estate
be delayed until property is sold or divided?   _____

§ 4943: Calculate permitted stock holdings to identify
excess business holdings. [§ 16.1]   _____

§ 4944: Review PF's investment listings to evaluate
presence of jeopardizing investments. [§ 16.2]   _____

§ 4942: Minimum Distribution Requirement

Evaluate calculation of minimum investment return:

Is method of valuation consistently applied?   _____

Are nonreadily marketable asset appraisals updated?   _____

Are exempt function assets excluded?   _____

Can > $1\frac{1}{2}$% cash reserves be justified?   _____

Complete Part XII & XIII to determine whether minimum
distribution requirements are satisfied.   _____

Determine if adjustments to "qualifying distributions"
are needed for the following.   _____

Sale of exempt assets previously classified as distribution?   _____

Amounts not redistributed in a timely manner by
another private foundation or controlled organization?   _____

Set-asides not used for an approved purpose?   _____

§ 4945: Did the PF spend money for any of the following:

Political campaign?   _____

Lobbying or a grant to finance lobbying?   _____

Unapproved individual grant?   _____

Grant to another PF or non-(c)(3) entity?   _____

If so, attach expenditure responsibility reports.   _____

(Continued)

Exhibit 8.2. *(Continued)*

Verify questions in Part VII *Statement Regarding Activities* on Form 990-PF [Exhibit 27.5] are answered correctly. *No* is not the right answer to all questions. _____

Should the foundation consider conversion to a public charity? [§ 12.6] _____

Could PF qualify as a private operating foundation.? [§ 15.5] _____

Violations of § 4941/4945 sanctions

Is Form 4720 required? _____

Can penalty be abated for reasonable cause under § 4962? _____

Has violation been corrected? [§ 14.12] _____

ANNUAL TAX-COMPLIANCE CHECKLIST

NON 501(c)(3)s

Organization: _____

Completed by _____ Reviewed by: _____

Date _____

Organizational Issues

Federal tax exemption

New organization: Has Form 1024 been filed? If not, consider need for proof proposed operation qualifies for exemption and proper listing for IRS filing status. _____

All organizations: Review Form 1024 and determination letter for exempt purposes originally represented to the IRS and to verify category of exemption. Satisfy your current activities in keeping with expressed purposes. _____

State and local taxes

Obtain a copy of state tax exemption(s) letter or prepare application for exemption(s). [§ 18.9] _____

Does the organization use the proper form to claim exemption? _____

Exhibit 8.2. *(Continued)*

Must the EO collect sales tax on goods or services sold?
Are timely returns filed? Is tax deposited on time? _____

Does the organization pay real or personal property tax? _____

Would use of property qualify it for exemption? _____

For property classed as exempt, is it devoted to exempt
use or has it been converted to commercial use? _____

Charter and bylaws

Were there any changes to the charter or bylaws this year? _____

If so, obtain copy for attachment to Form 990. _____

Were there any substantial changes in structure or purpose
that require reporting to the IRS? _____

   Change reported on Form 990? [§ 27.9]

   New 1024 required? [Exhibit 28.1]

Review the minutes of director's meetings. Do they
reflect the exempt purpose of the EO's activities? _____

Operational Issues

Private Inurement or Benefit

Does the EO provide benefits to persons that control,
manage, or fund it? [§ 20.6] _____

Is the amount of compensation paid to officers,
directors, and staff or price paid for goods or
services reasonable? [§ 20.4] _____

Are loans made to officers or directors? [§ 20.7] _____

Does the organization benefit an identifiable class of
exempt constituents? [Chs. 6–10] _____

Does the organization sell services or goods produced
by its staff or members? [§ 8.4] _____

Validity of Financial Information

Has a compilation, review, or audit checklist been
completed to ensure proper financial reporting and
adherence to accounting principles? _____

(Continued)

Exhibit 8.2.   *(Continued)*

Exempt activities

Do activities further the purposes for which EO was determined to be exempt (as described in Form 1024 or subsequently reported to IRS?   _____

Are files maintained to document or provide an archive of the nature of activities? For example: copy of educational programs, peer review boards, member services, etc.?   _____

Does the EO lobby? If so, is it germane to purposes?   _____

Has the organization participated in any political campaigns? Does campaigning further the exempt purpose? [§ 23.1]   _____

Should Form 1120POL be filed? [§ 23.3]   _____

Are expense allocations and expenses shared with related 501(c)(3), (4), (5), or (6)s accurately calculated?   _____

If a social club, can it meet the gross revenue tests? [§ 9.4]   _____

Does EO have unrelated business income? [§ 21.5] If so, complete Form 990-T [Exhibit 27.7] and UBI checklist.   _____

Does the EO make payments for personal services. If so, complete *Employee vs. Ind. Contractor Status* [Checklist. 25-1].   _____

Does the EO have a policy for distinguishing between employees and contractors? [§ 25-2]   _____

Does EO comply with Federal and state payroll withholding and reporting requirements? [See Checklist 25-2]   _____

Are payroll taxes deposited in a timely fashion?   _____

Has the IRS ever examined the organization? Review reports for compliance with any changes.   _____

Filing Requirements

FORM 990EZ: EOs with gross receipts < $ 100,000 and assets < $250,000 [Appendix 27-1]   _____

FORM 990: EOs with gross receipts > $100,000 or assets > $250,000 file long form [Appendix 27-2]   _____

Exhibit 8.2.   *(Continued)*

If the EO is exempt from filing, consider filing. Address is kept current and statute of limitations begins. _____

Is the EO a chapter or affiliate of a central organization holding a group exemption? If so,

   Must the chapter file its own 990? _____

   Will the central EO file a group 990? _____

   Have changes in address been reported to central? _____

Was an extension of time requested? [Form 2758] _____

If the return is being filed late, has penalty abatement been requested? _____

Does the EO need to change its fiscal year or its accounting method for tax purposes? _____

Can change be made automatically? _____

Notice of Nondeductibility

Fund solicitations must "conspicuously" disclose payments that don't qualify for charitable deduction. _____

Are nondeductible member dues attributable to lobbying reported to members? _____

Do accounting records identify lobbying expense? _____

Has EO chosen to pay proxy tax instead on Form 990-T? _____

Public Inspection Requirements

Has the EO furnished Forms 990 and 1024 to persons asking to inspect them? _____

Exhibit 8.3.   Annual Tax-Filing Requirements for Nonprofit Organizations.

ANNUAL INFORMATION RETURNS

Form 990	Return of Organization Exempt from Tax. Filed annually by most § 501 organizations with gross receipts > $100,000. § 501(c)(3) also file Schedule A. Reports due by 15th day of 5th month following end of fiscal year.
Form 990EZ	Short version filed by organization with gross receipts less than $25,000 and assets < $250,000.
Form 990 PF	Filed by all private foundations annually by 15th day of 5th month following the end of the fiscal year.
Form 990T	Income tax return to report unrelated business income and calculate tax due annually. Also reports lobby proxy tax.
State Reports	A copy of Form 990 or a version of it is filed in some states.

EMPLOYMENT TAXES

Form 941	Employment tax return reporting taxes withheld and due filed quarterly on April 30, July 31, October 31, and January 31.
Form 5500	Exempt organizations with employee benefit and pension plans must annually report its participant statistics and other details.
Depository Receipts	Federal, and some state, taxes are paid directly to a bank, not mailed to the IRS where tax due is > $500.
Form W-2	On calendar year basis, employees total wages and taxes are reported to individual employees on this form by January 31.
Form W-4	Completed (for exempt's files) by each employee that evidence number of exemptions claimed for income tax withholding.
W-9	Completed (for nonprofit's files) by each independent contractor claiming the nonprofit need not withhold tax from them.
Form 1099	Nonemployees fees, interest, rent, or other compensation paid to independent contractors is reported annually by January 31. If the nonprofit does not have Form W-9 verifying the social security number, backup withholding of 20 percent of each payment is required.

Exhibit 8.3. *(Continued)*

Unemployment Tax	Both federal and state unemployment taxes may be due, depending upon the exemption category, number of employees, and registry as a reimbursing employer.

Other State Reports

Sales Tax	Sales of goods and services may be subject to sales tax. State and local exemptions and reporting requirements vary. Exemption from paying sales tax on purchases of goods to conduct exempt programs may be exempt under state law.
Local Property	Some states collect tax on real and intangible personal property.
Other State Filings	Many nonprofits are exempted from state income and corporate franchise taxes upon submission of evidence of federal exemption. In such states, a variety of other periodic filings, including a version of Form 990 are filed annually to maintain ongoing exemption.
Solicitation Registration	Organizations that conduct fund-raising campaigns may have additional filings.

(c)   Other Filings

A nonprofit organization has a number of periodic filing requirements as outlined in Exhibit 8.3.

Accurate employment tax reports are particularly important. The penalties for failure to pay over taxes withheld from employees are very stiff. The money withheld from employees does not belong to the nonprofit and it certainly should not be spent for any other purpose. Lastly those nonprofit officers responsible for the failure to properly pay employment taxes are held personally liable for the tax.

NCIB Standards
in Philanthropy

The **National Charities Information Bureau** was founded in 1918 by a group of national leaders who were concerned that Americans were giving millions of dollars to charitable organizations, particularly war relief organizations, that they knew little or nothing about.

NCIB's mission is to promote informed giving. NCIB believes that donors are entitled to accurate information about the charitable organizations that seek their support. NCIB also believes that well-informed givers will ask questions and make judgments that will lead to an improved level of performance by charitable organizations.

To help givers, NCIB has been evaluating national charitable organizations against its Standards for 77 years. Its present Standards are the result of a study in the late 1980's by a distinguished national panel, in an exercise that spanned two years and took hundreds of comments into account.

NCIB believes the spirit of these Standards to be universally useful for all charities. However, for organizations less than three years old or with annual budgets of less than $100,000, greater flexibility in applying some of the Standards may be appropriate.

NCIB STANDARDS IN PHILANTHROPY

Governance, Policy and Program Fundamentals

1. Board Governance: The board is responsible for policy setting, fiscal guidance, and ongoing governance, and should regularly review the organization's policies, programs and operations. The board should have
   a. an independent, volunteer membership;
   b. a minimum of 5 voting members;
   c. an individual attendance policy;

d. specific terms of office for its officers and members;

e. in-person, face-to-face meetings, at least twice a year, evenly spaced, with a majority of voting members in attendance at each meeting;

f. no fees to members for board service, but payments may be made for costs incurred as a result of board participation;

g. no more than one paid staff person member, usually the chief staff officer, who shall not chair the board or serve as treasurer;

h. policy guidelines to avoid material conflicts of interest involving board or staff;

i. no material conflicts of interest involving board or staff;

j. a policy promoting pluralism and diversity within the organization's board, staff, and constituencies.

2. Purpose: The organization's purpose, approved by the board, should be formally and specifically stated.

3. Programs: The organization's activities should be consistent with its statement of purpose.

4. Information: Promotion, fund raising, and public information should describe accurately the organization's identity, purpose, programs, and financial needs.

5. Financial Support and Related Activities: The board is accountable for all authorized activities generating financial support on the organization's behalf:

a. fund-raising practices should encourage voluntary giving and should not apply unwarranted pressure:

b. descriptive and financial information for all substantial income and for all revenue-generating activities conducted by the organization should be disclosed on request;

c. basic descriptive and financial information for income derived from authorized commercial activities, involving the organization's name, which are conducted by for-profit organizations, should be available. All public promotion of such commercial activity should either include this information or indicate that it is available from the organization.

6. Use of Funds: The organization's use of funds should reflect consideration of current and future needs and resources in planning for program continuity. The organization should:

a. spend at least 60% of annual expenses for program activities;

b. insure that fund-raising expenses, in relation to fund-raising results, are reasonable over time;

c. have net assets available for the following fiscal year not usually more than twice the current year's expenses or the next year's budget, whichever is higher;

d. not have a persistent and/or increasing deficit in the unrestricted fund balance.

Reporting and Fiscal Fundamentals

7. Annual Reporting: An annual report should be available on request, and should include

   a. an explicit narrative description of the organization's major activities, presented in the same major categories and covering the same fiscal period as the audited financial statements;

   b. a list of board members;

   c. audited financial statements or, at a minimum, a comprehensive financial summary that 1) identifies all revenues in significant categories, 2) reports expenses in the same program, management/general, and fund-raising categories as in the audited financial statements, and 3) reports all ending balances. (When the annual report does not include the full audited financial statements, it should indicate that they are available on request.)

8. An organization should supply on request complete financial statements which

   a. are prepared in conformity with generally accepted accounting principles (GAAP), accompanied by a report of an independent certified public accountant, and reviewed by the board; and

   b. fully disclose economic resources and obligations, including transactions with related parties and affiliated organizations, significant events affecting finances, and significant categories of income and expense; and should also supply

   c. a statement of functional allocation of expenses, in addition to such statements required by generally accepted accounting principles to be included among the financial statements;

   d. combined financial statements for a national organization operating with affiliates prepared in the foregoing manner.

9. Budget: The organization should prepare a detailed annual budget consistent with the major classifications in the audited financial statements, and approved by the board.

Glossary of Financial Terms and Abbreviations

Accession: An addition to permanent collection of museums, libraries, historical societies, or similar organizations, either by gift or by purchase.

Account: An individual record or category established for each type of asset, liability, fund balance, expense, or revenue embodied in the nonprofit's accounting system. Revenue accounts for a school, for example, might contain an account for donations, student tuition, book store sales, investment income, and event revenues. See Section 6.3 for a sample Chart of Accounts that reflects a typical list of accounts for a particular organization.

Accountability: Responsibility to keep records that evidence and to report the sources and uses of resources owned, received, and expended by an organization. A nonprofit is accountable in a public fashion, not only to those that provide its funding, but also to its exempt constituents, and the governmental bodies that grant it exempt or other special status.

Accounting: A system of accumulating, summarizing, and reporting financial transactions and the results thereof in terms of the organization's financial position (what it owns and what it owes) and the changes that occurred during the reporting period to increase or decrease those net assets. See Chapter 6.

Account Payable: A debt or obligation due or owed to be paid to suppliers or vendors for goods purchased or services rendered.

Account Receivable: Money due to the organization from services rendered, donations or dues promised, grants awarded, loans made, or employee advances (not yet accounted for) due but not yet paid.

Accrual Method: A system of accounting for financial transactions according to when the obligation to pay or receive actually occurs, rather than when cash is paid out or received (Cash Method). Preferred method for realistic reports on a nonprofit's financial condition as explained in Section 6.5.

Accrued Expense: Obligation accumulating, but not yet required to be paid (such as a maintenance contract due at end of year or month, salaries, property taxes, interest on mortgage), which is recorded currently (usually monthly) to assure an accurate statement of the nonprofit's liabilities or debts.

Acquisition Indebtedness: Moneys borrowed to acquire or substantially improve property, before or after acquisition of property; also debt that would not have been incurred but for acquisition of a property, even though funds are used for another purpose.

Action Organization: A nonprofit organization whose purposes can only be accomplished through the passage of legislation; an action organization cannot qualify for exemption under § 501(c)(3).

Advanced Ruling: A tentative IRS opinion regarding eligibility to be treated as a "public charity," issued to certain new charitable organizations in response to filing Form 1023. When the projected sources of revenue and proposed fund-raising methods indicate the nonprofit will receive the requisite amount of support from the general public, a five-year tentative, or advanced, ruling is issued. During this period, donors can rely upon this public status classification.

Agency: An organization or group that functions on behalf of another. A nonprofit organization receiving United Way funding, for example, is referred to as a united way agency.

Agent: An organization or person holding funds as custodian or fiscal agent for another organization or person. For example, a church might serve as agent for the collection of food donated for victims of a disaster. See Section 7. 4 for discussion of such arrangements or affiliations.

AICPA: American Institute of Certified Public Accountants.

Appraisal: An opinion, or evaluation, of the fair market value of property, usually conducted by a person professionally trained as an appraiser or by a person or company who specializes in selling or dealing in similar types of property.

Asset: A resource of measurable financial value owned by the organization—such as cash, investment securities, grants receivable, land, equipment, inventory, and collections; also anything that is owned that has exchange value.

Audit: An examination of financial records by an independent CPA in accordance with procedures designed to ascertain the validity and accuracy of the financials and enable the CPA to render a formal opinion on the nonprofit's status. See Section 2.6 for discussion of range of financial reporting services a CPA performs.

Audit Report: A CPA's report issued to express an opinion about an organization's financial condition; it can be unqualified, qualified, or disclaimed.

Audit Trail: The link between original source documents or transactions—such as the checks, invoices, sales reports, and other tangible documentation—and the balances reported in the accounting records and reports.

Balance Sheet: A financial statement, as of a particular date, of the nonprofit's assets, liabilities, and fund balances with titles and amounts thereof, now also called a Statement of Net Assets.

Bequest: A personal-property donation received upon death pursuant to a will; real property is *devised.*

Bookkeeping: The recording of detailed (each check, each deposit, each gift, and so on) financial transactions in a systematic fashion—in accounts—designed to accumulate the information for accounting purposes. See Section 6.1 for the elements of an accounting system that a bookkeeper would create or prepare.

Budget: A financial plan of action for future periods. Also the financial goals for the next year(s) expressed in numbers—how much revenue will the organization collect from what source, how much will be spent on what program or administrative cost. See Chapter 4.

Capital: The resources of a nonprofit organization providing the financial base or underpinning for operations; also called net assets (total assets less liabilities), net worth, or wealth. In a for-profit business, capital is also called stockholders' equity. See Section 1.4(a) regarding capitalization of a nonprofit.

Capital Addition: A donor-designated or restricted gift, grant, bequest, gain, or other income on investments dedicated either permanently or for some period of time to the purpose stipulated by the donor.

GLOSSARY

Certified Public Accountant: A person licensed by one or more states to engage in the public practice of accounting and qualified to examine the financial affairs of entities and issue opinions thereon in accordance with professional standards set out by the AICPA.

Charitable Class: That group of individuals that a nonprofit, classified as exempt under IRC § 501(c)(3), is organized and operated to benefit—the poor, the sick, the educable, the earth, the animals, and so on.

Charitable Donation: Any gift to a charitable organization qualifying for federal income tax deduction under IRC § 170.

Charitable Organization: A nonprofit organization dedicated to and operating to pursue one of eight "charitable" purposes, as defined in IRC § 170, including religious, charitable, scientific, testing for public safety, literary, educational, fostering national or international amateur sports competition, and preventing cruelty to children or animals.

Charitable pledges: Pledges received are included in revenue when the pledge is made or promised, rather than when paid in cash or other assets, if there is "sufficient evidence in the form of verifiable documentation that a promise was made and received." See Section 6.7.

Collection: Works of art, books, memorabilia, botanical or animal specimens, or similar items used for educational display or study.

Consideration: Money or other property received or given in a financial transaction.

Contribution: Gift of money or other property for which the giver receives nothing in return; also called transfer without consideration or donation.

Contributed services and facilities: Also referred to as *probono* services, these are the services and facilities provided to a nonprofit organization at a reduced price or without charge. The value of such gifts are reported as revenue, with the corresponding amount reported as an expense, when specific conditions exist as outlined in Section 6.7.

Current assets: Properties owned by a nonprofit that are readily available to satisfy its obligations (pay the bills), including cash, marketable securities, inventory held for sale (student books or drugs for patients), and amounts due to be received within one year (tuition receivable, Medicare reimbursements, or member receivables).

GLOSSARY

Current ratio: The proportion of current assets in relation to current (also called short-term) debts or liabilities due to be paid. A ratio of 1.0 or higher is highly desirable. See Section 7.1.

Deaccession: The disposition of collection items previously accessed.

Depreciation: The portion by which the cost of permanent assets—a building, a vehicle, a computer—declines (due to deterioration or obsolescence) over the accounting periods expected to benefit from its use; recorded as operational cost.

Depreciation Reserve: The cumulative sum of depreciation written off (expensed) during the period of time the assets (currently held) have been owned.

Designated Funds: Unrestricted moneys set aside by the board of directors or trustees for specific purposes. Such a restriction is not permanent.

Determination Letter: An opinion of the IRS concerning the nonprofit organization's tax-exempt status. Primary evidence furnished to anyone seeking proof of an organization's qualification as a federally tax-exempt organization. See Section 8.4.

Direct Cost: An expense specifically associated with and identifiable by program, project, or activity. See *Indirect Cost* for comparison.

Disqualified person: Persons and entities in certain relationships to a nonprofit who are subject to restraints on financial transactions with the organization for federal tax purposes. As defined in IRC § 4946, for private foundations, substantial contributors, officers, directors, trustees, and their relatives and businesses they own may be treated as disqualified.

Encumbrance: A binding contractual obligation committing the organization to purchase or acquire goods or services.

Endowment: A legal restriction requiring that the principal sum donated be kept intact, with only its income being expended. See Section 5.7.

Excise Taxes: Federal penalty taxes can be assessed for performance of prohibited acts by private foundations and public charities electing to lobby; they are found in IRC §§ 4940–4955.

Exclusively: A charitable organization must be organized and operated exclusively for its exempt purposes, but the presence of limited noncharitable activity is allowed. Thus, in the federal IRC § 501(c) exemption context, the term means not solely, but primarily.

GLOSSARY

Exempt Constituents: A nonprofit's constituents are those persons it was organized and is operated to benefit or serve. For philanthropic nonprofits, this group is called a "charitable class." The recipients of the nonprofit's services or the members it is organized to serve—members of a profession, a country club, a particular neighborhood.

Exempt Function Assets: Property or resources used by an exempt organization in connection with conducting its programs and operations.

Exempt Organization: A nonprofit corporation, trust, or association qualifying for exemption from federal income tax and most state and local taxes. The IRC § 501(c) lists 26 different categories of exempt organizations. The standards for granting exemption vary from state to state and from state to federal. Some exemptions are automatic; others require filing to receive recognition of exemption So for many reasons, not all nonprofit organizations are exempt organizations. See Chapter 8.

Expendable Funds: That portion of fund balances not already spent on fixed assets and available for use in satisfying obligations (except for endowment, pooled income, or permanently restricted funds).

Feeder Organization: A nonexempt trade or business operated for the benefit of a tax exempt organization as defined in IRC § 502.

Financial Management: The administration of financial affairs through planning, budgeting, recording, reporting, and analyzing an entity's flow of funds. It can also mean safeguarding resources or properties owned by the organization, using the funds for the purposes to which they were dedicated, accumulating necessary information concerning work performed, and submitting whatever reports are required by funders and governmental authorities.

Financial Statements: Basic financial statements suitable for a nonprofit would include (1) balance sheet or statement of net assets, (2) statement of activity and changes in net assets, (3) statement of cash flows, (4) statement of functional revenues and expenses, and (5) notes and opinion (if issued by CPA). See Section 6.6 for examples.

Fixed Assets: Assets acquired for permanent, long-term use, such as buildings or land (not used to pay for current operations or debts). Also can include equipment and furnishings.

FMV: Fair market value, or the price a willing buyer would pay a willing seller if neither is required to buy or sell and both have reasonable knowledge of all the necessary facts.

GLOSSARY

Functional Accounting: Departmental, category of service, or project classification for income and expense items, with financial reports reflecting revenues and costs by such classes of activity. For illustration see Section 6.3(b).

Fund Accounting: Nonprofit accounting method that groups assets and liabilities by the purpose to which they are dedicated. Fund balances are the equivalent of stockholders' equity, retained earnings, or capital accounts of a for-profit entity.

Fund Balance: Net worth, or what would be left if all assets were sold and all debts paid; comparable to stockholders' or owners' equity.

Fund Types: Under the standards of the Financial Accounting Standards Board of the AICPA, nonprofit organizations identify their net assets, or fund balances, according to any restrictions placed upon the use of unexpended funds by the entity or person providing the funding. See Section 6.7. For financial reporting purposes, funds are generally grouped into the following categories:

- *Permanently Restricted Net Assets* include the amount of those gifts or contributions subject to perpetual or everlasting conditions imposed by the donor on their use. The donor restrictions are those that cannot be removed by the organization's board or advisors and do not expire with the passage of time, such as an endowment gift. Gifts for construction of a building may be permanently restricted. Such gifts are sometimes referred to as not being currently expendable.

- *Temporarily Restricted Assets* are those assets whose use by the organization is limited by donor-imposed stipulations that either expire by the passage of time or can be fulfilled and removed by actions of the organization. Formerly such gifts were not shown as revenue in the year received but instead as liabilities entitled "deferred revenues."

- *Unrestricted Net Assets* is the category for all other resources of the nonprofit organization freely available for use in accomplishing the organization's purposes and subject only to the control of the organization's board or officers.

GAAP: Generally accepted accounting principles, promulgated by the Financial Accounting Standards Board, a division of the Financial Accounting Foundation created by the AICPA. See Section 6.7.

Grant: Gift or donation received for either a restricted or unrestricted purpose.

Indirect Cost Rate: Ratio, or percentage of add on, used to "fully cost" program services by calculating the proportionate share of indirect costs. Some funders limit the rate of reimbursement for such costs to a certain rate—a grant might provide for payment of direct costs plus 15 percent, for example.

Indirect Costs: Costs not readily identifiable with a particular aspect of organizational operation (sometimes called overhead or administration).

Examples are the salary of the executive director, the accounting department, and occupancy. A program officer's salary or teacher supplies would instead be direct costs.

In-Kind Gifts: Donated services and goods furnished without charge. Due to the difficulty of assigning monetary value, such gifts are not necessarily reported for financial purposes. On Form 990, gifts of goods may be reportable, although those donated services that are not deductible for tax purposes are not. See Section 6.7.

Institution: A church, school, hospital, or medical research/education organization afforded special status as a "public charity," regardless of sources of support.

IRC: Internal Revenue Code of 1986, or as subsequently amended.

IRS: Internal Revenue Service.

Journals and Ledgers: Accounting system components in which financial data is summarized. A nonprofit organization's system would contain, at a minimum, a cash journal, a general journal, and a general ledger. Other journals or ledgers would be used to separately accumulate information about transactions germane to the particular organization's types of revenue and expenditures, such as accounts receivable ledger, property and equipment ledger, and sales journal. See Section 6.1.

Liability: Any obligation, debt, or claim on organization's assets.

Liquidity: The capability of an organization to meet financial obligations as the debts are due. Simply put a nonprofit organization with sufficient liquid assets can pay its bills in a timely manner with assets that debtors are willing to accept (cash).

Lobbying: Direct contact with members of legislative bodies (and for some purposes the executive office) to urge the introduction or passage of legislation. Grassroots lobbying is urging the general public to lobby. Exempt organizations are subject to special limitations and reporting requirements concerning lobbying.

Management Letter: A report prepared by the independent CPAs at the end of an audit or review engagement to present any weaknesses in financial management and procedures and to make recommendations to correct the deficiencies.

MIR: Minimum investment return. MIR is equal to five percent of the average monthly value of a private foundation's assets held for investment purposes and not dedicated to charitable purposes. On a cumulative five-year running-average basis, a private foundation must make charitable expenditures or grants equal to its MIR.

Mission: A nonprofit organization's mission is its reason for being—its primary focus or purpose for operation. The mission can also be called the exempt function or the reason why the organization is given exempt status by governmental units.

Net Assets: The difference between an organization's assets, or properties it owns, less its debts or liabilities. New accounting theory recommends the financial statement on which this amount is presented, be called a *Statement of Net Assets,* also permitted to be called a balance sheet as it was in the past.

NOL: A net operating loss. Such losses realized in an unrelated business may be eligible to be carried backward and forward against income from the business.

Nonprofit Organization: An entity formed without profit motive to accomplish the common goals of its creator(s). Legally a nonprofit can be organized as a corporation, a trust, or an unincorporated association of individuals. One type of nonprofit is called a charity and is established to conduct programs that benefit a charitable class—those that need to be educated, those that are sick or poor, or the earth that needs to be protected from toxic chemicals. Other categories of nonprofits benefit a particular group of persons—a neighborhood association, a business league, or a social club, for example. Note all nonprofit organizations qualify for federal or state tax exemptions. See *Exempt Organizations.*

NPO: Nonprofit organization.

PF: Private Foundation, as defined below.

Pledge: A promise to contribute a certain amount to a nonprofit, with specific timing and possibly a particular type of property (such as an art object pledged to be given upon death). See Section 6.7 and *Fund Balances.*

POF: Private operating foundation.

Prepaid Expenses: Expenditures paid ahead of time to be reported as an expense of current activities; also called deferred expense and reported in the asset section of the balance sheet.

Private Foundation: Charitable organization whose revenues come from income earned on its endowment and donations from a small group of contributors, usually a family. Private foundations (PFs) are subject to special rules governing its activities.

Private Inurement: Economic benefit or preference given to those that control an organization, its board, its key officers, and managers. IRC § 501(c)(3) prohibits private inurement of the exempt nonprofit's income or assets to such insiders.

Private Operating Foundation: A type of private foundation that expends its funds to carry out its own projects—restores and maintains historic buildings or provides training for the unemployed—rather than making grants to other organizations as defined in IRC § 4942(j)(3).

Program Services: Activities or projects accomplishing the purposes for which the nonprofit organization was established.

Prudent Person Rule: Standard of conduct in managing funds that belong to another. The American Bar Association says "a trustee (and member of a nonprofit board) is under a duty to the beneficiaries (exempt constituents) to invest and manage the funds of the trust (nonprofit organization) as a prudent investor would, in light of the purposes, terms, distribution requirements, and other circumstances of the trust." See Section 5.5.

Public Charity: Federally tax-exempt organization meeting definitions of IRC § 509(a)(1) or § 509(a)(2) and qualifying for favorable tax status afforded to Section § 501(c)(3) organizations. Churches, schools, and hospitals are treated as public charities without regard to their sources of support. Other charities who receive over 1/3 of their annual support from the general public also qualify. Donations to public charities are allowed higher deduction limits than private foundations and are not subject to the special constraints placed on private foundations activities.

GLOSSARY

Qualifying Distributions: Grants, program service costs, or asset acquisitions made by a private foundation that satisfy IRC § 4942 tests for annual charitable giving or mandatory payout.

Substantial Contributor: One who contributes the greater of $5,000 or 2 percent of the cumulative total contributions the organization has received.

Set-Aside: Board designation or restriction of funds for specific future activity or asset acquisition. Such an action does not cause the funds to become permanently restricted for financial reporting purposes. In the private foundation context, the mandatory annual charitable payout requirement can be satisfied by a set-aside plan (may need to be approved by the IRS in advance).

Statement of Activity: This shows the results of operations for the all organizational funds and programs; formerly called *Statement of Revenues and Expenses* and in a for-profit context is called the Income Statement. The report distinguishes between program-service costs and supporting services (management and fund-raising). All nonprofits are encouraged to also present total expenses in both functional and natural categories—personnel, occupancy, interest, grants to others, and so on. See Exhibit 6.5.

Substantial: A measurement used with a variety of exempt organization issues to test qualification, usually expressed as percentage. Amount is usually 85 percent or more but may vary with as little as fifty percent allowing qualification.

Support: Donations, dues, or other property conveyed to a nonprofit organization as a voluntary payment without consideration or economic benefit being provided by the organization in return for the gift; see also *Contribution.*

Supporting Organization: A category of charitable exempt organization created and operated to benefit one or more other public charities, and controlled by or responsive to such charity. Supporting organizations are usually privately funded.

Supporting Services: Sustaining activities auxiliary to operating programs, such as accounting or fund raising, also called management and general or administrative department. See also *Program Services.*

Title-holding Company: A corporation the sole purpose of which is to hold beneficial legal title to property on behalf of another organization. For tax purposes, such an entity qualifies for exemption under § 501(c)(2) if it holds property for another exempt organization.

Transfer: Movement of fund balances from one fund to another, usually because of an intended change in use of an asset or to reimburse funds expended by one fund on behalf of another.

UBI: Unrelated business income.

UBIT: Unrelated business income tax.

Unrelated Business: Revenue producing activity that does not promote or advance a nonprofit's exempt purposes that is conducted in a commercial manner. Unrelated business income is subject to income tax, unless one of many exclusions apply as explained in Section 5.2(b).

Unrestricted gifts: Gifts received without explicit stipulation by the donor or "circumstances surrounding the receipt of the contribution that make clear the donor's implicit restriction on use," are reported as unrestricted. An organization's governing body or officers cannot cause funds to be reported as restricted.

Working Capital: Net assets available to pay current operating expenses; also current assets less current liabilities.

Yield: The overall economic return earned on an investment, including the current dividend or interest paid plus or minus the increase or decrease in the principal value as explained in Section 5.7.

Bibliography

American Bar Association, Section of Business Law, Nonprofit Corporations Committee, *Guidebook for Directors of Nonprofit Corporations*, edited by George W. Overton. New York: ABA, 1993.

American Institute of Certified Public Accountants, New York:

Account Standards Division, "Accounting for Joint Costs of Informational Materials and Activities of Not-for-Profit Organizations that Include a Fund-Raising Appeal," Statement of Position No. 87-2, 1987. (In process of revision)

Accounting Standards Division, "The Application of the Requirements of Accounting Research Bulletins, Opinions of the Accounting Principles Board, and Statements and Interpretations of the Financial Accounting Standards Board to Not-for-Profit Organizations," Statement of Position No. 94-2, 1994.

Accounting Standards Division, "Reporting of Related Entities by Not-for-Profit Organizations," Statement of Position No. 94-3, 1994.

Auditing Standards Division, "Compliance Auditing Applicable to Governmental Entities and Other Recipients of Governmental Financial Assistance," Statement on Auditing Standards No. 68, 1991. (In process of revision)

Committee on College and University Accounting and Auditing, "Audits of Colleges and Universities, Including Statement of Position Issued by the Accounting Standards Division," Industry Audit Guide, 2nd ed., 1975. (In process of revision)

Committee on Not-for-Profit Organizations, "Audit Guide for Not-for Profit Organizations," to be published in 1995.

Committee on Not-for-Profit Organizations, "Audits of Not-for-Profit Organizations Receiving Federal Awards," Statement of Position No. 92-9, 1992.

Committee on Voluntary Health and Welfare Organizations, "Audits of Voluntary Health and Welfare Organizations," Industry Audit Guide, 2nd ed., 1988. (In process of revision)

BIBLIOGRAPHY

Health Care Committee, "Audits of Providers of Health Care Services, Including Statement of Position Issued by the Accounting Standards Division," Industry Audit Guide, 1990. (In process of revision)

Subcommittee on Nonprofit Organizations, "Audits of Certain Nonprofit Organizations," including "Accounting Principles and Reporting Practices for Certain Nonprofit Organizations," Statement of Position No. 78-10, 2nd ed., 1988. (In process of revision)

AICPA Statement of Position 90-9, *The Auditor's Consideration of the Internal Control Structure Used in Administering Federal Financial Assistance Programs.*

The Chronicle of Philanthropy. Washington, DC: weekly journal.

Colvin, Gregory L., *Fiscal Sponsorships, 6 Ways to Do It Right.* San Francisco, CA: Study Center Press, 1993.

Desiderio, R. J., and S. A. Taylor, *Planning Tax-Exempt Organizations.* New York: Shepard's/McGraw-Hill, 1988.

The Exempt Organization Tax Review. Arlington, VA: Tax Analysts, Monthly journal.

Financial Accounting Standards Board, Norwalk, CT:

Statements of Financial Accounting Standards No. 93, "Recognition of Depreciation by Not-for-Profit Organizations," 1987. (Amended by No. 99, "Deferral of the Effective Date of Recognition of Depreciation by Not-for-Profit Organizations," 1988.)

Statements of Financial Accounting Standards No. 116, "Accounting for Contributions Received and Contributions Made," 1993.

Statements of Financial Accounting Standards No. 117, "Financial Statements of Not-for-Profit Organizations," 1993.

Statement of Financial Accounting Standards No. 124, "Accounting for Certain Investments Held by Not-for-Profit Organizations," 1995.

Foundation Management Report, 7th ed. Washington, DC: Council on Foundations, 1993.

Foundation News. Washington, DC: Council on Foundations, published bi-monthly.

Gross, M. J., Jr., W. Warshauer, Jr., and R. F. Larkin, *Financial and Accounting Guide for Not-for-Profit Organizations,* 5th ed. New York: John Wiley & Sons, 1995.

Hill, Frances R., Barbara L. Kirschten, Robin Atkinson, Wendell R. Bird, and Bonnie S. Brier. *Federal and State Taxation of Exempt Organizations.* Boston, MA: Warren, Gorham & Lamont, 1994.

BIBLIOGRAPHY

Hopkins, Bruce R. *Charity, Advocacy, and the Law.* New York: John Wiley & Sons, 1992.

———. *The Law of Fund-Raising.* New York: John Wiley & Sons, 1991.

———. *The Law of Tax-Exempt Organizations* 6th Ed. New York: John Wiley & Sons, 1992.

———. *The Nonprofit Counsel.* New York: John Wiley & Sons, Monthly newsletter.

———. *Starting and Managing a Nonprofit Organization Legal Guide.* New York: John Wiley & Sons, 1989.

The Journal of Taxation of Exempt Organizations. New York, NY: Warren, Gorham & Lamont, Bi-monthly journal.

McLaughlin, Thomas A., *Streetsmart Financial Basics for Nonprofit Managers,* New York: John Wiley & Sons, 1995.

National Association of College and University Business Officers *Financial Accounting and Reporting Manual for Higher Education.* Washington, DC: NACUBO, 1990.

National Center for Nonprofit Boards publishes a variety of pamphlets including *Nonprofit Governance Series* (16 booklets), *The Financial Responsibilities of Nonprofit Boards, Nonprofit Committees: How to Make Them Work,* (1992) and *Hiring the Chief Executive: A Practical Guide to the Search and Selection Process,* (1993). Washington, DC: NCNB.

National Committee for Responsive Philanthropy. Washington, DC: NCRP, Quarterly newsletter.

National Health Council, Inc., National Assembly of Voluntary Health and Social Welfare Organizations, United Way of America, *Standards of Accounting and Financial Reporting for Voluntary Health and Welfare Organizations,* Rev. ed. 1988.

New York University Conferences on Tax Planning for § 501(c)(3) Organizations. New York: Matthew Bender. Published annually.

Nonprofit Sector Series, Washington, DC: Independent Sector and San Francisco, CA: Jossey-Bass.

O'Connell, Brian, *The Board Member's Book.* New York: The Foundation Center, 1986.

———. *Nonprofit Management Series.* Washington, DC: Independent Sector, 1988.

Oleck, Howard L. *Nonprofit Corporations, Organizations, and Associations* 5th ed. Englewood Cliffs, NJ: Prentice-Hall, 1992.

Oleck, Howard L. and Martha E. Stewart, *Nonprofit Corporations, Organizations, and Associations.* Englewood Cliffs, NJ: Prentice-Hall, 1994.

Olenick, Arnold J. and Philip P. Olenick, *A Nonprofit Organization Operating Manual, Planning for Survival Growth.* New York: The Foundation Center, 1991.

BIBLIOGRAPHY

Paul Stretfus' Exempt Organization Tax Journal. Pasadena, MD: Monthly journal.

Rachlin, Robert and H. W. Allen Sweeny. *Handbook of Budgeting,* 3rd ed. New York: John Wiley & Sons, 1993.

Smith, Bucklin & Associates, *The Complete Guide to Nonprofit Management.* New York: John Wiley & Sons, 1994.

Turk, Frederick J. and Robert P. Gallo, *Financial Management Strategies for Arts Organizations.* New York: American Council for the Arts.

U.S. Department of the Treasury, Internal Revenue Service. *Exempt Organizations Continuing Professional Education Technical Instruction Programs.* Washington, DC: U.S. Department of the Treasury. (Available annually from IRS Reading Room, Washington, DC.)

———. Exempt Organizations Handbook. 1992. Internal Revenue Manual 7751. Washington, DC:

———. Private Foundations Handbook. 1992. Internal Revenue Manual 7752. Washington, DC:

U. S. General Accounting Office, *Government Auditing Standards* (GAAS) *(The Yellow Book),* revised in 1994.

United Way of America. *Accounting and Financial Reporting, A Guide for United Ways and Not-for-Profit Organizations,* 2nd ed. rev. Alexandria, VA: United Way Institute, 1989.

Wacht, Richard F., *Financial Management in Nonprofit Organizations.* Atlanta, Georgia: Business Publication Division, Georgia State University, 1984.

Index

INDEX

INDEX

INDEX

INDEX

INDEX

INDEX

INDEX